The Grand Theatre, High Street, Croydon

Demolished 1959

A photograph of the Norman Partridge (1970) . . .

. . . painting of the Theatre hanging in Fairfield Halls

# 60 Years of Jazz in Croydon......

...... and beyond

1930's - 1990's

Ian King

John Rickard

Kings Jazz Review
The London Borough of Croydon

This book is dedicated to all lovers of old-style jazz, but particularly those from Croydon

Allders department store in North End . . . the focal point

of Croydon's Jazz Week . . . at 11 am Tuesday, 21 March, 1995

First published in Great Britain in 1995 by

KINGS JAZZ REVIEW
18 Canning Road
East Croydon
Surrey CR0 6QD

Copyright © Ian King and John Rickard 1995

All rights reserved.
No part of this publication may be reproduced, stored in a retrieval system, or transmitted, in any form or by any means, electronic, mechanical, photocopying, recording or otherwise, without prior permission of the copyright owners.

Printed and bound by **Space Workshops**, Cherry Orchard Road, East Croydon

ISBN  0 9520787 0 8

# Contents

**Foreword** by Alan Elsdon ..................................................... viii

**Acknowledgements** ........................................................... ix

**Croydon Coat Of Arms** ...................................................... x

**Introduction** ..................................................................... xi

1   Early History ................................................................ 13
2   The 1930's ................................................................... 17
3   The 1940's ................................................................... 23
4   The 1950's ................................................................... 30
5   The 1960's ................................................................... 52
6   The 1970's ................................................................... 78
7   The 1980's ................................................................... 89
8   The 1990's ................................................................... 101
9   Extra Time .................................................................. 109
10  Coda ........................................................................... 121

**Appendices**

[i]     The North End (Civic) Hall ............................. 123
[ii]    Fairfield ........................................................... 127
[iii]   Kings Jazz Review .......................................... 139

**Index** (Excluding Appendices) .......................................... 155

# Foreword

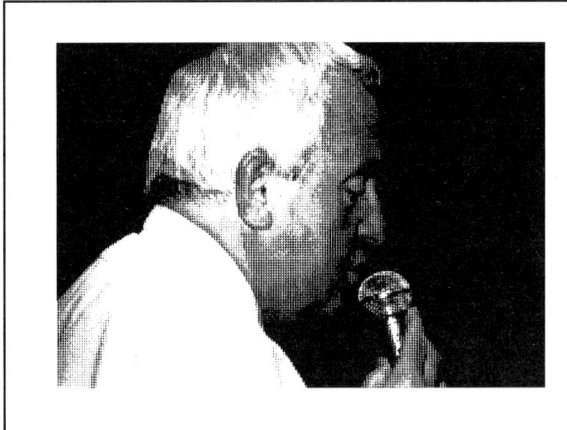

Alan Elsdon

If ever there was a "labour of love," this book qualifies for that sentiment in all departments. It charts the emergence and development of the jazz movement in Croydon over a sixty year period from the viewpoint of two avid and life-long jazz fans.

Don't be alarmed by the localised title, as there is little that is parochial about its content. Rather, it is a story board of the development of revivalist jazz in most major towns and cities in Europe.

The book gives a brief local history of Croydon, including fascinating early photographs of the area and the town's former jazz venues, then a potted history of the development of early jazz and its sources. The Authors then chart the course of the music, by decades, up to the 90's.

I first played in Croydon during the 50's with the bands of Cy Laurie, Graham Stewart and Terry Lightfoot, and then with my own band throughout the 60's to the present day. I have many fond memories of playing in the area and the Star Hotel was my favourite venue. I can recall playing with the Alex Welsh Reunion Band in November, 1982, at the Fairfield Halls, a concert hall as good as any in the country renowned for its fine acoustics.

The jazz fans were great, knowledgeable and incredibly loyal, with many of them travelling miles to listen and dance to their favourite bands.

I can remember visiting Dave Carey's Swing Shop in Mitcham Lane, which was a two-hour bus journey for me in those days, to buy rare American 78 rpm records at 12/6d a throw - a large sum of money then, and a far cry from the vast numbers of tapes and CD's available today.

Browsing through the various decades of the Croydon scene - one thing that becomes crystal clear, is that good, melodic, swinging jazz still continues to have a very wide appeal. With its great fans, good venues, several very fine bands resident around the town and a host of talented soloists in the area, Croydon is up amongst the best of them.

Long may it be so !

# Acknowledgements

Whilst much of the printed and photographic material used in this book has come from the personal collection of the authors, we would like to acknowledge, with grateful thanks, the invaluable assistance of the following :-

The Croydon Advertiser, whose records in the archives of the Local Studies Library proved to be a veritable goldmine of information. Material appearing on pages 18, 19, 20, 21, 28, 39, 44, 45, 52, 65, 68, 76, 82, 83, 86, 87, 99, 103, 104 and 123 to 125 has been reproduced by kind permission of the Croydon Advertiser Group Ltd., and the co-operation of the Editor, Malcolm J. Starbrook, is appreciated.

Jazz enthusiasts who either submitted items from their personal memorabilia or offered their recollections of times gone by: James Asman; Mike Atterbury; Ken Batty; Ray Bolden; Campbell Burnap; Charles 'Nobby' Clark; Phil Dearle; Alan Elsdon; Vic Gibbons; Chris Groom; Denny Holloway; Jim Keen; Graham Langley; Alan Littlejohn; Mike Pointon; David Sinclair; Vic Smith; Alan Tullett; Dick Waterhouse; George Webb.

Our special thanks to Sally MacDonald, Principal Museum Officer, Croydon Arts, for her encouragement throughout the project, and to Derek Barr, Chief Executive of Fairfield for allowing us access to his records.

Last, but by no means least, our thanks to Donna Rickard for tackling, with enthusiasm, the daunting task of checking the index.

# CROYDON

The Arms of the London Borough of Croydon.

In the pictorial language of heraldry, the coat of arms of the
London Borough of Croydon recalls earliest recorded "local government" of Croydon.
The Domesday Book states that in 1086:-
"Archbishop Lanfranc holds in demesne CROIDENE."
"The Abbey of St Peter of Chertsey holds Watendone."
"The Abbey of St Peter of Winchester holds Sandestede."
The Arms commemorate the three lords of the ancient manors of Croydon,
Coulsdon and Sanderstead. Canterbury is represented by the flowering cross of John Whitgift and by the two crosses from the arms of the See of Canterbury which hang from the collars of the lion and horse which support the shield. Chertsey Abbey contributes the crossed swords and keys to the head of the shield.
The black lion is from the arms of Hyde Abbey (the later name of the Abbey of St. Peter of Winchester) to represent the Manor of Sanderstead. The shield's second supporter is from the arms of the Earls of Surrey, the ancient feudal lords of the County of Surrey.

*Introduction by Ian King*

Why a book on jazz in Croydon?

Unlike many fans in the early period of jazz, my interest did not come about by listening to records or attending the rhythm clubs which came into being during the 40's and 50's, with members holding their meetings in church halls and pubs, but in a much different way.

In 1949 I was working in Nantes, a town in the Muscadet region of France, situated on the River Loire. In those days the piano accordion held pride of place in the bistros and cafés of the surrounding villages, bringing back memories of my Scottish homeland. There was often news of visiting American jazzmen, but little or no chance for me to get to see them, although I was aware of the Hot Club de France, resident in Paris at the time.

When I returned to England in 1950, the two week's compulsory training with the armed forces on "Z" reserve was still in force, and so what better way was there than to carry out this duty as a clarinet player with the Queen's Surrey TA regimental band, then housed in Croydon at the Mitcham Road barracks.

It turned out to have been one of the best decisions I had taken in my life. The musical training was second to none and I was always in my element when grappling with the card music dots on every marching parade. In those days there were many parades, and how very swell affairs they all were.

The open air concerts in Croydon still hold very fond memories, especially when the band played on the lawn of what is now the Queen's Gardens, stretching out in front of the town hall on Sunday afternoons.

Several years later, before the Queen's Surrey military band was disbanded due to cut backs, I happened one evening to be walking past the Castle pub in Tooting Broadway, and I heard a completely new sound of music coming from within the building. Pleasure in those days for me was a mixture of listening to the Odeon Würlitzer Organ at the cinema, or going dancing at the Streatham Locarno or the Orchid Ballroom in Purley, where the swing and dance bands played. But in the relatively quiet main thoroughfare of Tooting Broadway, there was a new sound.

I entered the pub and immediately fell in love with the music of Ken Colyer.

From that day to this, the jazz that I subconsciously hear constantly within me is a hybrid of those three set musical cultures, 'Paris Hot Club-Sousa-Colyer,' and all other forms of music take second place save, perhaps, the bagpipes.

In complete contrast, my co-author, John Rickard, is a Croydon man, born in Thornton Heath where he lived for 30 years before job relocation took him away from the area.

At the age of 15, John first heard the strange new sounds of jazz on the radio, from Hilversum in Holland, and was immediately hooked. His love affair with Traditional jazz was confirmed when he attended a concert given by Graeme Bell's Australian Jazz Band on one of their visits to Croydon in 1948, and following the purchase of a Parlophone recording of Freddy Randall's band playing *At The Jazz Band Ball* (he still has it to this day) there began a deep interest in the music which has never waned.

Our paths crossed on 18 September 1989 when we met at the Ken Colyer Trust All Stars concert being held in the Arnhem Gallery, Fairfield Halls, promoted by the Croydon Jazz Society. John and his wife Donna had just returned from New Orleans and I suggested to him that he should write an article for Kings Jazz Review on their experiences in the Crescent City, and this he did.

Time passed by and with Kings Jazz Review approaching its fifth year of publication, I was toying with the idea of publishing a book, using the material so far produced for that period, but I kept putting the idea out of my mind. Then one day in the Spring of 1992, I saw an article in the Croydon Advertiser on the London Borough of Croydon's Heritage Grant Scheme, and I immediately had talks with John, who was still writing short stories on jazz for the magazine, as to whether we should give it consideration.

As a result, the idea for this book was born.

# EARLY HISTORY

"Way Down Yonder In New Orleans"

# 1

## Early History

Although Croydon can claim to have formed the second jazz club in Europe after World War II, sadly much of the town's recorded history of jazz is vague, especially the dawn period around the 30's and early 40's.

It is thus inevitable that our story will not be replete but hopefully sufficient interest will be generated for others with jazz memories to follow in our footsteps so that one day the documentation of Croydon's early jazz history will be told in full. We make no apologies for much of the modern element of jazz being omitted; again, perhaps one day this vacuum will also be filled.

The genesis of jazz can be placed into three stages.

Firstly, in America, the period between the 18th and 19th centuries when the folk music being sung by Americans and Europeans in the Southern States was profoundly influenced by the African slave population; secondly, the development of their music through the plantation call and response form, pertinent also in Afro-American church music and railroad songs; thirdly, the merging of this sound with the English, Irish and Scottish ballads and the military band music.

After many refinements, the eventual musical sound became known as, simply, *jazz*.

## IN THE BEGINNING . . . . AND AFTER

It is not possible to state the exact time that jazz was born as it came into being over a period of time and involved a mixture of many different forms of music played by various performers, each of whom affected the process with his own personality.

Into this musical brew went the old African tribal rhythms, the vocal refrains of the *hollers* that could be heard in the cotton fields and the railroad work songs of the Negro slaves of Southern America, as well as gospel music that was being sung in their churches. This melting-pot of music was additionally flavoured by the sounds of the military bands, the folk dance stomps, the *ragged* music which became known as ragtime, and the sad sounds of the blues. The Spanish and French tinged music of the Creole added to these ingredients produced a heady mixture of individual but linked elements, out of which came colourful, syncopated sounds. Thus began the evolution of jazz.

The man usually acknowledged as being the first true jazz musician was cornettist Buddy Bolden and it is almost certain that he played ragtime and not the finished jazz form. Bolden's sound can only be imagined through the memories of other musicians who played with him, as he never recorded. (It is rumoured that there was a cylinder recording of the Bolden band but, alas, it remains only a myth as it has never been found).

If Buddy Bolden led the way there was certainly no shortage of players who were keen to master the new music and musicians such as clarinettists Lorenzo Tio Jnr. and Frank Lewis, cornettist Manuel Perez and valve trombonist Willie Cornish are legendary names of the earliest period of jazz

This first generation of musicians played a rough, earthy style of jazz and close upon their heels came the second wave, amongst whom Joe Oliver, Johnny Dodds, Kid Ory and Louis Armstrong would all become famous.

Although it is generally accepted that jazz was originally mainly played by black musicians, others were quickly drawn to it and perhaps the founder of the white jazz tradition was 'Papa' Jack Laine who formed the Reliance Brass Band as early as 1892.

The first band to make a jazz recording (1917) was a white group known as The Original Dixieland Jazz Band (ODJB), consisting of Nick La Rocca (leader, cornet); Larry Shields (clarinet); Eddie Edwards (trombone); Henry Ragas (piano) and Tony Sbarbaro (drums) and they undoubtedly had a great influence on the progress of jazz.

There were a number of White and Creole musicians with leanings towards the new music who were trained musically in the European classical tradition. The development of the New Orleans style of playing, where in the front line the cornet or trumpet provides the melody, the clarinet improvises above and below the range of the leader, and the trombone produces sweet, legato, controlled sounds and harmonic support, was greatly affected by them. Even with this approach, the white bands were not necessarily ahead in the progress of jazz. The black musicians were freer in their movements and they played more to the rhythmic and personal expressions of their vocals, which served them then solely as "instruments" for making music.

Although they have never completely abandoned it, the whites soon learned to throw off the mantle of playing strictly to written compositions and adopted the looser style of the Southerners. With the black influences being less apparent in their playing they were able to make the new music more in keeping with their white American audiences and it was because of this blending together that jazz achieved significance for its various styles of play.

Time passed and from isolated community beginnings the various musical elements went through a complex re-shaping process, eventually emerging as a "new" sound - the sound of *jazz*.

\* \* \* \* \*

By some trick of fate the evolution of jazz was to be centred on a large, bustling port on the Mississippi river, a city like no other in the United States of America.

New Orleans enjoyed a prime geographical position and was the major port of call in the Southern seaboard. But it was also an *open* city and of all the red-light districts which flourished in America at the turn of the century, the most infamous was in New Orleans. Known to its inhabitants as, simply, The District, it was created by the Mayoralty of New Orleans in January 1897 in an effort to contain the spread of prostitution, with its inevitable aftermath of crime. The area took its name from Alderman Sidney Story who prepared the groundwork for the eventual legislation and it will always be well remembered as Storyville.

For the next twenty years Storyville flourished and its brothels, gambling dens, saloons and barrelhouses provided employment for jazz pianists (professors) and other musicians, as we know that King Oliver, Freddy Keppard and Louis Armstrong played there before it was officially closed down in November 1917.


THE NORTH AMERICAN FLOW . . . .

Following the closure of Storyville there was a mass migration of jazzmen to cities such as St Louis and Kansas City, which could be reached by the riverboats, and even further afield. The main destination, however, was Chicago, another raucous town with an abundance of nightclubs and bars ready made for jazz to be introduced to an eager audience. Very soon a distinctive, Chicago-style, jazz evolved, and players such as Wild Bill Davison (cornet), Bud Freeman (tenor saxophone) and Eddie Condon (banjo/guitar) emerged.

And so over the years jazz spread across the States : cornettist Bix Beiderbecke and the Wolverines in Chicago; the Red Nichols-Miff Mole, trumpet - trombone partnership; Chicagoans in New York including Muggsy Spanier, Max Kaminsky and Dave Tough; on the West Coast where Lu Watters formed his soon-to-be-famous Yerba Buena band, with Bob Scobey (trumpet) and Turk Murphy (trombone).

But this was only the beginning and the impact of jazz was soon to be felt in other parts of the world.

# THE 1930's

"You Tell Me Your Dreams"

# 2

THE 1930's

Whilst Croydon has always been a town where music can be heard, it would have been extremely difficult to find a live jazz band to listen to in 1930.

On the 11th January, 1930, the Croydon Advertiser & Surrey County Reporter carried advertisements for a *Grand Military Dance* at the Royal Engineers Drill Hall in Union Road, West Croydon (admission 2/- [10p]) and "A Dance" in Ruskin Hall, Wellesley Road (tickets 1/- [5p]). Jan Ralfini and His Band were appearing at the Locarno in Streatham Hill, whilst the Croydon Empire was presenting Jack Gold and His Band. Admission to the latter ranged from 1/2d (6p) to 1/10d (9p).

Jazz appreciation at this time was restricted mainly to dance bands and to the recordings made by New Orleans musicians which somehow began to find their way to this country.

Some Croydon area music venues of the period included Pembroke Hall, West Croydon (February 1930 - *Jolly Paragon Dance* with the New Regent Dance Orchestra); the Palais de Dance, Thornton Heath (January 1930 - Al Tabor and His Trans-Atlantic Band); the Davis Theatre, where Al Jolson and Davy Lee appeared in *Say It With Songs* in March 1930; the Winter Gardens in Scarbrook Road; the Selhurst Picture Theatre in Windmill Road; The Scala, North End and the Hippodrome in Crown Hill.

In February 1930 Billy Cotton and His Savannah Band (*every night excluding Monday - DANCING & CABARET*) could be seen at the Streatham Hill Locarno, whilst Thornton Heath Sports Club presented a *Select Dance* at the Greyhound's new ballroom, with Goddard's Band for the then upmarket admission price of 3/6d (17 p).

But jazz was taking hold elsewhere in a world which would welcome the visits of a number of major musicians who ventured across the Atlantic to help spread the word to this country, Europe and beyond.

Amongst the American stars who came to the UK in the 30s were Louis Armstrong (July 1932); Duke Ellington (June 1933); Cab Calloway (March 1934) and Benny Carter (January 1937), to be followed by other famous names such as Coleman Hawkins, Thomas "Fats" Waller and the Mills Brothers.

Jazz fans who had only been able to listen to records of these jazz artists were now able to actually see them in the flesh and the impact which they made in the development of jazz in this country was inestimable.

But darker times were just around the corner and in September 1939 Great Britain went to war with Germany, so beginning a conflict which would last for six grim years.

*The Croydon Advertiser & Surrey County Reporter incorporating
the Croydon Guardian and Croydon Express*

SATURDAY, MARCH 15 1930

**DAVIS THEATRE CROYDON**
Managing Director: ISRAEL DAVIS     'Phone: CROYDON 3156
WEEK COMMENCING MARCH 17th
ALL TALKING  Frederick Lonsdale's Brilliant Play.  ALL TALKING
**THE LAST OF MRS. CHEYNEY**
Featuring NORMA SHEARER and BASIL RATHBONE
Showing at 3.15, 6.15, 9.5
—ON THE STAGE—
JACK THOMPSON, The Famous Composer of "Come Sing to Me," etc., in Selections from his Repertoire.
MICKEY MOUSE CARTOON

---

**THE Greyhound Theatre, Croydon**
'Phone: 1102, 0004, 3000.
**THE ANNUAL ST. PATRICK'S NIGHT**
**DINNER, DANCE and CABARET**
MONDAY, MARCH 17th.
Special Engagement of WILLIAM E. LOWRIE'S "EMPIRE" DANCE BAND.
Also of Croydon's Favourite in Cabaret,
**GORDON MARSH AND THE MARSHMALLOW GIRLS.**
Dancing 8 p.m.  Dinner 9 p.m.  Carriages 3 a.m.
Evening Dress Indispensable.
Tickets 10/6
All Profits to CROYDON GENERAL HOSPITAL.
Early Application is earnestly advised.
Extension of License will be applied for.

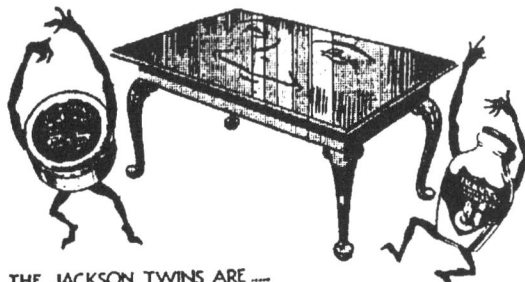

THE JACKSON TWINS ARE....

# A tonic for tired tables

"Ha ha!" cried Jackson's Furniture Cream. "Table tired and listless, eh? I'm the Tonic for that!"
But Jackson's Wax Polish wasn't listening. He'd already started polishing the floor. Making it shine as it never shone before!
Splendid fellows!

Bring the Jackson Twins into your home. Set them to work all over the house. They'll work miracles!

*Insist* on having Jackson's—both kinds. Jackson's Lavender Furniture Cream in the delightful lavender jars. And Jackson's Wax Floor Polish in the large orange tins.

JACKSON'S LAVENDER CREAM
10d 1/6 2/6

JACKSON'S WAX POLISH
...1/-...

76 Years' Reputation. THOS. JACKSON AND SONS, LTD. MITCHAM.

18

# The Croydon Advertiser

### And Surrey County Reporter
### The Croydon Guardian and the Croydon Express.

FRIDAY, SEPTEMBER 8th, 1939

## THE KING'S MESSAGE TO HIS PEOPLES

The King broadcast the following message on Sunday evening:

*In this grave hour, perhaps the most fateful in our history, I send to every household of my peoples, both at home and overseas, this message, spoken with the same depth of feeling for each one of you as if I were able to cross your threshold and speak to you myself.*

*For the second time in the lives of most of us we are at war. Over and over again we have tried to find a peaceful way out of the differences between ourselves and those who are now our enemies. But it has been in vain. We have been forced into a conflict. For we are called, with our allies, to meet the challenge of a principle which, if it were to prevail, would be fatal to any civilised order in the world.*

*It is the principle which permits a State, in the selfish pursuit of power, to disregard its treaties and its solemn pledges; which sanctions the use of force, or threat of force, against the sovereignty and independence of other States. Such a principle, stripped of all disguise, is surely the mere primitive doctrine that might is right; and if this principle were established throughout the world, the freedom of our own country and of the whole British Commonwealth of Nations would be in danger. But far more than this—the peoples of the world would be kept in the bondage of fear, and all hopes of settled peace and of the security of justice and liberty among nations would be ended.*

*This is the ultimate issue which confronts us. For the sake of all that we ourselves hold dear, and of the world's order and peace, it is unthinkable that we should refuse to meet the challenge.*

*It is to this high purpose that I now call my people at home and my peoples across the seas, who will make our cause their own. I ask them to stand calm, firm, and united in this time of trial. The task will be hard. There may be dark days ahead, and war can no longer be confined to the battlefield. But we can only do the right as we see the right, and reverently commit our cause to God. If one and all we keep resolutely faithful to it, ready for whatever service or sacrifice it may demand, then, with God's help, we shall prevail.*

*May He bless and keep us all.*

The following is an extract from the Croydon Advertiser and Surrey County Reporter.

The King's message on the left is exactly as printed by the Croydon newspaper of the day.

### WAR DECLARED
### How Croydon Took the News
### The First Thrill

At eleven o'clock on Sunday morning, September 3rd, 1939, Britain and Germany were again at war. Most people in Croydon, warned by the grave statements in the Sunday morning newspapers, listened to the radio announcement and so heard that all efforts for peace had finally failed.

Those who had not switched on their wireless sets heard the war declaration from friends, and the news quickly spread through the borough. It was not long after that Croydon had its first war thrill, for while the situation was still being discussed and considered, the warning wail of the air raid sirens was heard. Happily it turned out to be a false alarm but its effect was rather interesting psychologically. While many rushed to their shelters or sought the protection of basements, others indulged in obvious curiosity and stood at their garden gates gazing for a sight of the expected invaders. It cannot be too seriously emphasised that all who can do so should take shelter on hearing the air raid alarm signal. In the case of a raid many casualties could result from indulging in curiosity.

### Splinters and Debris

The necessity for shelter is shown by the fact that the direct results of a high explosive bomb extend over a very limited area, usually not more than a thirty foot circle round the centre of the hit. By far the greatest number of casualties are usually caused by secondary effects, splinters (including splinters of shells from anti-aircraft guns), blast and the fall of debris.

Anyone who has an Anderson shelter is virtually secure from anything except a direct hit, providing they are properly erected and "earthed." Those who have no shelter can obtain a considerable degree of protection by digging a trench in the garden with eighteen inches of earth cover.

It is stated that the ordinary house offers a good deal of protection. The side walls, or one or two floors overhead, will stop most splinters. Well constructed buildings are not easily brought down unless a big bomb falls near them. The best place inside the house is the basement, or if there is not one, on the ground floor. Choose a passage or a room with a small window as the place of refuge, especially if it looks out on a narrow passage. Small or narrow rooms are better than large ones. On no account look out of the window during an air raid.

### Clear Out Attics

We would once again emphasise the warning that all attics, loft and lumber rooms should be completely cleared. See that access is easy. If an attic or loft has no staircase, keep a pair of steps standing under its trapdoor.

# THE 1940's

*"Lonesome Road"*

| AIR RAID SHELTERS FOR HOME OR BUSINESS *WITHOUT DELAY* H. T. Perryman 139, STAFFORD ROAD, WALLINGTON | **A.R.P.** SANDBAGGING SHELTERS BASEMENT STRENGTHENING H. D. EBBUTT & SON, 12 & 13, Wandle Road, Croydon 1157 | September 22, 1939 |

September 22, 1939

**BLACK-OUT**

TO SHOPKEEPERS & HOUSEHOLDERS
LET FRAZERS YOUR WINDOWS

Phone or call for details:—
**131a, STAFFORD ROAD, WALLINGTON 1436**

Photograph of The Croydon Empire (left). Opened 1896; became the Eros Cinema 1953; Demolished 1960's

Photograph of a Norman Partridge (1945) painting of The Croydon Empire on display in the Ashcroft Theatre, Fairfield Halls (right).

## THE 1940's

During the early years of the war many musicians joined the Forces and a number of bands were formed within them.

Established bandleaders such as Lew Stone, Billy Cotton and Ambrose were joined by George Melachrino and Billy Ternent, whilst Ivy Benson formed her All-Girls Band. The voices of Sam Browne, Denny Dennis and Al Bowlly would help to brighten the gloomy days which lay ahead.

With the ceasing of hostilities in 1945 the country gradually returned to normal.

In that year several star bands played either at the Croydon Empire or the Unique Ballroom, including Joe Loss and His Orchestra - *In The Mood* (February); Harry Roy and His Band (August); Billy Ternent and His Ace Broadcasting Band (September) and Eric Winstone and His Orchestra (October).

But the infectious sounds of jazz could not be contained within the many American cities in which it was being played and, inevitably, it spread beyond those shores to countries eager to welcome the new sound.

In this country a young London pianist, George Webb, listened avidly to the few records which filtered across the Atlantic and in 1942 formed a band to play Traditional jazz. This band was to lead the way in the British post-war revival in splendid style.

Webb had absorbed the sounds of the Oliver/Armstrong two-cornet lead; had listened to the re-creations of the Watters/Scobey partnership, and had decided that within this music, plus the dynamic playing of Louis Armstrong's Hot Five and Lil's Hot Shots, in particular *Drop That Sack* and *Georgia Bo Bo,* lay the only way forward. He gathered around him seven like-minded enthusiasts, to begin a residency in the Red Barn, a public house in Barnehurst, Kent, which would echo the music of the Crescent City.

When the George Webb Dixielanders broadcast on the BBC in 1945 they created tremendous enthusiasm amongst the listening public who found it difficult to believe that the authentic sounds of New Orleans were being made by a group of British musicians.

It is worth noting that the band members on that historic broadcast were :-
George Webb (piano); Owen Bryce and Reg Rigden (cornets); Wally Fawkes (clarinet); Eddie Harvey (trombone); Buddy Vallis (banjo); Art Streatfield (tuba); Roy Wykes (drums).

The road ahead was now clear and where the inspirational George Webb had led the way, others would now follow.

The George Webb Dixielanders in the Decca Recording Studio, Broadhurst Gardens, 5th May, 1945

George Webb, piano; Buddy Vallis, banjo; Bill Bailey, drums; Wally Fawkes, clarinet; Reg Rigden, cornet; Owen Bryce, cornet; Eddie Harvey, trombone; Art Streatfield, sousaphone. Also present were :- Tony Short and James Asman.

In 1943, some 13,000 miles from London, a similar situation was developing. The city of Melbourne was the scene of another classic band formation, coincidentally also led by a pianist, Graeme Bell, who would go on to create the first jazz club in Australia (1946).

Bell had played in and around Melbourne for perhaps ten years until, aided by his trumpet-playing brother Roger, he achieved a great ambition by putting together a band to play New Orleans jazz.

Graeme Bell and his Australian Jazz Band soon became the premier outfit 'Down Under,' and after appearing in a World Youth Festival in Prague, Czechoslovakia, in 1947, the band made the first of several visits to England in 1948.

The Bell band took the country by storm, providing a great stimulus to the English jazz revival started by George Webb. They came to Croydon on a number of occasions, appearing at the Civic Hall and the Croydon Empire.

Graeme Bell and his
Australian Jazz Band
l to r
Pixie Roberts (cl)
Lou Silberiesen (bs)
Roger Bell (tpt)
Ade Monsbourgh (tmb)
Russ Murphy (drms)
Jack Varney (bjo)
Graeme Bell (pno)

Although the German forces occupying Holland in 1944 forbade the playing of jazz, two Dutch amateur musicians, Frans Vink (piano) and Peter Schilperoort (clarinet, saxophones) formed The Hague Orchestra of the Dutch Swing College (DSCB) early in 1945.

Schilperoort had admired American jazz since his student days in 1939, when he had listened to ex-patriot American students playing in the New Orleans style which they had learned from listening to records made by the jazz pioneers back home.

From humble beginnings the DSC flourished and soon after the War ended had formed their own club, regularly broadcasting on radio "Free Holland" and later from Hilversum. They cut their first post-war record in July 1948, *Apex Blues* and *Strange Peach,* and this would be followed by hundreds of recordings as the band became nationally and internationally famous.

Peter Schilperoort, who was knighted by Queen Juliana of the Netherlands in 1970, died on the 17th November, 1990, but the DSC are still going strong, making them Europe's longest playing jazz band.

They have made several visits to Croydon's Fairfield Halls.

# SPOTLIGHTS IN TOWN

Peter Schilperoort

Savoy Cinema

Crystal Palace Football Club : 1946

Back row

l to r

FRED KURZ;
JIMMY GUTHRIE;
JACK LEWIS;
DICK GRAHAM;
ARTHUR HUDGELL;
BILL BASSETT.

Front row

l to r

HOWARD GIRLING;
GLYN LEWIS;
FRED DAWES
(Captain);
BILLY NAYLOR;
BERT ROBSON.

Trumpeter Freddy Randall and clarinettist Bruce Turner circa late 1940's at . . . . .

. . . . . Pembroke Hall, Wellesley Road, Croydon . . . . .

. . . . . later to be occupied by the Pembroke Theatre in the 1960's

APPEARING IN CROYDON . . . . .

5th February, 1945
  "In The Mood" Joe Loss & His Orchestra at the Croydon Empire.

3rd August, 1945
  Harry Roy & His Band at the Croydon Empire.

14th September, 1945
  Billy Ternent & His Ace Broadcasting Band.

12th October, 1945
  Eric Winstone & His Orchestra.

23rd January, 1948
  Ted Heath & His Music with Paul Carpenter.

23rd February, 1948
  Harry Parry & His Sextet.

\* \* \* \* \*

5th March, 1948

Humphrey Lyttelton

In 1946, a new face appeared on the jazz scene when George Webb's Dixielanders lost the services of trumpeter Reg Rigden. To preserve the double-trumpet lead, George brought in a young, relatively unknown trumpet player who would soon become an international star - Humphrey Lyttelton.

"Humph," as he became affectionately known, would remain with the Dixielanders until November 1947, and in 1948 he formed his own band, later making a number of appearances in Croydon. With clarinettist Wally Fawkes, teenaged trombonist Keith Christie, and Lyttelton, the band had an all star front line. During that year, across the water in France, Hugues Panassié and the Hot Club de France founded a Traditional jazz festival in Nice, on the Mediterranean coast. The Lyttelton band appeared there with world famous trumpeter Louis Armstrong, and this set the stage for the town to claim the first international jazz festival.

As the 1940's drew to a close, the gloom which had settled on the country during the grim years of the war gradually began to recede; there did indeed seem to be a few silver linings in those grey clouds.

A jazz revival was sweeping the country and its effects were being felt in the music venues of Croydon. There is little doubt that for the town's jazz lovers the glorious, earthy sounds of Traditional jazz played a part in enabling them to look forward to the 1950's with a great deal of cautious optimism.

# THE 1950's

"Goin' Home"

# 4

THE 1950's

England had not completely thrown off the effects of the War as the country moved into the fifth decade of the century. Rationing still existed for meat and dairy products; many cities had a landscape littered with derelict bomb sites; there were shortages of steel and coal, and by 1951 income tax would be 9/6d in the pound. A little nearer to home, a Crystal Palace Football Club season ticket in the stand at Selhurst Park was £5·5s.

The local music scene continued to be dominated by dance bands, although jazz could be found by those keen enough to search for it.

During 1950 the Advertiser carried many advertisements of interest to the dance fan (Don Scott's dance orchestra, Bensham Lane, West Croydon; Vane's "Ye Old Tyme Dance" at Wallington Public Hall, with Harry Palmer and His Orchestra - admission 3/6d.) whilst Billy Cotton and His Band, with Alan Breeze, appeared at the Croydon Empire.

Maurice Winnick's orchestra had a weekly residency at the Orchid Ballroom, Purley, a venue which would later host the talents of Freddy Randall, Ted Heath and Stanley Black; the famous R.A.F. band, the Squadronaires, appeared there on the 27th November, 1951. But jazz notices began to be seen in the local press and although advertisements such as "RITZ BALLROOM, THORNTON HEATH (ask for The Pond) - Marjorie Verris and Her All Ladies Orchestra, with her Boy Friend "Henry" on drums" were still carried, it is noticeable that prominence was given to a series of jazz concerts at the venerable Croydon Empire. However, to the obvious dismay of the local jazzers, a Shirley Parish Hall grand dance advertisement forbidding jiving also appeared in the Advertiser. It is to be hoped that it was not seen by Graeme Bell, who, with his Australian Jazz Band, pioneered jazz for dancing during his London residency at the Leicester Square Jazz Club, London W1, which was held in a room above the Café de l'Europe in the late 40's.

```
A  GRAND DANCE
at Shirley Parish Hall
DECEMBER 22nd

CHARLES MACK & HIS BAND

NO JIVING ALLOWED
Dancing from 7·30PM. Admission 3/6d
```

Nonetheless, it would be a decade or more before jazz-dance became in any way accepted. There were still many American servicemen staying in this country for some time after the war, and they introduced the local girls to jitterbugging, a style of dance which they had practised back home when the Swing movement of Goodman and Miller became the rave in the States in the late 30's. The ban on allowing American musicians to visit Britain was still in force during their stay here, and so they had no alternative but to listen to British musicians and the style of jazz they played.

After an existence of some thirty years, this ridiculous Musicians Union ruling came to an end in 1954.

## CROYDON EMPIRE (1951)
### SUNDAY OCTOBER 7th 7.30 PM

The famous BBC feature
"JAZZ CLUB"
with Royal Festival Stars

**GRAEME BELL'S AUSTRALIAN JAZZ BAND**

CYRIL SCUTT'S BOOGIE BOYS
LAZY ADE'S LATE HOUR BOYS
NEVA RAPHAELLO
GEORGE MELLY

BOOK NOW AT BOX OFFICE: 5/6ᵈ, 4/6ᵈ, 3/6ᵈ, 1/6ᵈ. CRO.1941.

---

### SUNDAY OCTOBER 28th 7.30 PM

"BAND SHOW"
Featuring Europe's greatest trumpet star
**KENNY BAKER**
& His Famous Band
BOX OFFICE: 4/6ᵈ 3/6ᵈ 3/- 1/-

---

### SUNDAY NOVEMBER 4th 7.30 PM

**HARRY GOLD AND HIS PIECES OF EIGHT**

BERT TAYLOR    JIMMY DAY
LAURIE GOLD BOOGIE BOYS

---

### SUNDAY NOVEMBER 18th 7.30 PM

TITO BURNS' FAMOUS SEXTET
with

TERRY DEVON

# The New Addington Rhythm Club

Shortly after WW II, Frank Getgood and Charles 'Nobby' Clark were the two most important figures involved in the promotion of jazz in Croydon and it is doubtful whether jazz would have ventured South of the River Thames in the way it did had it not been for their dedication to the music.

Their story came to light when on the morning of 21 April 1993, in the Rendezvous Bar of Fairfield Halls, Charles spoke about the early days of jazz in Croydon.

Charles Clark and Brian Anderson were old school friends and both used to listen to the same jazz radio programme presented by Spike Hughes at 5pm on Wednesday evenings. They saved their pocket money to buy the latest jazz records and whenever they could afford it they rushed down to the Croydon record shops to pick up the latest arrivals. Their record collection soon grew quite large and they became members of the New Addington Youth Club.

One day in 1948, whilst travelling on a bus into Croydon, Brian met Frank Getgood who was reading the Melody Maker. They chatted and the conversation ended with a commitment to find a way to liven up the Croydon music scene. They decided that they would form a rhythm club.

The local Community Hall, which was merely a wooden shack, soon became the venue where the newly formed New Addington Rhythm Club held its meetings every other Sunday and at first it was a case of just listening to records. Then a band called Norman Hill's College Boys (NHCB) was formed, and during the 1951 Festival of Great Britain it was decided to hold a concert in the Civic Hall, Crown Hill, Croydon. The three bands which took part were the NHCB, Mike Daniels' Delta Jazzmen and Mick Mulligan's Magnolia Jazz Band, with vocalist George Melly. It was a great beginning to a challenging venture which laid claim to Croydon being the first town in England to hold a Traditional Jazz Festival with the formation of a new club.

# The Croydon Jazz Club

In addition to the New Addington Rhythm Club the Croydon Jazz Club was formed in 1949. Concerts were held in the Pembroke Hall, Wellesley Road, but, alas, they were not to be a great success.

In 1952 the Club, now well established, moved to the Gun Tavern in Church Street, Croydon. There were a lot of arguments for and against jazz but fortunately all were eventually resolved in its favour.

"Jazz, it is needless to say, will remain a creation for the industrious and a dissipator of energy for the frivolous, a tonic for the strong and a passion for the weak," said one. "It takes talent and practice to play jazz," said another.

Still at The Gun during the time of the floods on the East Coast of England in the early fifties, Charles Clark and Frank Getgood spoke to Winifred Attwell, who was then appearing at the Croydon Empire. They asked her if she would join them, with a jazz group, as they wanted to put on a concert for the flood victims, and she was only too delighted to take part. As a result it turned out to be a great evening of brilliant Boogie Woogie piano. Sadly, Mike Daniels, who was to have appeared at the concert, lost his way to Croydon in the thick fog. In those days, when smoke belched out of every chimney pot on every house, the fogs following a Guy Fawkes night during the month of November were devastating.

There began to be troubled times at The Gun as the manageress did not take too kindly to jazz, with too many people gathering in the garden. The Club was soon on the move again, this time to the Volunteer pub in Cairo Road. The music was played in a tiny, smoked-filled room which had a wonderful atmosphere, but here, in contrast to the Pembroke Hall, the place became too small for the growing number of jazz followers. The next move was to the Unique Ballroom in Bridge Place, just off St James's Road. The Ballroom was owned by a lady who did not like any jiving on her beautiful dance floor, and so yet again the Club made another move, to the Star Hotel in West Croydon, where it remained for 15 years until it closed its doors in 1968 with a farewell concert by the Ken Colyer Band.

Mike Daniels was the resident band at the Star Hotel for many years and many other bands also appeared there, including Cy Laurie, Max Collie, Eric Silk, Ken Colyer, Graham Stewart with Alan Elsdon, the Red Onions from Australia, Humphrey Lyttelton, Charlie Galbraith and Alex Welsh. The Clark-Getgood team also tried modern jazz, rhythm & blues and gospel but remained loyal to Traditional. Many unknowns appeared on the stage at interval times and went on to become famous, including Manfred Mann, Long John Baldrey and Joanne Kelly.

But such was the fervour for New Orleans, Dixieland and Traditional jazz in those days that when Ken Colyer returned from the Crescent City his dedication to the music was so great that he was reported as saying, "Where Bunk Johnson played a wrong note in a number, I will play that wrong note."

Following the trend started by Graeme Bell, the Clark-Getgood partnership also visited youth clubs to stage jazz for dancing.

Sadly, Frank Getgood died on the 4th of October, 1974.

The Wilton Arms, (Re-named Muddy Waters in 1994)
High Street, Thornton Heath

The Unique Ballroom is today part of a garage and car showroom complex in St James's Road, West Croydon. It served Croydon well in the field of Swing band entertainment and still retains its ornate lighting and spring inlaid dance floor in remembrance of its glory days.

Traditional jazz did get a foot in its doors, albeit only for a short spell.

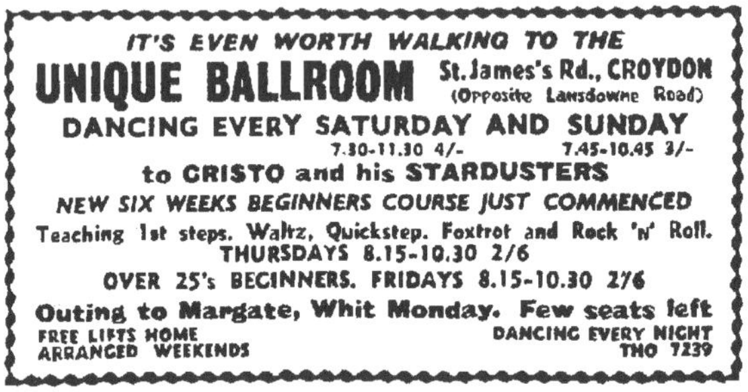

The Fox and Hounds, formerly the Derby Arms, North End, Croydon

## THE NEW ADDINGTON RHYTHM CLUB'S FIRST CIVIC HALL CONCERT

**THE CIVIC HALL,
CROWN HILL,
CROYDON.**

THE NEW ADDINGTON RHYTHM CLUB

present their

**FESTIVAL JAZZ
CONCERT.**

SATURDAY, JUNE 2nd, 1951.

MICK MULLIGAN and his
MAGNOLIA JAZZ BAND with
GEORGE MELLY.

MIKE DANIELS' DELTA JAZZMEN
with PHYLISS KEYES.

NORMAN HILL'S COLLEGE BOYS
with DIGGIE WOOD and
COLIN THOMPSON.

COMPERE : OWEN BRYCE

Programme............6 d.

---

If you have enjoyed the music this evening why not come along to the NEW ADDINGTON RHYTHM CLUB to-morrow night and fortnightly? There is plenty of room for dancing.

Sessions are held at the COMMUNITY CENTRE NEW ADDINGTON. 130 Bus from EAST CROYDON STATION will take you to the door.
Members 2/-, Guests 2/6.

Resident band: Norman Hill's College Boys. Sessions start at 7.30pm.
June meetings : 3rd & 17th. July 1st, 15th & 29th.

National Federations of Jazz Organisations (Hon. Presedent Marquis of Donegal) . Full particulars from N.F.J.O. Secretary James Asman, 18, Timbercroft Lane, Plumstead, S.E.18.

Tickets for the N.F.J.O. Festival Jazz Concerts on July 14th & 16th at the South Bank Concert Hall can be purchased through the New Addington Rhythm Club at to-morrow night's meeting.

Printed by T. Billington New Addington

## 1951

### Programme

The Bands' programme will be selected from the undermentioned numbers.

**NORMAN HILL'S COLLEGE BOYS.**
Clarinet Marmalade, Fidgety Feet, Buddy Bolden's Blues, China Boy Washington & Lee Swing, Weary Blues, Georgia Cake Walk, Wang Wang Blues, Summer Time, Sugar Walks Down the Street, Revolutionary Blues, Bessie's Blues, Strange Blues, Just a Closer Walk.

**MIKE DANIELS, DELTA JAZZMEN.**
Apex Blues, Bucket got a Hole in it, Mahogany Hall Stomp, Basin Street Blues, Panama, Nobody knows the way I feel this morning, Fish Face, Dixie, Strutting with some Barbecue, South, King Size Papa, Tar Paper Stomp, Big Butter and Egg Man, Decent Woman, Little Lawrance, Cater Street Rag. Tishomingo Blues, Jet Black Blues, Get Out of Here and Go on Home.

**MICK MULLICAN'S MAGNOLIA JAZZ BAND.**
Do What Ory say, Graveyard Words, Original Jelly Roll Blues, Snake Rag, Sunset Cafe Stomp, Trouble in Mind, Nobody But My Baby, Georgia Bo Bo, The Rock Island Line, Froggie Moore, Hotter than That, Kitchen Man, Red Hot Poker Rag, Black and Blue, Of all the Wrongs, Judge, Jelly Roll, 1919 Rag.

|  |  |
|---|---|
| 7.30 | NORMAN HILL'S COLLEGE BOYS with Diggie Wood & Colin Thompson. |
| 8.10 | MIKE DANIELS' DELTA JAZZMEN with Phyllis Keyes. |
| 8.35 | INTERVAL |
| 8.45 | MICK MULLIGAN'S MAGNOLIA JAZZ BAND with George Melly |
| 9.15 | MIKE DANIEL'S DELTA JAZZMEN |
| 9.45 | MICK MULLIGAN'S MAGNOLIA JAZZ BAND |
| 10.15 | GRAND FINALE |

Sunday August 5th - Saturday August 11th

Addington Community Association

presents FESTIVAL WEEK

Further details at Rhythm Club meetings

Mike Daniels' Delta Jazzmen with Beryl Bryden . . . . .

. . . . . en route to the Civic Hall from West Croydon

Charles "Nobby" Clark, standing; Mike Daniels, trumpet; Charles Connor, clarinet; Bill Cotton, banjo; Fred Hunt, piano; Beryl Bryden, vocals; Red Townsend, drums. Unknown, Bass and Trombone.

Photographs - Croydon Times, 7th June, 1952 . . . . .

CIVIC HALL, CROYDON.

FRIDAY, September 19th.

New Addington Rhythm Club
presents

Jazz Concert

HUMPHREY
LYTTELTON
AND HIS BAND
with guest singer NEVA RAPHAELLO

Mike Collier
and his Band

*Programme 6d.*

---

CIVIC HALL, North End, CROYDON.

NEXT ALL STAR CONCERT WILL BE HELD ON

Sunday, October 12th 7.0p.m.

★Featuring ★ FIVE STAR ★ Attractions★

MIKE DANIELS' and his band
CHARLIE GALBRAITH'S jazzmen
GRAHAM STEWART'S jazzband
CYRIL SCUTT'S Boogie-woogie trio
BERYL BRYDEN (guest vocalist)

TICKETS:- 5/- 4/- 3/- 2/-
TICKETS OBTAINABLE FROM THE CIVIC HALL
AS FROM THIS EVENING.

GREAT NEWS!
CROYDON JAZZ CLUB
RE-OPENS WEDNESDAY SEPTEMBER 24th.
7.45p.m. AT THE "GUN TAVERN" CHURCH
STREET. RESIDENT BAND MIKE DANIELS'
DELTA JAZZMEN Meetings every WEDNESDAY
7.45-10.30p.m.

1952

## Programme

(To be selected from the following, but is subject to alteration).

PERSONNEL:-
HUMPHREY LYTTELTON (Trumpet and Clarinet), WALLY FAWKES (Clarinet), JOHNNY PARKER (Piano), FREDDY LEGON (Guitar and Banjo). GEORGE HOPKINSON (Drums). MICKY ASMAN (Bass). NEVA RAPHAELLO (Vocals).

| | |
|---|---|
| Brownskin Mama | London Blues |
| Buddy's Habits | St. Louis Blues |
| Ce mossieu qui parle | Snag It |
| Doctor Blues | Straight from the Wood |
| Down in Honky Tonk Town | Get it |
| L'annee passe | Sweet Substitute |
| Big Cat Little Cat | The Onions |
| Cake walking Babies | Tia Juana |
| 1919 Rag | Get out of here and go on home |
| Wa Wa Wa | Trog's Blues |

In accordance with the requirements of the Council.
5. All entrances shall be available as exits.
12. Persons must not be permitted to sit or stand in any gangway.
20. All exit and entrance doors must be thrown open for the use of the audience at the end of each performance.

PERSONNEL:-
MIKE COLLIER (Trombone). PETE HULL (Clarinet and alto-sax), JOHNNY BERRY (Piano), VIC FORINO (Drums), GERRY SALISBURY (Trumpet), ERIC WILSON (Bass). BILL ROWLANDS (Guitar), JO LENOARD (Vocals).

| | |
|---|---|
| Washington and Lee Swing | Deed I Do |
| Sweet Georgia Brown | Changes |
| Lady be Good | Shine |
| Who's Sorry Now | One hour |
| Someday Sweetheart | Dr. Jazz |
| I can't give you anything but love. | |

New Addington Rhythm Club
Community Centre, New Addington.

Sunday, Sep. 21st. 7.30--10.30p.m.

Mike Collier and his Jazzmen
Graham Stewart and his Band

**MICK MULLIGAN'S MAGNOLIA JAZZ BAND**

Mick Mulligan (trumpet)
Bob Dawbarn (trombone)
Johnny Parker (piano)
Pete Hull (clarinet)
Johnny Lavender (banjo)
Bill Cotton (banjo)
Norman Dodsworth (drums)
Owen Maddock (tuba)

With the Croydon Empire now having joined the Civic Hall in staging regular jazz shows, plus the impetus provided by the New Addington and Croydon Jazz Clubs, the town was now well and truly on the jazz map.

Mike Daniels' Delta Jazzmen had a residency at the Gun Tavern and many well-known bands played at venues in the town.

Croydon's jazz followers were entertained by the talents of bands such as Alex Welsh, Mick Mulligan, Eric Silk and Freddy Randall; Dave Carey, who ran the splendid "Swing Shop" in Streatham, was also a visitor.

From a jazz point of view, this was indeed boom time.

January 1958

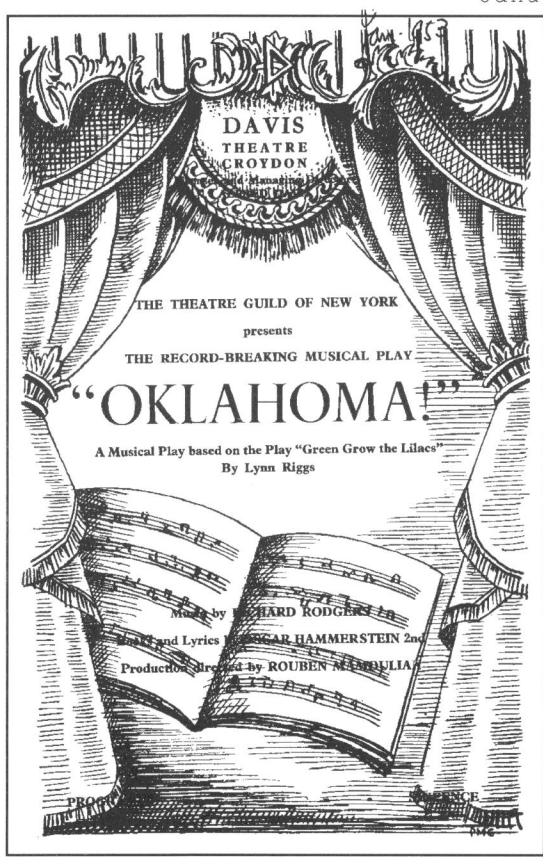

DAVIS THEATRE - CROYDON
Licensee and Managing Director: ALFRED DAVIS

*The Cast in order of their appearance:*

| | |
|---|---|
| Aunt Eller | JENNIE GREGSON |
| Curly | JOHN ELLIOTT |
| Laurey | BARBARA ANN RODGERS |
| Slim | ROGER SINCLAIR |
| Ike Skidmore | GLENN MARTEN |
| Will Parker | GORDON HUMPHRIS |
| Jud Fry | JACK RAINER |
| Ado Annie Carnes | BILLIE LOVE |
| Ali Hakim | HARRY ROSS |
| Gertie Cummings | LAURA HEDLEY |
| Ellen | JOAN STEER |
| Kate | MONICA BRENT |
| Sylvie | DIANA FIELD |
| Armina | JOYCE MORETON |
| Terry | VALERIE THOMAS |
| Jess | ALEXANDER MORROW |
| Aggie "Pigtails" | GEORGINA ROURKE |
| Andrew Carnes | RICHARD DUNN |
| Cord Elam | ANTHONY COPPOCK |
| Chalmers | FRED DIXON |
| Joe | CHARLES HANDLEY |
| Sam | HAROLD FLETCHER |
| Laurey | OENONE TALBOT |
| Curly (In the Ballet) | TONI REPETSKI |
| Jud | TONY STEEDMAN |

*Singers:* ROGER SINCLAIR, HAROLD FLETCHER, FRED DIXON, JOHNSON ASHLEY, DOUGLAS PEARSON, CHARLES HANDLEY, MONICA BRENT, JOAN STEER, JOYCE MORETON, VALERIE THOMAS, MURIEL ROYSTON, MARJORIE NIGHTINGALE, EILEEN FRENCH.

*Dancers:* TONY DALLMAN, ALEXANDER MORROW, GEOFFREY STRONG, MAURICE STEWART, LAWRENCE HAIG, DAVID LATOFF, GEORGINA ROURKE, DIANA FIELD, YVONNE DALMAIN, RITA KINGSLEY, JOAN ROCHELLE, ANNE ROBERTS, MARGARET WILSH, PHILUMINA SEPHTON, PAT DOWNHAM, ANN TAYLOR, ELIZABETH TAYLOR.

STAGE AND SCREEN PRESENTATIONS AT THE DAVIS THEATRE

June 1953

### Ken Colyer

During the 1950's the paths of two major names in British jazz were to cross, and Croydon would benefit by their frequent visits to the town.

Ken Colyer had been a founder-member of the Crane River Jazz Band, which included a young clarinettist, Monty Sunshine. This band played classic style New Orleans jazz, but, in his quest always for perfection, Colyer decided to visit the Crescent City in 1953 to hear the music first hand.

The story of his New Orleans adventure is now legendary . . . . . joined the Merchant Navy . . . . . jumped ship in Mobile, Alabama . . . . . bus to New Orleans . . . . . sat in with many Negro veterans, including George Lewis . . . . . briefly imprisoned before deportation back to England . . . . .

Upon returning to London, Ken found that another bandleader who was beginning to attract attention, trombonist Chris Barber, had liaised with Monty Sunshine in forming a new band, which was now ready for him to lead. With Tony "Lonnie" Donegan on banjo, Jim Bray on bass and Ron Bowden on drums, Ken Colyer's Jazzmen proved to be one of the best Traditional jazz bands of the period and Croydonians were indeed fortunate that they made a number of visits to their town.

Unfortunately, however, the life of this fine band was to be short lived. Differences of opinion between Ken and the others led to the band breaking up early in 1954, with Barber taking over the leadership and Pat Halcox occupying the trumpet chair. However, this event proved to be a significant turning point in the history of British jazz.

Chris Barber

The Chris Barber band went from strength to strength, whilst Ken Colyer formed another group which would achieve great success, with a long lasting, dedicated following - Bernard "Acker" Bilk (clarinet); Eddie O'Donnell (trombone); William "Diz" Disley (banjo); Dick Smith (bass) and Stan Greig (drums).

With many changes in personnel over the years, the Barber and Colyer bands are still playing superb jazz, the latter under the auspices of the Ken Colyer Trust - formed to perpetuate the memory of "The Guv'nor."

## Denny Holloway remembers the old times.

I must be getting old. On a gig recently, we were playing jazz at a wedding, and there was time for a few beers.

When you play jazz for a wedding there is generally time for lots of beers. I blame the bride's mother. She usually books the band and in a final act of spite, she chooses jazz, knowing that her future son-in-law is an avid U2 fan.

Since the rest of the party are also U2 fans, the jazz band is kept under wraps until the last half hour, by which time everyone thinks they're having fun and don't care anyway.

During such a break we musicians got down to the normal discussion of jazz and bands we had played with.

The trombone player, hearing that I originated from Croydon, asked me if I remembered The Star at Broad Green.

I marvelled at the question. Firstly, his speech and face were quite blurred by that time and it was wondrous that he managed to phrase it at all. And secondly I was amazed that someone else shared the memories of that wonderful outpost of jazz after so long a time.

I remember The Star as if it was 1950. Run by a real jazz enthusiast called Frank Getgood. It was the home of the Croydon Jazz Club and the prime venue for Trad jazz for some time.

Regular bands appearing on the Friday sessions were Mike Daniels' Delta Jazzmen, Mick Mulligan with George Melly, Graham Stewart, Alan Elsdon, and even a young Humph made the odd appearance.

This was a time before the Lord Napier was presenting jazz. Faces like Sandy Brown, Dave Keir and Acker would show up on the odd occasion, adding to the excitement for us erstwhile jazz musicians.

Frank Getgood also opened the New Addington Jazz Club for a short time, held in a scout hall in that area, and there I had the privilege to hear George Melly sing *Rock Island Line*, a song which had been his speciality long before Lonnie (Donegan) had a hit with it.

A regular visitor was a young trombonist who would plead to be allowed to sit in. The bands were always unwilling to agree and they were justified in their lack of confidence. He was awful.

Perseverance paid off, however, and now, forty odd years on, Chris Barber continues to play delightful trombone while some who dared to mock still can't even spell trombone, let alone play one.

The Star was mainly Trad. The Gun Tavern in Church Street, Croydon, tried a bit of everything; Trad, Modern - you name it, we tried to play it. Dick Charlesworth cut his musical teeth in that back room behind the Gun prior to the commercially successful *City Gents*.

Local jazzers learned their craft and the mixture of styles opened new avenues for exploration.

The Trad uniform was making us itch so we traded the duffle coat for a smart drape jacket, stopped calling everybody "Dad" and called them "Man" instead. And we were transformed into Modern Jazz fans.

At the time the rising trumpet star was Clifford Brown. Every horn blower wanted to play like him, but few could.

One memorable occasion at The Gun featured Bert Courtley, with his wife Kathy Stobart on tenor sax. On that occasion, Bert played as close to Clifford Brown as anyone could. I stayed silent for a while and have been a committed Mainstreamer ever since.

Around the same time, the old Davis Theatre in Croydon High Street was a popular venue for visiting big bands.

Am I alone in remembering the Johnny Dankworth Seven with one of the first appearances of Cleo Laine? Or Louis Armstrong during that amazing European tour with Jack Teagarden? Or Nat King Cole with Count Basie?

You couldn't buy that for a £1,000 today, but then it cost a mere half-crown. That's 12 pence to you Modernists!

It goes back further. In 1947 there was the Ted Heath Band every Wednesday at the Croydon Palais, where my trumpet playing ambitions were fired by a young Kenny Baker.

Typical of our jazz fraternity, Kenny took the time to encourage perseverance on my part. I suppose his trouble could not have been in vain - I'm still playing the thing.

In about 1953 Modern jazz seemed to take ascendancy over Trad. The Gun, for a while, became the main venue and The Star featured Modern on Wednesday nights with a regular rhythm section, relying on a host of visiting musicians to fill the front line.

Here I first saw Jimmy Deuchar and Derek Humble who were part of the Tubby Hayes Band. Now, that was a band. Tubby was the in-face in the British jazz scene and it was sheer heaven to see the whole band later at the Orchid Ballroom in Purley.

Les Condon, Jimmy Deuchar, Jackie Sharp and Benny Green were in that band.

The Crooked Billet at Penge had Tuesday sessions run by pianist Don Hunt, now better known as musical director for Bruce Forsyth. In Sydenham, Mac McKrell presented his quintet, with Ron Johnson on trumpet, at the Fox and Hounds.

Now and again there was a special performance of the Bell/Holloway Big Nine - a serious attempt at putting some form of discipline into our playing. It worked - but only just.

At the Park Lane ballroom in Central Croydon, the proprietor Ed Waller was always willing to give a lift to local musicians.

He was the first, for instance, to feature skiffle when a local group, "Pete Stewart," regularly played there. An old friend, Jim Weller, had a band there for a while, with Geoff Hoare on trombone. High Society Jazzmen, Monty Sunshine, Denny Holloway's Jazzmen - we all got a shot at it.

Unlike today, jazz gigs were plentiful then. With foresight we could have all retired rich. But that is not the nature of the animal. It was fun, though, and I look forward to returning one day.

When I left Croydon, the place of my birth and upbringing, to turn professional, it was a big wrench.

In and around Croydon during the early 50's

### EMPRESS BRIXTON (TEL BRI 2201) 6.30 & 8.45
WEEK COMMENCING MONDAY, 18th JANUARY

**WAKEY! WAKEY! ...**

# BILLY COTTON
★ AND HIS BAND ★
with ALAN BREEZE, DOREEN STEPHENS & CLEM BERNARD
AND HUGE SUPPORTING COMPANY

JANUARY 25th    MAX MILLER

---

### THE ORCHID BALLROOM
PURLEY    UPLands 1174/5
DANCING NIGHTLY (except Monday) 7.30—11.15
SUNDAY CLUB 7.30—11.00
Sunday Afternoon Instructional Tea Dance 3—5.30 p.m.
EVERY WEDNESDAY "DANCERS PARADISE"
Wednesday 20th, Third Heat (Quickstep)
Four Dance Open Amateur Competition
Olde Tyme Thursday Evening and Saturday Afternoon
RESIDENT M.C.s: MR. & MRS. CHAS. CRATHORN

TUESDAY, 26th - GUEST BAND - VIC LEWIS
Occasional Licences applied for
LES AYLING AND HIS ORCHESTRA

### GRANDISON BALLROOM
Admission 3/6    NORBURY    Licensed Bar

**POPULAR SATURDAY DANCES**
CONTINUOUS DANCING 7.30 to 11.30 p.m.
SUNDAY CLUB - - - 7.30 to 11 p.m. 2/6
MONDAY, BEGINNERS' BALLROOM, 7.30 to 9 p.m. 3/-
MONDAY, Intermediate Ballroom, 9 to 10.30 p.m. 3/-
THURSDAY, Latin American class, 8 to 10.30 p.m. 3/-

---

### GREYHOUND HOTEL
CROYDON
Dancing from 7.45 p.m. to 11.45 p.m.
BERT JOHNSON
AND HIS METRO BAND
Tickets 5/-
Obtainable at Croydon Police Station
Don't be disappointed. Get them beforehand

---

### GUITARS
We have a large stock of
SPANISH, CELLO, SKIFFLE,
CUTAWAYS, ELECTRIC

Wonderful new
AMPLIFIER from 10½ gns.
H.P. Terms arranged
GREAT NEW
BROADWAY DRUM KIT
In RED GLITTER For Only
£25-9-6

### POTTER'S MUSIC SHOP
7, South End, CROYDON
CROYDON 7961

---

### KENNARDS, CROYDON

Blue Room Orpheans Orchestra
M.C.: BILLY HEARN

30 SPOT PRIZES Including Nylons, etc.

Admission 3/6    Buffet

---

DAVE CAREY offers you 20 years'
Jazz Experience at

# THE SWING SHOP
1B MITCHAM LANE, STREATHAM, S.W.16

Where you will find the finest stocks in Great Britain of
**JAZZ RECORDS, BOOKS and PHOTOGRAPHS**
Also a wide range of Gramophone and Musical Instrument
Accessories etc. etc.

---

### PAYNE'S
MUSIC SHOP
and Recording Studio
(Prop. Pete Payne)

**DELTA RECORDS**

Mike Daniels - Mick Gill
Roy Vaughan - Rene Franc
John Haim - Joan Roberts

Your favourite Jazzmen on Delta
label 9/- each from all Jazz Clubs
and Record Shops, or direct (6d post)

**POSTAL SERVICE**

Foreign discs, H.M.V., H.M.V. Special
List, Parlo's, Delta, Esquire, Tempo,
Hard to get Brunswick and Decca's

213 Bromley Road
Catford, London, S.E.6
Hither Green 3134

## SWING MISCELLANY
### by 'Offbeat'
*The latest news about people and places concerned with swing music in Croydon*

Congratulations to The Hot Rods of Thornton Heath for winning two rounds of the National Skiffle Competition organised by the "Daily Sketch." They were runaway winners at the Savoy, Croydon, in the local finals, despite such strong opposition as that from The Nomads, of Croydon. At the recent district finals, at Bexleyheath, they won again and are now all set for the regional finals at Kingston on 28th of March.

The Hot Rods are seven-strong and have been playing together for five months. They are led by 17 year old Rodney Lyward, and this is their first big success.

Congratulations also to The Cellarmen - winners of a skiffle competition organised by J. Hadad Promotions at the Civic Hall, Croydon, recently. Their prize was five guineas and a recording test.

Incidentally, the system of audience applause applied to skiffle contests, as a guide, is invaluable; as a final judge it can be grossly unfair. While appreciating the difficulties of arranging for accurate skiffle judgment, I do submit that an audience can never be the final judge, for many reasons.

The system of volume of applause is wide open to well-intentioned cheating. Skifflers should insist on a fairer deal before entering competitions.

Hip-swinging Buddy Holly and the Crickets led the bill at the Davis rock 'n' roll concert last week. A thoroughly bad mannered section of the audience did justice to an incongruous supporting team, which included Gary Miller and Ronnie Keene and his Orchestra - billed as Britain's new musical sensation.

It's billing like this that gets the audience mad. The bad manners, justified as they may have been at times, were certainly not called for during Mr. Holly's boldly professional performance - a lusty, swinging, uplifting display of "rock," which I thoroughly enjoyed. It is, however, a sad commentary on any audience when the artists feel it necessary to refer to them as "jackasses" and "idiots."

Forthcoming entertainers at Croydon include Mario Lanza, Paul Anka, the blind singer Al Hibbler, with the Ted Heath Orchestra, and (as forecast in this column a month ago) "Jazz at the Philharmonic." This splendid stage show takes place at the Davis Theatre on 11th May. Ella Fitzgerald will be there.

Croydon Jazz Club members will be interested to see the results of their day's filming at Twickenham in the "Six Five Special," to be released shortly. At a recent private showing, I saw several of them jiving frantically to the music of Don Lang and company.

\* \* \* \* \*

Inevitably jive has just gained another victory over ballroom dancing. The well-known Park Lane Ballroom has just ended its Saturday ballroom dancing and taken up "Jazz Saturday" nights.

At the first session last week, Ian Bell and his Jazzband attracted more than 200 people. The average attendance for a ballroom night was 80.

"We have changed our Saturday policy owing to lack of support," says Mr Ed Waller, the manager. "There is a decline in ballroom dancing. Jiving gets the people in." Jiving certainly does. Both Mr Waller and Mr Frank Getgood (of the Croydon Jazz Club) are aware of the potential that jazz offers. Now, in Croydon, we have jazz on Friday, Saturday and Sunday. The new jazz night on Saturday stimulates the mild "jazz war" between the town's leading promoters.

"There is already enough jazz in Croydon," says Mr Getgood. "Many of our dancers do not come from Croydon at all," says Mr Waller.

Broad Green seems to like the Hot Rods skiffle group. After winning their heat in a national skiffle contest at the Savoy Cinema, this entertaining young Thornton Heath group has returned to the cinema this week for a series of nightly performances. I understand that they have also entered for the Croydon Jazz Club skiffle competition, to be held at the end of next month.

Josephine Stahl, the 16 year old Norbury vocalist, has just completed her recording test for Columbia and is anxiously awaiting the result. Her manager arranged for her to cut a long-playing record with a private company last week. He played the record at the Park Lane Ballroom on Saturday - and received six immediate orders for it. At £2 a time, this is surely a remarkable pointer to Miss Stahl's ultimate success. The ever-popular "Riverboat Shuffle, organised by the Croydon Jazz Club, will take place this year on Saturday, 13 July. The trip will be from Westminster to Hampton Court, where a special jazz session will be held at the Thames Hotel there.

Terry Lightfoot's Jazz Band and Mike Daniels and the Delta Jazzmen will be playing.

The new Modern Club at the Star Hotel, Broad Green, is progressing well, and Denny Holloway's brand of jazz is attracting audiences that increase by about 20 each week. Croydon Advertiser - 1958.

## 1958

CROYDON JAZZ CLUB
present

# CHRIS BARBER'S JAZZ BAND

with

OTTILIE PATTERSON :: MONTY SUNSHINE TRIO

| CIVIC HALL | SUNDAY |
| CROYDON | MARCH 2nd, 1958 |

SOUVENIR PROGRAMME — SIXPENCE

---

## Programme

*Items will be selected from the following:*

### Chris Barber's Jazz Band

*Personnel:* Chris Barber (trombone); Monty Sunshine (clarinet); Pat Halcox (trumpet); Eddie Smith (banjo); Graham Burbidge (drums); Dick Smith (bass).

A Pound of Blues
Big House Blues
Bobby Shaftoe
Bourbon St. Parade
Bye and Bye
Climax Rag
Deep Bayou Blues
Doctor Jazz
Double Check Stomp
Fidgety Feet
High Society
Ice Cream
It's Tight Like That
I Can't Escape from You
Lawd, You Sure Been Good To Me
Mama Don't Allow

Market Street Stomp
Maryland, My Maryland
Oh Didn't He Ramble
Ole Man Mose
Olga
Panama Rag
Rent Party Blues
Rockin' in Rhythm
Saratoga Swing
The Martinique
Tiger Rag
Weary Blues
Willie The Weeper
Whistlin' Rufus
Yama Yama Man
Yes Lord I'm Crippled

### OTTILIE PATTERSON

Careless Love
Doctor Clayton's Blues
Beale Street Blues
Good Time Tonight

I Love My Baby
K. C. Rider
Lonesome Road
Stop Now, It's Praying Time

### PAT HALCOX (trumpet solos)

Blue Turning Grey Over You

You Took Advantage of Me
Shine

### MONTY SUNSHINE TRIO

Burgundy Street Blues
Hush a Bye
St. Philip Street Breakdown

The Old Rugged Cross
Wild Cat Blues
When You and I Were Young, Maggie

### CHRIS BARBER (Solos)

Chinatown, my Chinatown

Sweet Georgia Brown
Sweet Sue

*Band introduced by* FRANK GETGOOD

---

## CHRIS BARBER and HIS BAND

The phenomenal rise to fame of the Chris Barber Band has surely been one of the most astonishing things in the whole history of British jazz music. Only quite a short time ago the band, outside the better jazz clubs, was virtually unknown, but Chris Barber and his Band are now almost a household word.

There is, of course, a reason for this popularity. This band play a relaxed, smooth sounding type of jazz which is easy to listen to, entertaining, and, moreover, good to dance to.

The leader himself is somewhat of a perfectionist. His early days, the musical ones that is, were spent gigging around gaining invaluable experience with most of the better traditionalist jazz bands. Chris, no doubt, liked what he heard and what he played, but he always felt during this embryo period that this type of jazz should be better presented and that it would do no harm if better musicianship were added to the already evident enthusiasm.

His approach to the problem was in no way slapdash. Vacating his secure, but unjazzlike job with an insurance company, he enrolled at the Guildhall School of Music where he studied trombone and bass for three years to improve his musicianship. Thus fortified musically, and no doubt spiritually, his next step was to find some good musicians to work with him. Barber had played for a time with Ken Colyer's Jazzmen and it was from this band that he enlisted Monty Sunshine, a clarinettist whose methods he had always held in the highest regard.

It is interesting to note that Barber's initial band was the first full time professional traditional band to be formed in this country. Much of their success was, and still is, due to Barber's insistence on a 'book' that was different. The old jazz standards have never been ignored but the band manage to include in every programme a number of fine old jazz tunes, such as those composed by Duke Ellington, suitably arranged to suit the Barber instrumentation. The result is always something fresh and new, progress—in fact—within the traditional framework.

Another reason for the band's popularity has been the singing of Ottilie Patterson. Ottilie, a young girl of Irish-Latvian parentage, has a rare feeling for the blues and can put over a jazz song with rare zest and power. Her vocal production has improved immensely since she first joined the band, and like the rest of the group she has always shown great keenness to better their music which is the keystone of the Barber Band's success. Rehearsal and attention to detail have enabled the band to produce that clean internal balance and finely integrated ensemble work which is their trade mark. Listen to this band and it at once becomes apparent that a programme such as this is the result of much preparation and careful planning. The easy stage manner speaks of relaxation—the good musicianship is the result of hard work.

### Forthcoming Concerts at the Civic Hall

FRIDAY, MAY 23rd

**CHRIS BARBER'S JAZZ BAND**
(Tickets on Sale APRIL 11th)

SATURDAY, MAY 31st

**CROYDON TIMES**

**SURREY SKIFFLE CHAMPIONSHIPS**

ALL SEATS BOOKABLE

from Box Office, Civic Hall; or from Potter's Music Shop, 7 South End, South Croydon.

---

COME ALONG AND JOIN SURREY'S OLDEST AND FINEST JAZZ CLUB

## CROYDON JAZZ CLUB

EVERY FRIDAY, 8.0 – 11.0 p.m.

EVERY SUNDAY, 7.30 – 10.30 p.m.

### Star Hotel, London Rd., West Croydon

(opposite Savoy Cinema)

| Sun. | March | 2 | ... | SONNY MORRIS JAZZMEN. |
| Fri. | ,, | 7 | ... | ALEC WELSH DIXIELANDERS. |
| Sun. | ,, | 9 | ... | TERRY LIGHTFOOT'S JAZZMEN (Direct from Television's Six-Five Special on Saturday, March 8th) |
| Fri. | ,, | 14 | ... | TERRY LIGHTFOOT'S JAZZMEN. |
| Sun. | ,, | 16 | ... | Club Closed To-night only. |
| Fri. | ,, | 21 | ... | Mr. ACKER BILK'S JAZZMEN. |
| Sun. | ,, | 23 | ... | SONNY MORRIS JAZZMEN. |
| Fri. | ,, | 28 | ... | MIKE DANIELS DELTA JAZZMEN. |
| Sun. | ,, | 30 | ... | RIVER CITY JAZZMEN. |

ADMISSION: Members 3/- Guests 4/-
Life Membership 2/-

*JOIN AT OUR NEXT CLUB MEETING*

Holders of this Programme at tonights 6 p.m. performance will be admitted to this evening's session at the Croydon Jazz Club at a special rate of 2/-.

If you wish to be kept informed of future activities promoted by the Croydon Jazz Club, send your name to FRANK GETGOOD, 2 Gatestone Court, Central Hill, S.E.19.

## Reminiscing With Mike Pointon

Blue Crow Jazzmen
Lantern Hall
Croydon c.1957

l to r
Pete Crowcombe
George Grute
Mike Stanley
Mike Pointon
Unknown
Bill Stagg

Although born in Edmonton, North London, in 1941, Mike Pointon spent much of his early years living in Thornton Heath and he attended Elmwood School in Hackbridge. Together with classmate Bill Stagg, Mike listened to the records of Ken Colyer and Chris Barber before attending his first ever live concert in 1956, at Croydon's Civic Hall, where the Colyer band was appearing with the Terry Lightfoot Jazzmen.

The desire to play an instrument soon became ingrained in Mike and he took up the invitation of John Latus, another school friend who was learning to play the trumpet, to join a group including Dick Morrissey (clarinet), who were forming a workshop for aspiring musicians at Wallington, Surrey. The Skiffle craze was beginning to emerge at this time and Mike Pointon "messed around" on washboard and tea-chest bass as well as attempting to teach himself play a trumpet which John Latus had lent him.

Regular Friday visits were made to the Star Hotel, where the resident band was the River City Jazzmen whose clarinettist, Douggie Richford, lived near Mike.

Being an avid follower of the Ken Colyer band, when his musical dabblings turned to the trombone, Mike found a "role model" in Ken's trombonist, Mac Duncan. The urge to purchase a trombone was strong and he eventually persuaded his parents to invest in a second-hand instrument. Frequent visits were made to Dave Carey's Swing Shop in Streatham and Potter's Music Shop in Croydon to look for records by such favourite trombonists as Kid Ory, Honoré Dutrey and Roy Palmer, and from listening to these recordings Mike began to have an idea of the sounds that he would like to hear made by a few of his friends with whom he was thinking of forming a jazz band. The Addiscombe Music Shop was another source for Mike's endless search for records.

Mike had met clarinettist Pete Crowcombe and Mike Stanley (trumpet) at the Star Hotel, and with Bill Stagg (banjo) and George Grute (bass) from Elmwood School, the Blue Crow Jazzmen were formed. An invaluable influence on the young would-be jazzmen during this period was 'Mrs M' who lived near the school. She introduced them to the recordings of George Lewis, Red Allen, Bunk Johnson and Tommy Ladnier, tolerated their rehearsals in her bungalow and remained a friend and mentor to them. The band now needed a drummer and Ron Berry filled the vacant chair in response to an advertisement pinned to the notice board in The Pond Music Shop, Thornton Heath, which was run by Frank Wilson who played trombone in Billy Cotton's Band.

Rehearsals were held in Crowcombe's Upper Norwood home, and the band played at a Youth Hostel in Duppas Hill before broadening its scope to appear at the Lantern Hall, Sydenham Road, West Croydon, and The Star Hotel, Broad Green. The latter venue was the home of Frank Getgood's Croydon Jazz Club and the Jazzmen occasionally played there during the intervals. Mike recalls using the hired rooms of various pubs for band practice, including the Derby Arms, Volunteer Inn, Prince Albert, Duke of Clarence and The Gun - and even for a while in a cellar beneath a pet shop in Surrey Street, Croydon.

An event which was to have a profound effect on the young trombonist occurred on Sunday, the 14th April, 1957 when he visited the Stoll Theatre in London to see George Lewis as a solo guest with the Ken Colyer band. Little was Mike to know at the time that by 1965 he would be touring with the great New Orleans clarinettist, with the Barry "Kid" Martyn band.

In 1958 the name of the band was changed to the Perdido Street Six, whose first public engagement was at The Star. By this time Mike Stanley had left the band to be replaced briefly by a young lady named Pat Aldridge who was a nurse at Mayday Hospital, again following an advert in Frank Wilson's shop.

The band had some success, but again Mike was restless and needed to move on. With Mick Collins on clarinet and Fred Barter on cornet he started the Mike Pointon Jazzmen who rehearsed in the Canterbury Arms, Sumner Road, and secured gigs in Chislehurst Caves on Saturdays and occasionally in the ballroom above the Pyramid Record Shop, Broad Green. Budding trumpeters who appeared in the band included Clive Peerless, Gerry Ingram and Dave Gedge (Gerry Ingram currently plays string bass).

It was during this period that Mike discovered the Bunk Johnson Appreciation Society whose members met regularly at the Porcupine pub in Great Newport Street, London, opposite Studio 51 - The Ken Colyer Club. With Jim Holmes (trumpet), Bill Greenow (clarinet) and Dave Evans (drums), yet another band was formed. Bill Stagg remained on banjo.

When the George Lewis band came to Britain in January of 1959, Dick Charlesworth, who had a Wednesday residency at the Purley Hall, went up to the Imperial Hotel in Russell Square, where the Lewis band members were staying. There, he managed to persuade Kid Howard, Jim Robinson and Joe Robichaux to return with him to Purley, and they sat-in with his band that evening. On the 25th January, 1959, the full Lewis band played at the Davis Theatre.

New Orleans had come to Croydon and suddenly the world seemed smaller. Mike had the chance to hear and meet the George Lewis Band in London, and, after meeting clarinettist Sammy Rimington, he was inspired to form a band in that style which became the Kid Martyn Ragtime Band, a key group in Britain's New Orleans revival.

Mike's final memories of the decade include a concert by Louis Armstrong and His All-Stars at the Davis Theatre on the 8th March, 1959, at which he had been greatly impressed by trombonist Trummy Young. He remembers, too, a recording session which took place at The Star Hotel to produce an album to raise money for the great Louisiana trumpeter, "Punch" Miller. The personnel of the band were as follows:- Keith Smith (trumpet); Sammy Rimington (clarinet); Graham Paterson (piano); Bill Stagg (banjo); John Rodber (bass); Colin Bowden (drums) and, of course, Mike on trombone.

Croydon holds many fond memories for Mike Pointon. The events which occurred and the people he met during this early period of his life formed a solid base for his later musical activities and he really is in his element when recalling these nostalgic jazz memories of yesteryear.

Sunday 26 September 1954, the year the Ivy Benson All Girls Band played the Corner House

The Croham Valley Stompers, personnel unknown, at . . . . .

. . . . . the New Addington Rhythm Club - circa 1950

As the 1950's drew to a close Croydon's jazz fraternity could look back at the decade with a great deal of satisfaction. Apart from the British bands which included Croydon on their jazz circuits, a number of eminent American stars had visited the town. Without doubt the Davis Theatre management could rightly be proud to have staged the Glenn Miller Orchestra, directed by Ray McKinlay (2nd February, 1958); the truly star-studded presentation by Harold Davison of Norman Granz's *Jazz at the Philharmonic,* with Ella Fitzgerald, Oscar Peterson and Dizzy Gillespie (11th May, 1958), and the George Lewis New Orleans Jazz Band, with George on clarinet, Kid Howard (trumpet & vocals); Jim Robinson (trombone); Joe Robichaux (piano); Alcide "Slow Drag" Pavageau (bass) and Joe Watkins (drums), supported by Chris Barber's Jazz Band with Ottilie Patterson (Sunday 25 January, 1959), and the visit of Louis Armstrong and His All-Stars: Trummy Young (trombone); Peanuts Hucko (clarinet); Billy Kyle (piano); Mort Herbert (bass); Danny Barcelona (drums)and vocalist Velma Middleton on the 8th March, 1959, plus Alex Welsh and His Band with Alex on trumpet, Roy Crimmins (trombone); Archie Semple (clarinet); Fred Hunt (piano); Bill Reid (bass) and Johnnie Richardson (drums).

Outwith the Davis Theatre, jazz festivals of sorts had been held, and in 1958, under the banner *"Easter Jazz in Croydon,"* the Park Lane Ballroom presented Dick Charlesworth's Jazz Band, The Nomads, the Brian Taylor Jazz Band, the Clay Burns Quintet and the Saffron Valley Boys; Terry Lightfoot's band appeared at the Croydon Jazz Club and Pete Stewart's band at the Star Hotel.

These were heady days.

Louis Armstrong

George Lewis

Alex Welsh was born in Edinburgh on 9th July, 1929, and died in London on the 25th June, 1982. He formed his band in August, 1954 and it became an immediate success in the London jazz scene, appearing at the Royal Festival Hall; Alex on cornet, Roy Crimmins, Ian Christie, Fred Hunt, Neville Skrimshire, Frank Thompson and Pete Appleby. His Dixielanders had a success in 1958 with *Melrose Folio* and held an eight-month TV series "Sunday Break" that year. Jack Teagarden offered Alex a permanent job but he opted to stay with his own group who had stuck with him through his lean years. The 1959 tour with the Louis Armstrong All-Stars was the highlight in his career.

George Lewis, born in New Orleans of Creole parentage on the 13th July, 1900, died there on the 31st December, 1968. He started learning the rudiments of playing an instrument at the age of seven, was a natural musician and never learnt to read music. He joined the Black Eagle Band on 19th March, 1914, and played alongside Buddy Petit, Chris Kelly and Kid Rena until 1917, when he became a member of the Pacific Brass Band with trombonist Willie Cornish. He made his first recording on 11th June, 1942 for a private label, and later recorded with his own band, George Lewis and His New Orleans Stompers. Lewis has remained synonymous with the world-wide "revivalist" movement in jazz and has inspired countless in playing the basic pattern of New Orleans music.

Alex Welsh

# THE 1960's

"Back In Your Own Backyard"

# THE 1960's

As Croydon moved quietly into the 60's, the Croydon Advertiser informed us that Prince Monolulu [1] had been conditionally discharged after appearing at the local Magistrate's Court, accused of insulting behaviour; Council rent was forecast to rise between 6d (2·5p) and 5/- (25p) per week, and "Teddy Boys" caused damage at St James's Church Hall, St James's Road, on Boxing night when they were refused admission to a private dance. The Odeon Cinemas in Croydon and South Norwood were showing "The Five Pennies," starring Danny Kaye as the legendary cornetist Loring "Red" Nichols, ably supported by Louis Armstrong, and Johnny Howard and his Orchestra held the residency at the Orchid Ballroom. There were lunchtime classical music concerts at the Civic Hall, and Acker Bilk's Paramount Jazz Band appeared there on the evening of the 15th January, 1960. Frank and Peggy Spencer were teaching all forms of dance at their Royston Ballroom in Penge.

Jazz was at last beginning to get the recognition that it deserved. For too long the duffle-coated, pint of bitter Traditional jazz fan had suffered strange sideways looks from supposedly highbrow classical music lovers, but now began to be treated as almost normal.

The local newspapers played their part in this transformation and Traditional jazz made the headlines, albeit on page 30 of one edition.

A Page About One Of Croydon's Often Misunderstood Arts
by Anthony Brooks and illustrated by Gloria Timbs.

The Star Hotel, Broad Green, West Croydon

Most people know something, if only a very little, about classical music. Even if they take no great interest in it themselves, they respect - or at least tolerate - those who do. But with jazz there is often a tendency not only to refuse to listen to the music itself, but to condemn its loyal devotees. In the area covered by this newspaper there are several places where jazz and kindred music is played.

What goes on in this misunderstood world? Are jazz enthusiasts really as bad as some imagine? We tried to find the answers to these two questions, and the results of our inquiries appear as follows:-

(1) A colourful figure at the race courses.

## It's ritualistic - It's noisy, yet friendly - It's serious - It's Jazz

If you know that someone likes jazz, the fact does not really tell you very much else about him. He could be a barrister or a motor mechanic, he could be indifferent to any other kind of music or mad about Vaughan Williams. In many a long-playing record collection, Big Bill Broonzy lies comfortably next to Bach, and Brubeck jostles Bartok. Perhaps the most one could say about the jazz enthusiast is that he is probably fairly young and not likely to be completely and utterly unmusical..

"He," of course, means "she" as well. At most jazz concerts, the sexes seem to be fairly evenly balanced, though the first impression is always of a preponderance of girls. This is partly due to the fact that those short standing-out skirts take up a lot of room, and partly to the tendency of little groups of earnest young men to hide away in corners where they can listen to the jazz undisturbed by frivolous women-folk who want to dance.

That jazz is a serious business is evident from the faces of jazz concert audiences. As at a chamber music recital, no one is visibly having a whale of a time. It is clear then, that it is the music they have come for; it could hardly be for anything else, for the surroundings are usually not very attractive and the atmosphere and sheer noise are such as to inhibit anything in the nature of dalliance or ordinary conversation.

### Struggling to the bar

Conditions vary, of course. Of the clubs in this area whose resources are sufficient to attract the Big Names, one meets at the Star public house in Broad Green and the other at the Palm Court Hall in Purley, but there seems to be little difference in the demeanour or degree of enthusiasm of their respective members. Any difference there is can hardly be attributed to the provisions of the Licensing Act; when a really Big Name is playing, it takes as long to get out to the bar at Broad Green as it does to nip down the road for a quick one at Purley.

### Can't help dancing

Usually there is room for dancing. Opinions differ about the justification for this. Some go chiefly to dance - "You can't help it really, when it's got a good beat." Others regard it merely as a subsidiary pleasure, and the purists frown on any form of audience participation exceeding the silently tapped foot.

Those who do dance at jazz concerts seem to be rather good at it, particularly the girls. In this kind of dancing, as in ballet, the man is there largely to give point to the movements of the woman, to accelerate her spins, and support her when she would otherwise fall over. Properly done, it is quite fun to watch.

When the tempo is slow the style appears ritualistic and not ungraceful, like the courtship of flamingos. The dancers are rapt, concentrating, with no time for asking each other if they come here often. It has an advantage over ballroom dancing in that when the dance is over you don't have to lead your partner back to her place; you probably haven't moved from it.

What with the dancing and the crowd and the general hubbub at concerts, it is not surprising that there are few personality cults, as such, in the jazz world. It must be nearly impossible for a performer to get much of his personality across when most of his audience can't see him and his announcements are inaudible.

### Fans follow for miles

It is only the performance, tremendously amplified, that does get across, and it must therefore be technique or style that the fans follow (and some will travel miles to hear a particular band). This is praiseworthy, and distinguishes jazz from the more widely popular musical idioms of the day.

One other thing about the devotees of jazz deserves comment. Whatever local residents may think about their motor bikes, those who go to jazz concerts in Croydon are on the whole well-mannered, friendly, and no more boisterous than any tennis club dancers. Anyone could take his grandmother to a jazz concert with confidence; she might not enjoy it very much, but there would be nothing there to confirm her belief in the decadence of modern youth.

And, of course, the winkle-picker shoes - as well as the music, if it happened to be Traditional jazz that night - would make her feel at home straight away.

Croydon Advertiser, Friday 6th May, 1960.

But the early part of the 60's was a barren period for Traditional jazz, support for which showed a rapid decline, although the dedicated minority remained loyal to their chosen music.

Croydon blossomed with "Modern" jazz at this time. There was a tendency for its followers to seek their own venues, so as not to be associated with the Traditional groups, as the music strove to create its own identity in vocabulary and dress, whilst originating a genre pertinent to its own art form. There is nothing wrong in that approach, as success would depend on complete individuality.

During the Swing era of jazz in the 30's, several musicians broke away from the styles of jazz heritage created a decade or so earlier. It was the period also of the big bands and the dance orchestras playing sweet music. In turn, there were a number of jazz artists, both in America and in this country, who wanted to defy labels such as Traditional, Dixie and Sweet, and so they set about looking for new styles of playing. These styles jostled for recognition and each tried to retain the support which was crucial for its survival.

For the Modernists in Croydon, the Johnny Dankworth Band presented *Rockin' Down The River* on the M.V. Royal Daffodil which cruised on the river Thames from London to Mortlake and back (June 1960) and the Classic cinema in South Croydon screened *Jazz On A Summer's Day* (August 1961).

Traditional jazz fought back strongly and in 1962 the bands of Ken Colyer, Gerry Brown, Terry Lightfoot and Mike Daniels appeared at the Croydon Jazz Club. Eggy Ley could be heard at The Star Hotel, whilst the Bob Wallis and Jim Weller bands played at other venues in the town.

A major event which would dramatically alter the cultural face of the town occurred in 1962 when the Fairfield Halls opened. An arts complex of some style, Fairfield would provide entertainment across the whole spectrum, including prestigious plays at the Ashcroft Theatre. To the delight of Traditional jazz fans, early musical presentations included Acker Bilk and Dick Charlesworth.

Sadly, the opening of Fairfield saw the simultaneous closure and demolition of the old Civic Hall in Crown Hill. Possibly the last jazz concert to play the Hall was *Crazy, Man, Crazy,* featuring the New Addington Artisan Jazz Band, on the 19th November, 1962. Personnel:- Peter Savory (trombone); Don Chapman (trumpet); Geoff Foster (clarinet); Pete Stewart (banjo); Tony Wrightson (bass); Ron Berry (drums).

For many years the Civic Hall had been a haven for Traditional jazz fans. Although the concert hall setting was in complete contrast to the "back rooms and basements" of the town's other jazz venues, the atmosphere generated by a "full house" at the Hall would long be remembered by its many jazz patrons.

THE CIVIC HALL

The Civic Hall, originally called the North End Hall,[1] was opened on Sunday, 21 February, 1915, and Croydon now had a venue, with accommodation for 1,400 people, worthy of the Borough Council.

The Hall received slight bomb damage during WWII. It was taken over by Croydon Council in 1945 and thereafter would be known as the Civic Hall. It was very much a great asset to the town before being replaced by Fairfield Halls, which were opened by Queen Elizabeth, the Queen Mother, on Friday, the 2nd November, 1962. She attended the opening concert given by the BBC Symphony Orchestra.

The Fairfield Halls now became the main venue in the town for all styles of music. From the jazz standpoint, the superior acoustics, recognised to be the finest of any hall in the country, and plush setting enabled the management to attract many major stars and throughout the ensuing years a veritable "Who's Who" of jazz have graced the concert hall stage. [2]

(1) See Appendix [i]
(2) See Appendix [ii]

Croydon Jazz Club

presents

# KEN COLYER'S JAZZMEN

Friday 30 March
8 p.m.

## CIVIC HALL
CROYDON

Souvenir Programme 6d.

---

*Come along and join Surrey's oldest and finest Jazz Club*

## CROYDON JAZZ CLUB

Every Friday, 8—11 p.m.

### Star Hotel, London Road
West Croydon
(opposite A.B.C. Cinema)

*April 6th*
GERRY BROWN'S JAZZBAND

*April 13th*
ALAN ELSDON JAZZBAND

*April 20th*
TERRY LIGHTFOOT'S JAZZMEN

*April 27th*
MIKE DANIELS DELTA JAZZMEN

*May 4th*
TWO-BAND SESSION

*May 11th*
KEN COLYER'S JAZZMEN

Membership 2/-  Join at Club Meeting or S.A.E. to Frank Getgood, 272 Grange Road, S.E.19

*Printed by Viking Poster Service Ltd., Clyde Works, Clyde Road, Wallington*

**1962**

---

## PROGRAMME

### KEN COLYER'S JAZZMEN

PERSONNEL :  Ken Colyer, Trumpet
Sammy Rimmington, Clarinet
Jeff Coles, Trombone
Pete Ridge, Drums
Ron Ward, Bass
John Bastable, Banjo

*Items will be selected from the following :*

| | |
|---|---|
| All of Me | Maryland, My Maryland |
| Chimes Blues | Melancholy Blues |
| Closer Walk | Michigan Water |
| Corinne, Corinna | One Sweet Letter |
| Dallas Blues | Over the Waves |
| Didn't He Ramble | Runnin' Wild |
| Dippermouth | Sheik of Araby |
| Goin' Home | Snag It |
| Hilarity Rag | Swannee River |
| I Can't Escape | Tishomingo Blues |
| Yaka Hula | The Grey Goose |
| The Old Rugged Cross | Bogolousa Moan |
| John Henry | Walk Thru' the Streets |

---

## MEET KEN COLYER

Ken Colyer must surely be the most established traditional Jazz Band leader in Britain today. His never-deviating way of playing New Orleans Jazz, has won him fans from all age groups all over the world.

Born in Yarmouth in 1928, his first venture into the musical world was at the age of 14, playing the harmonica. Later, he joined the Merchant Navy and practised the trumpet during the 3½ years that he was at sea (sometimes to the great annoyance of his fellow crew members). During a temporary respite from the sea, he became the leader of a band featuring many names which are famous on the traditional jazz scene today. This band was called the Crane River Jazz Band, deriving its name from the area in which it was formed, namely Cranford, near London Airport. This band went very well and achieved great success during the Festival of Britain year, when they had the honour of playing before Her Majesty The Queen, then H.R.H. Princess Elizabeth, at the Royal Festival Hall.

After this, Ken left the country again in the Merchant Navy and managed, after many months, to achieve his ambition and visit New Orleans itself. It was here that he managed to sit in and play with the famous George Lewis Band, also meeting and playing with many other famous musicians whom he had admired for so many years.

On his return to England, Ken Colyer took over the leadership of a band which had such names as Chris Barber, Monty Sunshine and Lonnie Donegan. After a few months, Ken re-formed this band and the personnel had very few changes for the following five years.

Ken Colyer has established a reputation for playing only New Orleans jazz and although he has many "pop" numbers on his repertoire, the audience can always rely on this band to play these numbers in the New Orleans style.

57

By the summer of 1963, just eight months after its opening, Fairfield was established as the entertainment centre of South London, and so became the "top-spot" for jazz concerts.

Somehow or other jazz artists have never made a name for themselves by virtue of their appearances at Fairfield in the same way, for example, as saying that Sidney Bechet played the Drury Lane Theatre. Nevertheless, Fairfield Halls were a major force in bringing to Croydon audiences the aesthetically pleasing music of jazz. Concert goers in the 60's also had the opportunity of hearing the great exponents of Folk and Blues music, and famous names such as Sonny Terry and Sonny Boy Williamson thrilled attentive audiences with their exciting rhythm and phrasings of the authentic Blues. Because of its excellent acoustics the Fairfield Concert Hall was chosen as the only British venue for the American Blues Festival featuring Memphis Slim, Lonnie Johnson, Muddy Waters and Big Joe Williams.

Graham Langley, Secretary of the British Institute of Jazz Studies in Crowthorne, Berkshire, recalls that on Friday the 20th October, 1963, Sonny Boy, Big Joe, Otis and others walked through the doors of the Star Hotel at around nine in the evening, during the first concert of the new Rhythm & Blues Club, where the Yardbirds, with a young Eric Clapton, were appearing. The Americans finished up jamming with the Yardbirds until late in the evening and Williams was so impressed with the boys that he used them as the backing group on his solo tour of the UK and then recorded with them.

Fairfield also played host to the Swing bands of Count Basie, Tommy Dorsey, Gerry Mulligan, Duke Ellington and Woody Herman, whilst among the great singers presented were Sarah Vaughan, Ella Fitzgerald, Shirley Bassey and Ray Charles.

\* \* \* \* \*

The Georgian Club, Dingwall Road, East Croydon, was featuring Hooter Jazz every Wednesday evening during the summer of 1964. "Club members are essentially arty types," said Harry Lovatt, whose series of articles relating to the places that jazz-lovers congregated to listen to their favourite music and musicians were avidly read in the Croydon Advertiser of the day.

Duke Burns, who helped to run the Georgian Club, opined that there were only two kinds of jazz - good and bad - so instead of calling the music either Modern or Traditional, the name Hooter was chosen because the Club was situated over a garage. As the cars hooted horns, so likewise came the sounds of trumpets and saxophones, and so it seemed appropriate to name the music "Hooter" jazz.

The premises were used as a working man's club during the day, were in excellent decorative condition, and had the largest selection of bottled beers in Croydon. "Most club members are very serious-minded. They belong to no special sect - "mods" "rockers" or otherwise. They are all very appreciative of a good jazz session, a "blow" as it is known, and that is the essential thing they have in common," said Duke.

Burns had been in the music business since 1948, and his notion of jazz was that of a modern art form expressing various emotions. He had great ambitions for jazz in Croydon, referring to the town as "Little New York," and was certain that Hooter jazz would grow and that its roots would remain firmly in Croydon. Sadly, Hooter jazz did not thrive, but when the Georgian Club came into being, Duke had missed out on the "Trad" boom by a couple of years. Nonetheless, Hooter jazz was truly a Croydon creation and will be remembered as such to this day.

\* \* \* \* \*

Another of the Harry Lovatt visits gives us an insight to the "Big Swinging Sound" at the Duke's Head, South End, Croydon, where 16 enthusiastic musicians practised under the name of the Croydon Dance Orchestra (CDO), led by Don Wesson, who had the view that music was either dancing or non-dancing.

The main problem that CDO had was that they were not recognised by the Croydon Council and therefore lacked financial assistance. The band longed for a "spot" at Fairfield Halls but it is not known whether they achieved this ambition.

The two main functions of the group were to provide budding jazz artists with a chance to sit-in on a big band session, and to encourage "new lads" to play musical instruments. Their president was Johnny Dankworth and the band styled itself on the swing bands of the mid-30's. They remained an amateur outfit playing, for their own satisfaction, during a period when little chance of commercial success was in prospect. Now based in the Midlands, John Dankworth went on to fame in the Modern jazz world.

Still with the big band scene, Fairfield presented the Duke Ellington Band, directed by Ray Nance, on the 17th February, 1965. The star-studded line-up included Johnny Hodges, Paul Gonsalves, Cootie Williams and Cat Anderson (saxophones); Buster Cooper, Lawrence Brown and Russell Procope (trombones); Mercer Ellington (trumpet) and John Lamb (bass).

The Phil Brown Band were planning a move from their residency at The Gun to The Red Deer, South Croydon and soon afterwards they appeared at London's 100 Club.

Local pianist Roy Budd, who lived in Holmesdale Road, South Norwood, was voted most outstanding new star of 1965 in the Melody Maker jazz poll.

\* \* \* \* \*

Whilst the mid 60's showed a slump in the fortunes of Traditional jazz, its ever-faithful core of followers rallied together and prepared for a fight-back.

On October the 28th, 1966 the Croydon Jazz Club celebrated its 17th birthday by presenting Kenny Ball and His Jazzmen at their renowned venue, The Star Hotel. It was announced that the Alex Welsh Band would appear on the 4th November, with Humphrey Lyttelton and Chris Barber booked to appear at later dates.

The Star Hotel July 1994

Jazz promoter Frank Getgood was justly proud of the achievement of the club which he had founded with two friends and stated: "Since we started, every one of the important names in Traditional jazz in Britain has appeared there at some time or other. Three years after the club started the boom came. It went on and on for the next ten years or so. Then Bop and Rhythm 'n' Blues took their toll, and ever since "Trad" has been on the sidelines."

Frank was confident that Traditional jazz would continue to gain in popularity and predicted that it would not be too long before his club was as popular as it had been in the boom period, with regular Friday night sessions.

Fairfield Halls continued to go from strength to strength, presenting jazz of great quality, climaxing with a spectacular array of stars on the 22nd March, 1967, when Harold Davison brought his *Jazz From A Swinging Era* promotion to the concert hall during the show's third tour of Europe. Not since Norman Granz's *Jazz At The Philharmonic* and the 1965 Duke Ellington Band concert has so many top American jazzmen appeared together in Croydon, and the auditorium was packed to capacity, with many disappointed fans being turned away.

This was a major event in Croydon, and it is important to remember that the concert encapsulated American jazz artists who represented a great deal of the development of innovative styles from the early beginnings of jazz, and whose roots were in Chicago, Kansas City and New York. The concert was held at a time of great soul searching as to whether jazz should be seeking a new identity and changing its old titles and these three American cities played a major role in moulding an essential element of jazz as we know it today. It was of great credit to the critics through the ages that they chose to analyse and label the music, so enriching the history of jazz, for an art form without nomenclature would be fruitless, and in essence - disastrous.

The mould of New Orleans style collective improvisation soon began to change as jazz artists offered terse statements of theme upon which each would solo in turn, and from this new approach there developed the jam session, an amiable element in not only mastering the finer movements for new jazz creation, but in providing an avenue which both musician and listener alike could explore.

It was in such an atmosphere that the Fairfield concert took place, and the following notes are based on the information given in the special souvenir programme produced for the concert:-

EARL "FATHA" HINES (piano), was born on the 28th December, 1903, in Duquesne, Pennsylvania, and died in Oakland, California, on the 22nd April, 1983. His parents wanted him to become a concert pianist, but in 1923 he was playing jazz piano in Chicago and it was there that he met Louis Armstrong. On the 7th December, 1928, he recorded the duo masterpiece, *Weather Bird,* with Louis Armstrong, a King Oliver tune in which Hines showed the limitless scope of jazz piano. Through the influence of Louis, Hines developed the art of creating a trumpet sound on the piano. He composed *My Monday Date* and *Rosetta,* and recorded *Apex Blues* with Jimmie Noone and *Wild Man Blues* with Johnny Dodds. His LP, *Once Upon A Time,* recorded with Duke Ellington sidemen, was a popular seller in 1966.

ROY ELDRIDGE (trumpet), was born on the 30th January, 1911, in Pittsburgh, and died on the 26th February, 1989. He went to New York in 1930 to begin an intensive career working chiefly with the big bands of the day. He was perhaps the most dynamic trumpeter between the styles of Louis Armstrong and Dizzy Gillespie. For sheer power and drive he had few competitors among jazz trumpeters.

BUCK CLAYTON (trumpet), was born on the 12th November, 1911, in Parsons, Kansas, the son of a Cherokee Indian, and died on the 8th December, 1991. He was a regular visitor to Britain. His musical characteristics were a glowing lyrical tone, tender and mellow, with only occasional displays of the power he always kept under control. In the 1950's he did most to establish the Mainstream style of jazz when England was bedevilled with much feuding and fighting between the Traddies (rockers) and Modernists (mods). He was also a considerable arranger, usually in a kind of updated Swing-age style. *One O' Clock Jump* and *Hollywood Hangover* are two of his well known numbers.

VIC DICKENSON (trombone) was born in Xenia, Ohio, on the 6th August, 1906 and died in New York on 16th November, 1984. He was something of a rolling stone as a musician, moving from band to band, destination to destination. Leonard Feather called his playing "tongue-in-horn trombonist," as his refusal to be slotted into any pigeon-hole ensured that his playing was enjoyed and equally admired by musicians from various jazz camps. He played with Bennie Moten, Blanche Calloway and Claude Hopkins before he went with Benny Carter and the Basie band in the 1940's. He spent many years freelancing with small Dixieland groups and in 1965 had a successful tour of Britain.

BUD FREEMAN (tenor sax), was born in Chicago on the 13th April 1906, and died there on the 15th March, 1991. In the 1920's he established the tenor saxophone in jazz to the satisfaction of the likes of Eddie Condon. Well preserved and smart looking in his British suits, well-polished shoes, always cool and dapper, he was the perfect gentleman of jazz. For a man who came from the sharp-edged Chicago school, he blew, in these latter days, a disarmingly soft horn. Bud played in the Ray Noble, Benny Goodman, Tommy Dorsey and Red Nichols bands and went on numerous tours around the world, from South America to Britain.

EARLE WARREN (alto), was born in Springfield, Ohio, on the 1st July, 1914 and died in New York on the 4th June, 1994. He played piano and banjo in a family band before taking up the C-melody sax and alto. He was leading a 17-piece orchestra in Cincinatti when Count Basie heard him and asked him to join his band in 1937, whereupon he became the Count's chief director of the band as well as its lead altoist and ballad singer. He composed a number of tunes for the band including *Rockin' The Blues, Tom Thumb* and *9.20 Special*. He toured Britain in 1959 with Buck Clayton. Willie Smith fell very ill shortly before the concert and Earle took his place in the line-up.

ALBERT "BUD" JOHNSON (reeds), was born on the 14th December, 1910, in Dallas, Texas, and died in Kansas City, on the 20th October, 1984. He started his career as a drummer and later became master of all jazz reed instruments. He was linked in many ways with Earl Hines and was instrumental in the transition in the 40's, with the Woody Herman band and Dizzy Gillespie, from swing to be-bop, writing music for them and a few other bands. He recorded with Benny Goodman and toured the American service camps in Britain.

SIR CHARLES THOMPSON (piano) was born on 12 March, 1918, in Springfield, Ohio. His father was a Methodist minister and he played the organ. Influenced by the swinging style of Basie, he played with a variety of bands and his big break came in 1940 when he joined Lionel Hampton. He then worked with a long list of musicians - Lester Young at the Café Society in New York, Roy Eldridge, Don Byas, Charlie Parker, Coleman Hawkins (solo on *Stuffy* - 1945) and Illinois Jacquet. In 1947, whilst with the latter, he wrote *Robbins' Nest*, which has become a jazz standard.

BILL PEMBERTON (bass), was born on the 5th March, 1918, in New York City and died there on the 13th December, 1984. He had spent 10 years studying the violin before taking up the bass. He joined the Earl Hines band in 1966, and both Pemberton and Oliver Jackson went to Russia on a State Department sponsored tour with the Hines band.

He has backed pianists Art Tatum, Barbara Carroll and Dorothy Donegan; has been in combos led by Johnny Hodges and violinist Eddie Smith, and earlier in the big bands of Mercer Ellington, Lucky Millinder and Billy Kyle.

OLIVER JACKSON (drums), was born in Detroit on the 28th April, 1933 and died in New York, on the 29th May, 1994. He started by backing Yusef Lateef and Dexter Gordon and then moved to join Wardell Gray and to play in piano trios led by Teddy Wilson and others. He recorded with Charlie Shavers, Harold (Shorty) Baker, Ray Bryant, Roy Eldridge, Coleman Hawkins and Duke Ellington. He had a spell with guitarist Kenny Burrell's combo before joining Earl Hines for the 1966 visit to Russia.

\* \* \* \* \*

Many Traditional jazz fans were in the audience at Fairfield for this concert which must rank as one of the greatest jazz assemblies ever to have visited Croydon. When Bud Johnson came from the rear of the Halls playing *It's Magic* on soprano, walked down the aisle and onto the stage, it was indeed magic, and a perfect tribute to Sidney Bechet.

It became clear that those 10 giants of American jazz were plainly at ease performing under the nondescript label *Jazz From A Swinging Era,* but it would not have happened in the way that it did had each not been schooled through the many styles of jazz.

These musicians, together with a handful of others, had outstanding and remarkable talents, with intense individualism and personalities which enabled them to move away from the norm. Although having played alongside other musicians of different backgrounds, they were perhaps happier to perform in an atmosphere of informality, and it was to the benefit of all those in attendance that they came together that evening to swing at Fairfield.

This large poster of the concert is retained in the new Croydon museum

## Auld Lang Syne

The predictions made by Frank Getgood at the time of the Croydon Jazz Club's 17th anniversary, alas, did not come to pass.

On Friday the 2nd January, 1968, less than a year after the *Jazz From A Swinging Era* concert, the death knell rang out for Croydon's premier club.

Both the Croydon Times and Midweek devoted full page coverage to the event, and for those of us who had attended the Club regularly through its good and bad times, it was a stunning blow.

The Croydon Times.

Ken Colyer and his clarinettist, Tony Pyke.

Ian King with two attentive Colyer fans.

The Jivers.

The saddest event in the local music scene for many years was summed up admirably in the title of Sandra Grant's Midweek article. The headline for the closure of the second oldest jazz club in Europe simply read: *And When The Saints Went Marching Out.* The Croydon Jazz Club, based at the Star Hotel, Broad Green, West Croydon, closed in a wave of nostalgia with a packed house of 250 fans attending the last concert. In the main bar the teenagers listened to Long John Baldry on the juke box as the young 20 year olds and older, in complete disbelief at what they had read in the papers, flocked to listen to Ken Colyer's Jazzmen and a local group led by banjoist Pete Stewart, in the hope that it was not the end of another jazz era. "Hello, what's this I hear about the club closing then?" Old familiar faces were greeted with enthusiasm. "Hello, squire, good to see you again." "Had to come for the last night." Many had arranged baby sitters so that they could get to their old stomping ground - the Star Hotel.

Frank Getgood was heard saying that he should have had a last night every Friday, because the Christmas event attracted just 18 people, all of them regulars, and with those few numbers the club just could not last.

The evening ended at midnight with Ken and his Jazzmen playing a New Orleans funeral march, then Auld Lang Syne. It was the end.

The shock of wondering whether we would ever recover from the demise of what had become known as the greatest jazz club in the South of England brought to mind one of the most unlikely jazz parallels imaginable, that of the relationship between the Mexican Military Band during the 1880's and early 1900's to the bars and barrelhouses of New Orleans, and the Queen's Surrey Military Band to the wealth of local public houses on the fringe of the Band's Mitcham Road barracks headquarters in Croydon.

Whilst it is well documented that at the end of the American War of Independence various musical instruments discarded by the disbanded military bands became available to the citizens of the Southern States, a more obscure fact is that a similar situation arose when the Eighth Cavalry Mexican Band played at the World's Industrial and Cotton Centennial Exposition, which opened in New Orleans on the 16th December, 1884.

At the close of the Fair, surplus band musical instruments were available at bargain prices and were readily acquired by aspiring local musicians who eventually formed groups to play in the City's drinking houses. By the end of the 19th century and the beginning of the 20th, most musicians of New Orleans played in every type of job; the circus, saloons, restaurants, theatres and dance orchestras.

When the Queen's Surrey Band was disbanded in the late 50's, unlike its counterpart, the Mexican Band in 1880's New Orleans, there were no surplus instruments to be had in Croydon, but a few musicians continued the musical tradition and joined those already playing in the local public houses.

It is in this context that military bands exerted a measure of influence on jazz in both New Orleans and Croydon.

Most of the Croydon public houses stretching from the Jubilee Bridge, formerly the Pitlake Bridge, to The Pitlake Arms in Waddon New Road, and beyond, were frequented by jazzmen at one time or another. As a point of interest, the Pitlake Bridge led into the bottom end of Church Street before the flyover road construction work was carried out and the bridge given its new name, resulting in the razing to the ground of many fine old buildings.

The pubs that are no longer standing are as follows :-

The Volunteer Inn (Cairo Road);[1] The Globe and The George (Old Town); The Coach and Horses (Lower Church Street); The Six Bells and The Black Boy (Handcroft Road).

Among the pubs of interest to survive were :-

The Wellington (now The Paddock); The Derby Arms (now The Fox and Hounds); The Albert (now The Queen Victoria); The Canterbury Arms (now The Nowhere Inn Particular). Those with no change in name are The Rose and Crown (Reeves Corner); The Eagle (corner of Church Street and Tamworth Road); and The Tamworth Arms (Tamworth Place).

(1) Prior to 1851, this public house was known as The Atmospheric Arms. Shades of the *Atmospheric Blues* to come?

Courtesy The Jazz Archivist, Howard-Tilton Memorial Library, New Orleans

Payen's Mexican Military Band
The Mexican barracks are pictured in the background

The Queen's Surrey T A Regimental Band at camp in the late 1950's

Selhurst Park, the home of Crystal Palace Football Club, has occasionally played host to a number of jazzmen over the years. The Ron Russell Band would appear in the old Supporters' Club, on one occasion with the distinguished trumpeter Wild Bill Davison, but how strong the link is between football in general and jazz is hard to determine.

The Traditional jazz/football supporter numbers in the 60's were undoubtedly numerous, but not by any stretch of the imagination as great as the "pop" music brigade. Unfortunately the part of the pools revenue earmarked for the Foundation for Sport and the Arts has not benefited Traditional jazz at all.

Crystal Palace Football Club 1968

A quarter of a century on from when this Palace team photograph was taken came a year of great empathy between Crystal Palace and Croydon's Traditional jazz, but, unlike the former, whose players may well command transfer fees of many millions of pounds, this Croydon Jazz Club membership card remains firmly in the hands of its owner and is available for transfer under its reserved price of £2,000,000.

However, whatever may be realised for the card in years to come, let us for a moment all hop onto a 654 trolley bus to the Wallington Public Hall for a spot of dancing and a "Perm," or go even further back in history, say fifty years, with the team and the jazz fans of the day, riding on one of the South Metropolitan Electric Tramways and Lighting Company Limited trams, on the way passing cornfields to Wallington Aerodrome, there to watch the first aeroplane, a bi-plane B.E.2, touch-down at Beddington, the official name of the Aerodrome which later became Croydon Airport.

## Civic Hall, Croydon

★

**Croydon Jazz Club**

PRESENTS

## Monty Sunshine and his Band

WITH

### Beryl Bryden

Souvenir Programme     Friday,
6d.                    June 9th 1961

### Monty Sunshine's Jazz Band

| | |
|---|---|
| Monty Sunshine (Clarinet) | Rod Mason (Trumpet) |
| Geoff Sowden (Trombone) | Nick Nickolls (Drums) |
| Dickie Bishop (Banjo) | Gerry Salisbury (Bass) |
| Johnny Parker (Piano) | Beryl Bryden (Vocals) |

---

Traditional Jazz Fans come along and join Croydon's only Jazz Club. Formed in 1949 the Club features the bands of Mr. ACKER BILK, CHRIS BARBER, KENNY BALL, KEN COLYER, MIKE DANIELS, ALEC WELSH, etc.

### Every Friday 8 p.m.

STAR HOTEL, LONDON ROAD,
WEST CROYDON, (opp. A.B.C. Cinema)

Jazz for listening and dancing.

### Annual Riverboat Shuffle
### Sunday, 16th July

"Royal Princess" leaves Westminster Pier at 9.30 a.m. returning at 6.30 p.m. Dancing on deck—all day to :—

**KENNY BALL'S JAZZMEN**
**MIKE DANIELS DELTA JAZZMEN**
**ERIC ALLANDALE NEW ORLEAN KNIGHTS**

Tickets 21/- each. Licensed bar and refreshments available.

*Details of membership for the Croydon Jazz Club and tickets for the Riverboat Shuffle, S.A.E. to*
FRANK R. GETGOOD,
272, GRANGE ROAD, UPPER NORWOOD, S.E.19

---

## THE CIVIC HALL CIRCA 1961

**Tonight!**    **Tonight!**    **Tonight!**

### CONCERT!

Repeated by overwhelming demand for the hundreds who missed it and for the lucky ones who saw it.

Musical wonders beyond imagination with

### THE TEMPERANCE SEVEN

An epoch-creating achievement without counterpart or parallel!

Programme of events

---

The personnel:—

| | |
|---|---|
| CAPT. CEPHAS HOWARD | Trumpet and Euphonium. Leader of the Orchestra. (T.V. scene designer). |
| 'COUNT' CLIFFORD de BEVAN | Piano and Harmonium. Scores out the band's arrangements; responsible for musical standards. (Professional musician and arranger). |
| ALAN SWAINSTON COOPER (Henry MacHooter) | Clarinet, bass clarinet, phono-fiddle, soprano and swanee whistle. Responsible for musical policy. (Teaches sculpture). |
| JOHN R. T. DAVIES (Sheik of Wadi el Yadounir) | Trombone, alto and second trumpet. Also responsible for musical policy and recording. (Recording engineer). |
| RAY WHITTAM | Tenor & bass saxes. (Publicity Expert). |
| JOHN GIEVES WATSON | Banjo and spoons. In charge of wardrobe. (Teaches graphic design). |
| FRANKLIN D. PAVERTY (Steve Powers) | Sousaphone. Arranges the band's travelling. (Professional musician). |
| Whispering PAUL McDOWELL | Megaphone vocalist. Responsible also for band presentation and policy. (Abstract painter). |
| BRIAN INNES (Prof. Emeritus) | Grand Jazz Percussion Kit. The band's official spokesman. (Art Director). |

The 1960's had seen great musical changes taking place in the country. It was a decade of jiving, twisting, rock 'n' rolling; of large open air jazz festivals and, finally, the advent of the "pop" music concert.

With regard to the forerunners of the open air jazz concerts, Lord Montagu of Beaulieu organised the Beaulieu Jazz Festival which, with the Reading Jazz Festival, were major events. The latter, after a couple of years, was taken over by the rock 'n' roll and pop worlds.

It was a period of the duffle-coat, the winkle picker shoe, the teddy boy and the leather-coated rocker; such was the colourful choice of dress and variety of groups, all jostling for position to make a name for themselves in this glorious 60's age.

Resident in Liverpool was a young group, The Beatles, who had made a name for themselves in Germany. On their return they would be cosseted by Harold Wilson, the duffle-coated, pipe-smoking, labour prime minister, as a badly needed dollar earner. Whatever chance there was for the survival of Traditional jazz in Liverpool was soon lost in the deck of cards and quickly dealt to the bottom of the pack. How could one have predicted then that, three decades later, a recording of Beatle John Lennon playing in his first band, The Quarry Men, at a church social in Liverpool in 1957, would realise a six figure sum at Sotheby's, and what of Paul McCartney's lyrics to *When I'm Sixty-Four* realising a five figure sum? Is there much hope for a Croydon Jazz Club card to follow suit some day? Why not! The Beatles and one or two similar groups were soon to make a lasting impact on the British pop scene.

Elsewhere, Alan Elsdon signed to provide the music for a feature film and made his first visit to Scotland and then over the sea to Ireland. Kenny Ball visited America and had a hit with *Samantha* and *Midnight In Moscow;* Monty Sunshine with *Petite Fleur.* The Soviet Union had 3,000 amateur jazz groups; Czechoslovakia's Jazz Federation claimed 25,000 members in Prague alone, and Poland had 500 jazz followers.

Peter Clayton reviewed the Alexis Korner Rhythm & Blues Band at Croydon's Civic Hall:-

> *"Forty Days And Forty Nights" caught Acker Bilk's audience unawares when Alexis Korner decided to use it to open his spot in the programme at the Civic Hall, Croydon, on January 19, 1962. Blues Incorporated, Korner's new group, with which he hopes to stir up interest in contemporary Chicago-style Rhythm and Blues, was playing its first date in the London area, and it had a curious effect on an audience basically suspicious of the guitar in general and the electric guitar in particular.*
>
> *Alexis Korner himself, having decided to go the whole hog, gallantly used a rather glamorous looking solid (bodied). With him he had harmonica, piano, bass, drums and a singer named Andy Wren, who is handicapped at the*

moment by having to try to revise history and evolve Rhythm & Blues from a Rock 'n' Roll approach. As yet, he lacks the technique which Muddy Waters-style music demands, and for a crowd which looks upon Acker's very good band as the "Whole Truth," he came too close to some Elvisisms for their liking. Somebody, whose voice was stronger than his grasp of history, shouted "We came to a jazz concert!" But we gathered later that Blues Incorporated aroused a good deal of genuine interest also, and that the rather thoughtless yelling that occasionally came from a certain section of the audience nearly led to some bitter little scuffles.

Alexis found the whole thing encouraging. "An Acker Bilk audience is probably the toughest of the lot. They come to hear Acker, and if King Oliver himself was suddenly to be reincarnated and given the first half of the show, they'd want their money back. Modern R & B is practically unknown in this country, but I think that a lot of people who have recently been, or in fact still are, keen on Rock, will soon be at home with it."

He is clearly not aiming at a big jazz following, though genuine jazz fans will almost certainly be interested in what he's doing, since the line from primitive country blues, through the more sophisticated players like Big Bill, to the tough, thoroughly urbanized sound of present day Muddy Waters, is clear and unbroken.

The group is not quite a group yet, but it has in Cyril Davis a very exciting harmonica player. He also had the whole audience with him - with no dissenters - when he sang and played "Hoochie Coochie Man." Keith Scott, who has done a lot of solo work at the Colyer Club, was on piano, rolling a good, mean blues sound behind his leader's percussive hit parade guitar work. Colin Bowden was on drums, and while supplying the necessary drive, created undue monotony by clamping his foot firmly on the pedal of his hi-hat cymbals and bashing away on the upper one for most of the set. Bass player Graham Beazley helped to provide the insistent beat so necessary to the idiom.

Jazz News found him unduly saddened by the mixed reception; he need not have been, for the group did precisely what it set out to do. Alexis Korner played in an unfamiliar but thoroughly authentic way, giving a noisy, unstable but powerful lead. Croydon and Chicago are poles apart, but there's no reason why the gap shouldn't be narrowed.

One of the last jazz bands to play the Civic Hall was trumpeter Dave Keir's, whose sidemen included Jim Shepherd (trombone); Ronald Duff (piano); Bob Stamford (bass); Colin Miller (drums); Hugh Gordon (banjo) and an unknown clarinettist.

---

**ALEXIS KORNER'S**
**BLUES INCORPORATED**
THE MOST EXCITING EVENT OF THIS YEAR

**RHYTHM AND BLUES CLUBS**

No. 1: THE EALING CLUB, EALING BROADWAY, W.5.
(Immediately Opposite Tube Station)
"To the many people who MADE the opening, A BIG Thank You"
This week's Guests: DICK HECKSTALL-SMITH and ERIC LISTER (Saturday, March 24th at 7.30 p.m.)

"We're sorry we couldn't make the opening, but we'd like to wish the first R. and B. Club in this country every possible success". CHRIS BARBER and OTTILIE PATTERSON

The Coulsdon Jazz Club held its sessions every Saturday at the Youth Centre, Chipstead Valley Road. Regular bands appearing were Ron Rendall's Alhambra Jazz Band, Geoff Wilkins' Diplomats and Colin Kingwell's Jazz Bandits.

Scotland held its first jazz festival and so too did the Bexley Jazz Club, Kent, which operated on Monday evenings at the Black Prince Hotel.

Ronnie Ross and Ken Colyer represented British jazz in Berlin as part of the British Jazz Week.

Max Collie came from "Down Under" to replace trombonist Kevin Shannon, leader of Australia's Melbourne New Orleans Jazzband that played a session in the Star Hotel, Broad Green, West Croydon. The band once played to an audience of 60,000 in the Melbourne Music Bowl. The Lyn Dutton Agency was responsible for bringing this band to the U.K. plus Papa Bue's Viking Jazz Band from Denmark; the Dutch Swing College from Holland and the Clyde Valley Stompers from Scotland. The agency at one time represented Eric Allandale's New Orlean Knights; Micky Ashman's Ragtime Jazz Band; Avon City Jazz Band; Len Baldwin's Dauphin Street Six; Acker Bilk's Paramount Jazz Band; Ken Colyer's Jazzmen; Mike Daniels' Delta Jazzmen; Humphrey Lyttelton Band; Merseysippi Jazz Band; Terry Pitt's Jazz Band; Doug Richford's London Jazz Band; Eric Silk's Southern Jazz Band; Ken Sims' Vintage Jazz Band; Monty Sunshine Jazzband; Alex Welsh and his Band; artistes Doreen Beatty; Beryl Bryden; Nat Gonella; Mike McKenzie and Neva Raphaello. When asked which bands did he tip for stardom, Lyn Dutton replied, "Good jazz is like good whisky - it matures slowly. My bet is that the end of '62 will see little change in the popularity stakes." His predictions measure good to this day.

Gerry Brown's Jazzmen supported the great Louis Armstrong All-Stars at the Festival Hall on one of their British tours.

The Cy Laurie band came into being in the early 50's and a decade later had built up a fan club of 14,000 members.

**Jazzshows Jazz Club**
JJC EVERY NIGHT AT 7.30
100 OXFORD STREET, W.1.
Manager:
DON KINGSWELL

Wednesday, February 7th
DICK CHARLESWORTH
City Gents with Jackie Lynn
Thursday, February 8th
CLYDE VALLEY STOMPERS
Friday, February 9th
ED CORRIE'S Jazzband
Saturday, February 10th
ALEX WELSH and his Band
Sunday, February 11th
TERRY LIGHTFOOT New Orleans Jazzmen
Monday, February 12th
KENNY BALL Jazzmen
Tuesday, February 13th
GERRY BROWN'S Jazzmen
Full details of the club from:
The Secretary J.J.C.
22 Newman Street, London
W.1. Phone: LAN 0184

---

Dance or Listen in Comfort
At The
**PICCADILLY JAZZ CLUB**
41, Gt. Windmill Street
London, W.1.
(Panama Entrance)

Wednesday, February 7th
7.30 p.m. COUNT RUDOLPH JAZZ BAND
Thursday, February 8th
7.30 p.m. UNIVERSITY JAZZ NIGHT
Friday, February 9th
7.30 p.m. JOHN RENSHAW JAZZ BAND.
Saturday, February 10th
7.30 p.m. DAVE NELSON MARLBOROUGH J.B.
Sunday, February 11th
7.30 p.m. LONDON CITY STOMPERS
Monday, February 12th
7.30 p.m. LONDON CITY STOMPERS
Tuesday, February 13th
7.30 p.m. RIVERSIDE JAZZMEN
Every Sunday Afternoon
3.00-6.00 p.m. Uncle John Renshaw Elastic Band

Phone:
Members — GER 2491
Enquiries — REG 2011

Keith Smith's Climax Jazz Band was booked for an exchange concert with Berlin's Spree City Stompers. It was a period of many exchanges of musicians and bands from Europe and the U.S.A., following the end of the Musician's Union ban on transfers.

An excellent book entitled *Ain't Misbehavin,* the story of Colchester Jazz Club by Phil Brown and Bob Catchpole, was produced around 1990, the year of its 35th birthday. The club's slogan in the 60's at one stage was *400 on a bad night, 500 on a good one.* Well over a hundred different bands have appeared there over the years, with Tom Collins being the resident band, with Tom on trumpet; Terry Lewis (trombone); Roy Smith (reeds); Don Nevard (piano); Jimmy Moull (drums); Mel Cox (banjo); Stan Ratcliffe (bass). This was the line-up of the Tom Collins band at the Red Lion Hotel during the 1965 Colchester Arts Festival. At Bank Holiday periods, 700 members seeking to attend the Colchester Jazz Club concerts was then not unusual. George Allen is one name to mention among the many over the years who have helped to achieve this marvellous record.

The local press and the Daily Mirror contributed to the publication of the book.

Two decades earlier, just after the war, Manchester featured Dave Wilson's Dixielanders and two other bands, Smoky City Stompers, which included trombonist Ken Wray, and the Delta Rhythm Kings with trombonist Geoff Sowden. During this period the Red River Jazzmen, Ged Hone's Ragtime Jazz Band and Alan Dents Jazz Band were the principle groups.

It was the era in which Bob Wallis first featured the saxophone, played by Al Gay; Hugh Rainey took up the guitar, and a young lady in a Northern jazz club was heard to say to her boy friend, "Ere Alf, 'a thowt it war trad tonight!"

There was plenty in the way of jazz material to read, although "Coda," the Canadian magazine, was suspended for a while; the American "Metronome" was in temporary trouble, and "Downbeat," in 1994 into 60 years of publication, was little seen in this period - the 60's.

Here in Britain there was Jazz Journal, ('International' since 1983 when it was acquired by Eddie Cook, its publisher and editor-in-chief), now in its 48th Year; the Melody Maker which took many twists and turns, and Jazz News, a London based magazine which began in 1956 and, in order to broaden its horizons, changed its name to Jazz Beat, but closed in 1966. The adverts printed here appeared in the former publication. Jazz Times was produced by the West London Jazz Society and its gig guide section became Jazz Guide, a free publication with a circulation of around 10,500 today. John Wurr and Steve Lane were at one time associated with the magazine, which is now run by Bernie Tyrrell.

---

**MARQUEE**
THE LONDON JAZZ CENTRE
165, Oxford Street, W.1.

Wednesday, March 21st
★ FAIRWEATHER — BROWN ALL STARS
★ WALLY FAWKES BAND
(Members: 4/-
Guests: 5/-)

Friday, March 23rd
★ CHRIS BARBER'S JAZZ BAND with OTTILIE PATTERSON
(Members: 5/-
Guests: 6/-)

Saturday, March 24th
★ DON RENDELL QUINTET
★ RONNIE ROSS QUARTET
(Members: 6/-
Guests: 7/6d)

Sunday, March 25th
★ JOHNNY DANKWORTH
(See Display Advert. Below)

**DANKWORTH NIGHT at the MARQUEE**

Sunday, March 25th
at 7.30 p.m.
JOHNNY DANKWORTH ORCHESTRA
and the
RONNIE SCOTT QUARTET

RICHMOND JAZZ CLUB Station Hotel, presents the GORDON BAKER SIX plus Guests.

**TUESDAY**

MORDEN. MIKE DANIELS 'ELTA JAZZMEN with DOREEN BEATTY. 'The Crown' opposite Morden Underground.
BROMLEY JAZZ CLUB, "White Hart", High Street. ED CORRIE'S CONCORD JAZZ BAND.
BARNET, Assembly Hall, Union Street. KEN COLYER JAZZMEN.

The Jazz Book Club served the jazz fraternity well, and its first issue was *Mister Jelly Roll* by Alan Lomax, published some years earlier. In the previous decade Humphrey Lyttelton wrote *I Play As I Please,* which was one of the Club's issues in its first year in 1956, and he had another one, *Second Chorus,* issued four years later. Humph went on to widen his jazz style to embrace "Mainstream," also expanding his career to encompass more writing and broadcasting. He was later contracted to Black Lion Records, eventually producing his own Calligraph record label. Lyttelton's contribution to British jazz has been incalculable, and today he produces and presents *The Best Of Jazz* programme on BBC Radio 2, which not only entertains, but provides a wealth of jazz information, as well as running his own band which is in demand at many of the top jazz festivals in the country. The Club went on to provide an invaluable collection of jazz books and by 1966, when it ceased to operate, had produced 66 in all, among which were notables such as *Play That Music,* edited by Sinclair Traill; *Jazz: Its Evolution and Essence,* by André Hodier; *The Book Of Jazz,* by Leonard Feather; *My Life in Jazz,* by Max Kaminsky, and *The Real Jazz,* by Hugues Panassié.

*The Kings Of Jazz* series, priced at 5/- described the life and works of Bix Beiderbecke, Louis Armstrong, Duke Ellington and Bessie Smith.

It is an old New Orleans custom to hire a brass band to play at funerals and when Ken Colyer returned to Britain after his visit to the Crescent City, he formed the Omega Brass Band which gave its first performance at the Soho Fair. The band was so successful that eventually an LP was produced.

**REPRESENTING THE BEST IN TRADITIONAL JAZZ**

**CHRIS BARBER**

**JAZZ BAND with OTTILIE PATTERSON**

**TERRY LIGHTFOOT**

**AND HIS JAZZMEN**

BOTH RECORDING FOR COLUMBIA LANSDOWNE JAZZ SERIES

**FORRIE CAIRNS**

AND THE **CLANSMEN** with **FIONNA DUNCAN**

BOTH RECORDING FOR FONTANA

**HAROLD DAVISON AGENCY LIMITED**

EROS HOUSE
29-31 REGENT STREET, LONDON, S.W.1
Telephone REG 7961 (10 lines)
CABLES : HARDAV : LONDON

The Barnes, Richmond and Twickenham districts, situated on the River Thames, were famous for Traditional jazz and it would be just a matter of time before a festival and riverboat shuffle would be organised in the area during the vibrant days of the 60's.

Parades were held in Germany, Denmark and Sweden, as well as a number of towns in the North of England, but they were not introduced into Croydon until the late 80's, during one of the town's now famous Jazz Week festivals.

The London area also had its marching band and it performed regularly, with its line-up of Ken Colyer, Jim Holmes, Keith Smith (trumpets); Mike Pointon, Roy Mascal (trombones); John Defferay (tenor sax); Bill Greenow (alto sax); Bill Cole (sousaphone); Sammy Rimington (E-flat clarinet); Barry Martyn (bass drum); Dave Evans (snare drum). They performed sometimes at the Brentford football ground and at the first Richmond jazz festival.

Mike Cotton's Jazzmen appeared in the feature film *The Wild and the Willing*.

Pee Wee Russell played at the Thames Hotel in Kingston-upon-Thames and Ken Colyer had a regular date at Eel Pie Island, Twickenham.

The period also produced the Golden Disc, Pye Records LP's and The Golden Guinea label. Numerous bands played at the Tropicana in George Street, with the Ian Bird Sextet being the resident group. Modern jazz was being played at The Jazzhouse and The Blue Anchor, South End, where for three shillings and six pence one could listen to Vic Ash, Joe Harriott, Dick Morrissey and Bert Courtley. Another day, one could, by way of a little bit of shanks's pony, taking care not to trip on the granite cobble stones embedded where the tram lines used to be, go strolling in a southerly direction along the main Brighton Road, leaving Croydon under the light of a silvery moon; then you would probably be on your way to the village of Purley, that is to say if you just happened to be leaning on the classical side of Traditional jazz, or perhaps were seeking a partner to trip the light fantastic away at the Palm Court Ballroom, there to dance to Rob Charles' Rhythm Group. A perfect end to a perfect evening.

With the passing of time, the demise of Katharine Street's Central railway station, when the steam trains ran where the Queen's Gardens stand today, and the consequent growth of East Croydon station and its architecture can very much be compared to the move of the music hall and theatreland to the wide open space of Fairfield.

---

**'TROPICANA'**
18, George Street, Croydon
FIVE STAR LUXURY, DANCING, BUFFET, LICENCED UNTIL 2 a.m

| WED. 1 MAR. | **MIKE WESTBROOK BAND** Exciting, Dynamic, Avant-garde — Admission 5/- |
| WED. 8 MAR. | **DAVE GELLY - ART THEMEN QUINTET** Admission 5/- |
| WED. 15 MAR. | **TUBBY HAYES QUARTET** Admission 7/- |
| WED. 22 MAR. | **NORMA WINSTONE / IAN BIRD SEXTET / JOHNNY MARSH TRIO** The Bird Sextet has been given tremendous acclaim since its formation a few months ago. The Johnny Marsh Trio is a fine group and resident at The Old Place. Norma Needs No Introduction. Admission 5/6 |
| WED. 29 MAR. | **ALEX WELSH BAND** Popular Musicians, Popular Music and a raving success wherever they go. Admission 7/- |

---

**PALM COURT BALLROOM** — BANSTEAD ROAD, PURLEY.
The CLUBMEN and The ROB CHARLES RHYTHM GROUP
M.C. Jack Springall. Dance and jive in a friendly atmosphere.
Admission 3/6. Now in FULL SWING. 7.35 p.m.

The main entrance to the North End Hall/Civic Hall, in Crown Hill . . .

. . . and the exit, between Wilson's coffee shop . . .

. . . and Kennards, in North End, Croydon

To a large extent, the well being of any town is dependent upon its transportation and leisure, and as far as the latter is concerned, the pub is a great British institution. The placement of fine buildings, all readily identified with ornate signboards unique to each pub, has brought a special culture to the nation. The management and tenancy structures which feature their personality are outwith the scope of this book, yet both these facets invoke a special character and relationship to the British way of life and have in part been responsible for the way that Traditional jazz has evolved in this country through the 60's and up to the present day.

Surrey Street, that ancient, well loved Croydon market place, just a stone's throw away from the main street and well known beyond the boundaries of the town, also played an important part in keeping Traditional jazz alive, for it stood at the centre of the jazz fraternity, particularly so when television all but put paid to the cinemas. When the increased office population descended upon it at lunch-times, for their fruit and vegetable shopping and to catch up with the news, they could also enjoy the trading cries and friendly banter of the stallholders' when, as predicted, Croydon became the business *Boom Town of the Sixties*..

The Gun Tavern, a bygone venue for Traditional jazz and until recently for Modern jazz, which had moved to the Grouse and Claret in Cherry Orchard Road, is only a few doors down the road from the Surrey Street market. When the sun goes down in the evening all take on a different way of life, but it is to a market trader, whose local pub around 1968 was the Lord Napier in Thornton Heath, that we now direct our attention. It was there that a new and exciting chapter in the history of Traditional jazz in Croydon began, following the closure of the Croydon Jazz Club at the Star Hotel, Broad Green.

At this juncture we can draw two very important parallels. One is the closing and opening of The Civic Hall and Fairfield Halls respectively, the other, the death of Traditional jazz at The Star Hotel and its springing to life again at the Lord Napier. One brought about by Civic dignitaries, the other instigated by the ordinary citizens of the town.

The 1960's had witnessed many ups and downs in the life and times of Croydon's jazz lovers. The general slump in the popularity of the music towards the end of the decade was reflected in the town, with perhaps the lowest points being reached when the Civic Hall and the Croydon Jazz Club closed down.

History has shown that Traditional jazz and its followers nationwide are resilient, and the old spirit would prevail in their struggle for the survival of their kind of jazz. The Fairfield Halls and the Lord Napier were now proving to be a magnet for jazz musicians at the top of their profession, both from home and abroad, and the visitors from the U.S.A. and Europe were a welcome addition to the existing expertise of our own players.

The music would again come through a difficult period.

# THE 1970's

"Beautiful Dreamer"

# 6

THE 1970's

Close to Thornton Heath clock tower and on the left hand side of Parchmore Road leading to the crossroads at Beulah Road there stood several large family houses, one of which served as a music school, now replaced by purpose-built flats. How apt that some of us should return to an area where we once learned to play the scales on our instruments, unbeknown at the time that there stood nearby the Lord Napier public house which in 1970 comprised of two fairly large sized rooms. The main room, once the saloon, had had the old public bar wall that separated them knocked down to create a nice, comfortably sized room, which in the wintertime was heated by a large log fire. An ornamental wrought iron structure encircled the bar area, with nicely upholstered early period chairs and not-so-matching tables dotted around the room that had two doors leading off it into the back room. Darkened it was, smoke encrusted too, but there stood a lovely, green cushioned, large solid-legged table, facing upwards and lit by a skylight dome which was a sheer work of art. When it was light it was light, and when it was dark, it was *dark*. Fine, long, high-backed, pure leather seating arrangements extended along two of the walls, and at the far end of the room a threequarter size stained-glass, sash-corded window which let in, at times, some light. At this end of the room there was an exit which led into a small yard with entry into Bensham Grove, the street where the main entrance to the pub stood. It was, of course, the Billiard Room. The Lord Napier in the 70's was seen as the perfect place for our kind of jazz. Apart from two large New Orleans wall murals, one covering the blocked up window, and the now vanished billiard table, with round balls, a triangle to hold them in place and spiral cues, nothing much has changed. Today it is almost as it was in the 70's, not overlooking the fact that the skylight is now out of sight.

Vic and Iris Watts had become the landlords of the place, and it was Sam the Surrey Street trader who persuaded them to start up jazz at the Lord Napier. Sam then loved to sing and no doubt had his sights set on doing so, and what must have crossed his mind at the time was that there was no better place than the Lord Napier, his local, for this to happen.

In those early days at the Lord Napier, the handful of new clientele little but matched the number of snooker enthusiasts, and as one was asked to pay 2/6d to listen to jazz, Iris and Vic were persuaded to drop entry charges. As time passed, the number of jazz fans started to increase dramatically. The Yarra Yarra Jazz Band from Australia was popular at the time, and little did we realise that some of the jazz artists, like Sammy Rimington, would be making a name for themselves in later years.

Bill Brunskill had a residency at the Fighting Cocks in Kingston-upon-Thames, and he also started to play at the Napier. Soon, Sammy would be seen playing in the Brunskill line-up and Nat Gonella and other well known jazz artists would attend. At the pub, George Melly enjoyed it so much that he produced a TV documentary *Whatever Happened To Bill Brunskill*? giving it well deserved publicity. Friday evenings, when Bill Brunskill became a regular at the pub, the place was always packed out. Such was the demand, Bill soon became used to playing 15 or 20 minutes past 11 pm, the time scheduled for finishing his gig.

*Tears In Yours Eyes As Big As Buckets . . .*

Bill Brunskill's Jazzmen

PERSONNEL
Trumpeter and leader Bill Brunskill; Les Allen (reeds); Hugh Crozier (piano); Roy Dale (string bass); Bobby Parr (drums); Mike Sherborne (trombone); Bill Stagg (banjo).

On the 29th January, 1972, the *Tears In Your Eyes As Big As Buckets...* LP was recorded at The Lord Napier and Bill Stagg wrote the following liner notes:-

> Bill Brunskill has been associated with the British jazz scene for a quarter of a century, but seems to gain more popularity as each year passes.
>
> Bill has fronted his current band for about four years, but clarinet player Les Allen and drummer "Little" Bobby Parr are sidemen of his from some years earlier. Mike Sherborne joined Bill on a permanent basis in 1971 from Chez Chesterman's Band, but had in fact played on many gigs with Bill prior to this. He was formerly with Brian Green's New Orleans Jazzband and Keith Smith's Climax Band. Bill Stagg also played with the latter between 1962 and 1965 and was later a member of the jazz/comedy group - *The Lounge Lizards*. He has played with the Brunskill Band for most of its four year residency at the Lord Napier and was in fact responsible for the band starting the job in 1968. Bass player Roy Dale has also been with the band for most of the *Napier* residency, having previously played with many bands in the "Trad-Boom" days as well as with what might be termed "more tasteful" groups. The remaining member of the band, Hugh Crozier, joined in 1971 after playing in Steve Lane's Southern Stompers. Apart from his ensemble work, he is an accomplished soloist, and this side of his talent is well-known to regular patrons of the band's sessions.
>
> The current success being enjoyed by the Bill Brunskill Jazzmen is due largely to those people who regularly venture out to listen to the band, and the numbers selected for this record are some of those which are most frequently requested by these valued followers. It is to these people that this record is dedicated.

Yes, Yes In Your Eyes • Perdido Street Blues • Miss Otis Regrets • Bourbon Street Parade • All I Do Is Dream Of You • Ace In The Hole • Gettysburg March • Tishomingo Blues • Willie The Weeper • The Old Rugged Cross • When I Leave The World Behind.

An AJS Rocker ?

In those far off days public transport was the name of the game, but one could always spot a Harley-Davidson, a Brough Superior, a Sunbeam Sidecar, a British Small Arms (BSA), an Albert James Smith (AJS) and a Vincent standing outside, habitually waiting to ensure that owners of them went timely homeward bound.

They were, of course, motorcycles, mostly belonging to "Rockers."

The Gun Tavern

The Lord Napier

Among other famous bands beginning to appear under Vic's drive to spread the *Jazz At The Lord Napier* word was the Mac Duncan Jazz Band which held a Saturday night residency and produced an album in early 1971 under the Corona label, to delight their many fans. Alan Elsdon's band had a regular Tuesday night date, and on the 14th May, 1971, the Croydon Advertiser reported that he had found his long lost eight inch pocket cornet and was thrilled to bits with it. *The instrument, which is about 100 years old, cost Alan £17 in a junk shop and was the pride of his life.* It was sent to him slightly battered but otherwise in good condition by a committee member of a sportsman's club in Lancashire who had identified it as Alan's when a workmen found it there.

Alan and his cornet.

\* \* \* \* \*

The Croydon - New Orleans connection which began in the 50's was maintained through the 60's, including Chris Barber bringing Louis Jordan of Timpany Five fame to the Fairfield Halls, and continued into the 70's. Local jazz enthusiast Reg Hall recalls the following sessions at the Lord Napier:-

FATHER AL LEWIS, a New Orleans banjo player and singer, was recorded at the Lord Napier on 15 October, 1972. The personnel were Bill Brunskill (trumpet), replaced by Brian Minter (trumpet) on two tracks; Mike Sherbourne (trombone); Les Allen (clarinet); Hugh Crozier (piano); Father Al Lewis (banjo & vocals) including Bill Stagg (banjo) on two numbers; Terry Knight (bass) and Bobby Parr (drums). The session was issued on the Carrot label (Carrot 2).

THE OLYMPIA BRASS BAND OF NEW ORLEANS played at the Lord Napier on Monday, 20 November, 1972. The personnel were Milton Batiste (trumpet); Paul Crawford (trombone) Joseph Torregano (clarinet); Harold Dejan (alto, leader); Irvin Eisen from Germany (tuba); Andrew Jefferson (snare drum); Papa Glass (bass drum) and Anderson Minor (Grand Marshall). The band was recorded at a private session in the same location the following day, and tunes *New Second Line* and *Basin Street Blues/The Duck's Yas Yas* were issued on NoLa JBS(S)3.

PAUL BARNES, a New Orleans clarinet player who recorded with Papa Celestin, Jelly Roll Morton and King Oliver, played at the Lord

THOMAS JEFFERSON, New Orleans trumpeter and singer, played at the Lord Napier on Monday, 14 January, 1974, leading a pick-up band, the NoLa All Stars. He was recorded at a private session at the same location on 16 January, 1974, with Sammy Rimington (reeds); Jon Marks (piano); Max Leggett (bass) and Dave Evans (drums), and an LP was issued: Thomas Jefferson and his Dixieland All Stars, *If I Could Be With You,* on NoLa LP(S)10.

KID SHEIK, New Orleans trumpeter, was recorded in my house in Waddon, Tuesday, 14 September, 1976, accompanying English singer Bob Davenport on one song, *Keep Your Feet Still, Geordie Hinnie.* The rest of the pick-up band were Eric Webster (banjo); Alan Mears (bass) and Norman Emberson (drums). The track was included on an LP, *Bob Davenport And The Rakes 1977,* issued on Topic 12TS350.

\* \* \* \* \*

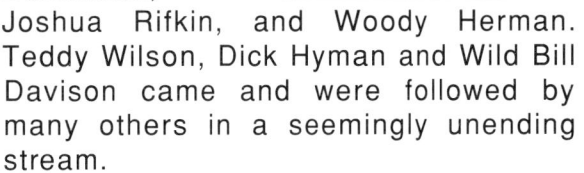

The procession of top-notch American jazzmen visiting the town appeared to be endless. Oscar Peterson, Dave Brubeck, Buddy Rich, The World's Greatest Jazz Band and Stan Kenton would be followed by Ray Conniff, Billy Butterfield, Joshua Rifkin, and Woody Herman. Teddy Wilson, Dick Hyman and Wild Bill Davison came and were followed by many others in a seemingly unending stream.

Kenny Ball

Jazz-loving Croydonians can look back at this fruitful period with some satisfaction - the chance to see and hear musicians such as these was rewarding. However, our own musicians were not to be outdone and Britain's best paraded their talents in Fairfield Halls to the delight of Croydon's ever increasing number of jazz-hungry fans.

83

Kenny Ball played the Fairfield Halls in May 1974 and his Jazzmen in the line-up at that concert were banjoist Ted Baldwin from Edgeware, Middlesex; trombonist John Bennett from Hackney, London; drummer Ron Bowden from Fulham, London; clarinettist Andy Cooper from Elgin, Morayshire, Scotland; pianist Johnny Parker from Beckenham, Kent, and bassist Vic Pitt from Wolverhampton. They recorded *Midnight In Moscow* a decade and one year earlier, for which Kenny Ball received a Gold Disc, presented to him by Louis Armstrong with the spoken words, "Mr Ball, you're sure on the ball."

However, prestigious venue or not, things did not always go according to plan at Fairfield, as jazz trombonist and radio presenter Campbell Burnap recalls:-

Regarding memories of Fairfield Hall concerts - well, I played there with Acker more than once, although nothing special comes to mind about *those* concerts.

However, I do remember being in the audience at a concert featuring Lee Konitz, Bill Evans and Philly Joe Jones, plus bassist Mark Johnstone, when there was some antagonism from the crowd. The quartet arrived late from Italy through flight delays and all one could hear was the overpowering drum work of Philly Joe! The public address system was up the creek, or badly-balanced, and most of the people wanted to hear the great Bill Evans' piano.

The band slunk off stage while the sound engineers fiddled around. Altogether a disappointing evening, with much muttering.

An entirely different night was back in the early 1970's when Sy Oliver and trombonist Warren

Campbell Burnap in concert

Covington brought a re-created Tommy Dorsey Orchestra over from America. I remember the orchestra filtering onto the stage - and the lights then being put out - *Pitch Black* ! - and then, as if by magic, a spotlight picked out the bell of leader Warren Covington's trombone (he'd slid quietly on stage) and he was playing *Song Of India* - à la Dorsey - très sweet! Wonderful show - biz effect ! ! (He was wearing a white suit, of course ! !)

On another night I went back stage to say hello to trombonist Vic Dickenson - over with the World's Greatest Jazz Band. I'd met him in New York in 1968 and had gone out to bars with him there. I just wondered if he remembered me. When I got to say hello again I realised that Vic had been smoking so much exotic stuff that he couldn't even remember who *he* was !! □

Another interesting turn of events, indeed dramatic, that happened at the Fairfield Halls as brought to light by Vic Gibbons, of Cromwell Management, and personal manager to Chris Barber's Jazz & Blues Band:-

> May 31st, 1975 was a particular highlight for Chris Barber whose band has played numerous sell-out concerts at the Fairfield Halls over the years. It was, to the day, 21 years since Chris Barber's Jazz Band had played their very first engagement as a professional outfit at London's 100 Club on May 31st, 1954.
>
> The 21st Anniversary concert that night at the Fairfield Halls saw the original six members reunited as part of the Anniversary celebrations for what was billed - and recorded as - *The Great Reunion Concert.* Even the addition of choir seats on the stage were not sufficient to satisfy the enormous demand for tickets and countless disappointed fans were turned away for what was to be a most memorable evening in more ways than one!
>
> May 31st, 1975 was also the date of a National Referendum where voters had the opportunity to decide whether or not to stay in or come out of what was then interpreted as being the "Common Market." The Fairfield Halls were one of the locations for the counting of votes after polling closed. It seems that even in those early days, long before talk of federalisation, central currency and other bureaucratic mayhem that has seen a growing dissent over the EEC (European Economic Community) that the seeds of doubt were already being sown in the mind of at least one individual who perpetrated a bomb scare at the Fairfield Halls. It turned out to be a false alarm, but not before the concert was brought to an abrupt halt shortly after the commencement of the second half, and in typical Dunkirk spirit the entire audience waited around the perimeter of the Theatre - most of them gathering in the artiste's car park until the all-clear was given. Monty Sunshine, in pied-piper/New Orleans parade style, led the audience back into the theatre once more and the concert was able to come to a happy conclusion.
>
> However, the event was being committed to tape for a subsequent live recording to be issued as a double LP. The tape was left running during the time that the building had been vacated, so consequently there was not enough of it left to record the rest of the proceedings after order had been restored and the balance of the concert played out to a deliriously appreciative audience. Consequently, those who subsequently purchased a copy of *The Great Reunion Concert* found that something like 70% of the recording was from the live show itself but the rest of the titles had to be re-recorded later under studio conditions as a result of the recording engineers failing to forsee such an eventuality and therefore running out of recording tape.
>
> The recording in question has subsequently been re-issued in 1994 to commemorate, would you believe it, the Band's 40th Anniversary, and whereas in 1975 there was just the one Fairfield Halls concert to mark the 21st Anniversary, today has seen a 100 plus date schedule of UK/European tours by those same founder-members of Chris Barber's Jazz Band. As one might expect, the venues included Fairfield[1]. Again the concert was sold out, but this time there were no interruptions.

(1) Fairfield Halls, under independent management from April 1st, 1993, became known as Fairfield.

# THE JAZZ CENTRE SOCIETY

From May until November, 1978, Rudolph's Jazzbar in the Red Deer, South Croydon, was the regular Tuesday venue for the Jazz Centre Society, and during its brief existence some notable jazz artists appeared there.

In the last few weeks of the Society the gig guide was as follows:-

| 5 | September | - | Stan Tracey Quartet. |
| 10 | September (Sunday) | - | Jim Mullen |
| 26 | September | - | Kathy Stobart Quintet. |
| 17 | October | - | Alex Welsh Band. |
| 31 | October | - | Don Weller/Terry Smith Quintet. |
| 14 | November | - | Bebop Preservation Society. |
| 28 | November | - | Jimmy Hastings Quintet. |

Unfortunately, however, audience levels fell dramatically during this period and the Society folded at the end of November, 1978.

JAZZ on Tuesday nights began at the Red Deer public house, Brighton Road, South Croydon, this week. First band to appear featured Harry South, piano, Don Weller, tenor sax, Gordon Serter, bass guitar, Henry Lowther, trumpet, Haydon Jackson, drums and Chris Pyne, trombone.

In early 1979 the South London Jazz Federation was formed by Croydon enthusiasts Peter Kymbrell and Ken Britchford. Jazz was presented at the following venues:-

The Racehorse, West Street, Carshalton (Sunday lunchtimes); The Cobblestones, Streatham High Road (Tuesdays); The Fountain, Garratt Lane, Tooting (Sunday evenings) and The Star, Broad Green (Mondays). The Federation's main musical organiser was Martin Blackwell (piano).

\* \* \* \* \*

At around this time The Croydon public house in Park Street, Croydon, presented Sunday lunchtime jazz, and artists such as Dave Aarons, Vic Ash, Jimmy Hastings and Olaf Vas played there.

Dick Wellstood

## The Dutch Swing College Band

l to r Dick Kaart; Henk Bosch Van Drakestein; Huub Janssen; Peter Schilperoort; Bert De Kort; Jaap Van Kempen; Bob Kaper

## Stephane Grappelli and the Diz Disley Trio

l to r Diz Disley; Philip Bates; John Etheridge

87

## The Monty Sunshine Jazz Band

l to r Geoff Downs; Johnny Johnson; Eddie Blashfield; Monty Sunshine; Ken Barton; Alan Gresty, at Fairfield Halls, January 25th, 1979
N.B. Micky Ashman (bass) depped for Johnny Johnson on the night

The decade was a period of continuing change for Croydon. The skyline of the town had begun to alter dramatically in the 60's and this would continue throughout the 70's. The increasing influence of television caused the closure of many cinemas, with only the Odeon (West Croydon), the ABC (Broad Green) and the Focus (Crown Hill) remaining in 1975.

But from a musical point of view it was a fruitful period for Croydon, and jazz had made a strong comeback after the disappointing times experienced towards the end of the 1960's.

It had not been easy, with the closure of two major venues causing some disarray amongst Traditionalists, and the death of Frank Getgood having deprived the town of a prominent figure in the promotion of jazz concerts, but the loyalty and tenacity of its followers saw the music through.

As the 70's drew to a close, Croydonians had become used to seeing top jazz stars from the UK, Europe and America; bands such as that of Frank Weir catered for the town's dancers, and classical music was frequently performed in a number of venues.

The Fairfield Halls complex was now the flagship for the jazz revival, closely supported by a number of pubs, which augured well for the future.

# THE 1980's

"When You're Smiling"

# 7

The 1980's

As the new decade began to get into its stride, Croydon's lovers of old-style jazz looked forward with eager anticipation to the visit of the Preservation Hall Jazz Band of New Orleans, scheduled to appear at the Fairfield Halls on the 11th September, 1980, in a concert promoted by Raymond Gubbay.

Croydonians at last had a rare opportunity to see and hear authentic New Orleans music played by seasoned veterans away from their St. Peter Street headquarters; names such as Kid Thomas Valentine, Willie Humphrey and Sing Miller were legendary, and here they were playing at Croydon's premier auditorium.

A packed house was treated to an evening of marvellous music which would long be remembered by those fortunate enough to be present on that historical night. Extracts from the souvenir brochure follow.

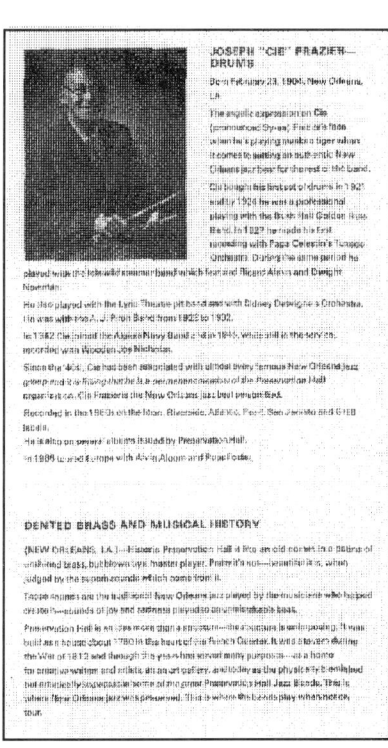

# The Preservation Hall Jazz Band of New Orleans at Fairfield Halls

## Thursday, 11 September, 1980

**WILLIE J. HUMPHREY, JR.—CLARINET**
Born December 29, 1900, New Orleans, LA.

He's soft-spoken, articulate, a teacher of harmony and theory, successful musician from New Orleans to Chicago to Broadway and on the big river boats. By choice he returned to New Orleans in his mellow years to play his beloved style—New Orleans jazz—that's Willie J. Humphrey, Jr.
Willie was born at the turn of the century and was taught music by his grandfather, a gifted musician whom Willie envies to this day. Willie still approaches each concert with the will, and the capacity, to make it "a little bit better" than the last one. He's proud of his New Orleans phrasing which many have tried to imitate, but only he can execute—that's Willie J. Humphrey, Jr.
His first job was with his father's band at a Poydras Market butchers' party. In 1919 he went first to St. Louis then to Chicago where he played with King Oliver and Freddie Keppard. Played with a Navy Band in World War II. In the '30s was with the Paul Barbarin band. He has recorded on the Riverside, Good Time Jazz, Southland and Atlantic labels. Has taught music since the mid-thirties but does little teaching now.

**THOMAS "KID THOMAS" VALENTINE —TRUMPET**
Born February 3, 1896, Reserve, LA.

If you dubbed Kid Thomas "Mr. Preservation Hall" you'd get little dispute from those in the know. It was his band that began the series of "rehearsals playing for the kitty", in the old art gallery that became Preservation Hall.
Kid Thomas is a tradition in himself. He was born way back in 1896 in Reserve, LA where his father was a trumpeter and instrument-keeper for the St. John's Parish Band. He played most of the instruments as a boy, but settled on the cornet. By 1915 he was playing cornet in clubs across the river and in 1923 he moved to Algiers and joined the Elton Theodore band. Within two years Kid Thomas was leading the band and because of his exciting, stomping style he developed a loyal, local following. In 1930 his band started a 20-year stint at the Moulin Rouge. He first recorded in England in 1964 and toured Japan with the late George Lewis in 1965. He has also toured Asia, Australia, behind the Iron Curtain, Europe and South America. Kid Thomas is a natural showman and his exuberant command of his horn, along with his ratty tone, bespeaks rough New Orleans jazz.

**NARVIN HENRY KIMBALL— BANJO**
Born March 2, 1909, New Orleans, LA.

Mastery of stringed instruments is in Narvin Kimball's blood—his father, Henry, was one of the all-time great New Orleans bass players. Narvin couldn't wait for his first instrument; before he was twelve he made something that resembled a ukulele out of a cigar box. Soon after he bought a real ukulele and when he was fifteen his father bought him a banjo.
By the time Narvin was seventeen he was a professional aboard the famous Capitol steamboat playing with Fate Marable. When the boat docked for winter he stayed with the band and continued his education at the same time. He attended Xavier University for two years. In 1927 he joined Sidney Desvigne's Orchestra and later played with Papa Celestin's Tuxedo Orchestra. The Ink Spots recorded his composition, "Don't Let Old Age Creep Up On You".
Narvin gave up music for five years during the depression because jobs were so scarce. In 1940 he got back into the business with the Desvigne group and stayed for several years. In 1947 he performed with jazz immortal Louis Armstrong. During the '50s and '60s he had his own band for a while and was in constant demand as a sideman. Today he's a solid and valued member of the Preservation Hall bands.

**FRANK DEMOND— TROMBONE**
Born April 3, 1933, Los Angeles, CA.

"It took me about ten seconds." That's the time it took for Frank Demond to make up his mind to drop a successful house-designing career in Newport Beach, California and go full time with Preservation Hall when he was made an offer six years ago. Frank was bitten by the New Orleans jazz bug in the late forties when he heard the Kid Ory group in L.A. He later sat in with the New Orleans musicians every time they came near the Coast. He usually played both banjo and trombone, but after he came under the spell of the late, great trombonist, Jim Robinson, he has concentrated on polishing his New Orleans horn technique. Home or away, large or small concert, Frank says he looks forward to every performance as a chance to improve. He has recently recorded with both the 'Kid' Thomas Valentine and Percy Humphrey bands.

**JAMES EDWARD "SING" MILLER— PIANO**
Born June 17, 1913, New Orleans, LA.

'Sing' Miller has carried his nickname since he was a tot surrounded by a family of musicians. His contribution to the family music was singing until he got his first instrument—a violin tuned like a ukelele. Later he mastered the banjo and string bass. 'Sing' was 16 when he got his first job as banjoist at the Oiwa Lounge in New Orleans—soon after he joined Kid Howard's band.
His piano career started in 1928 and 'Sing' is self-taught, that is if you discount a few organ lessons taken in school. He admits being influenced in his playing by Steve Lewis, Jeanette Kimball, Isadore Washington and Stack O'Lee, a neighbour who played blues piano.
'Sing' is a superb musician who chose not to stray far from New Orleans—he's had all the work he could handle in this hotbed of the New Orleans beat. Through the years he played in most of the name clubs in greater New Orleans. After Joe James' death, 'Sing' joined the 'Kid' Thomas band which became the vehicle for his association with Preservation Hall.
'Sing' is touched deeply by the loss of Jim Robinson and other New Orleans style musicians who have reached historic statue. But he will never give up his music. "It's my life," he says, "it keeps up myself-esteem."

**ALLAN JAFFE—TUBA**
Born April 24th 1935, Pottsville, PA.

Allan and his wife Sandy, are indeed the preservers of Preservation Hall. He was born in Pottsville, PA, —far from the delta. But after a varied and successful business, military, and musical career, he was drawn to New Orleans in 1960 by his lifelong passion for that sweet, sad, yet joyful style of music called New Orleans jazz.
The Jaffes found Preservation Hall little more than an informal, history-steeped gathering place for the ageing exponents of New Orleans jazz to keep their beloved style polishing.
The Jaffes not only kept Preservation Hall alive (without disturbing one loose, unpainted board), but have helped make the accomplished group of musicians world-famous through their global tours. Largely because of the Jaffes' efforts, of the Preservation Hall bands are as acclaimed in Tokyo, Tel Aviv and Copenhagen as in U.S.
Allan Jaffe was a member of the all-state high school band and won scholarship to Valley Forge Military Academy. He graduated from Wharton School of Finance.
While in army at Fort Polk, LA, that he had his interest whetted in New Orleans jazz, which was eventually to become his life.

*The band made two further visits to Fairfield Halls :-*

*Tuesday, 22 September, 1981 : Personnel as the 11/9/80,*
*but Percy Humphrey (trumpet) replaced Thomas Valentine.*

*Thursday, 23 September, 1982 : Personnel as the 22/9/81,*
*but Frank Parker (drums) replaced Cie Frazier.*

**London Borough of Croydon**
# Fairfield Hall, Croydon
Director: Michael Tearle, T.M.A., F.I.M.Ent.

*Michael Webber Promotions present*

## A TRIBUTE TO ALEX WELSH, with

# "JAZZ GALAXY"

### the Alex Welsh Reunion Band

Alan Elsdon & Digby Fairweather *(Trumpets)*
Roy Crimmins & Roy Williams *(Trombones)*
Johnny Barnes & Danny Moss *(Saxes)*
Brian Lemon *(Piano)*   Jim Douglas *(Guitar)*
Pete Skivington *(Bass)*   Laurie Chescoe *(Drums)*

## THURSDAY, 11TH NOVEMBER, 1982
### at 8 pm

---

Tickets from The Box Office
The Fairfield Hall, Park Lane, Croydon, Surrey   Tel.: 688 9291
£2.50, £3.00, £3.50 and £4.00

Credit phone — 681 0578 (Access and Barclaycard)

Many top jazz artistes contributed to the musical culture of 80's Croydon and fans continued to welcome, amongst many others, the visits of Alan Elsdon, Digby Fairweather, Neville Dickie, Bob Kerr, Cleo Laine and John Dankworth. Humphrey Lyttelton and Acker Bilk appeared frequently; Chris Barber's Jazz and Blues Band and the Pasadena Roof Orchestra, on an annual basis, and the Dutch Swing College Band, carrying on the Croydon/Arnhem link, graced the Fairfield stage on many occasions.

Elsewhere in Croydon, the skyline now resembled those of Chicago and New York, with the ever-growing multi-storey office blocks towering above the 60's Fairfield Halls building complex and the attractive, Victorian Gothic Revival, Grant's department store (built 1895-7), which closed its doors early in this decade and has not re-opened since.

At Selhurst Park, a season ticket in the Old Stand would cost between £85 and £102 to watch Crystal Palace play, and North End, in the centre of the town, would become fully pedestrianised.

Billy May

By 1984, Fairfield had welcomed Billy May, to conduct the Radio Big Band; *100 Years of American Dixieland Jazz* had been celebrated, and the wonderful Miss Peggy Lee had enthralled a packed audience. All had left their imprint on the musical culture of Croydon in the Eighties.

---

**Friday 23rd April 1982 at 8.00pm**
**The Radio Big Band** conducted by **Billy May**
Guest Singer **Matt Monro**        Introduced by **Don Durbridge**
**Producer Jack Dabbs**

---

*This concert will be broadcast on Saturday 15th May on Radio 2.*

**Radio Big Band**

Due to its heavy work load, the Radio Band is rarely seen outside of its home in the BBC's Maida Vale studios, so it is with great pleasure that we welcome its appearance at the Fairfield Halls this evening. The orchestra is heard regularly in many Radio 2 Programmes, including its own Saturday evening showcase, Big Band Special.

| | | | | | | |
|---|---|---|---|---|---|---|
| Trumpets | Nigel Carter | Horn | Jim Buck | Oboe | Chris Hooker |
| | Brian Rankine | Tuba | John Jenkins | Clarinet | Duggie Robinson |
| | John Barclay | Alto Saxes | Barry Robinson | Bassoon | Brian Whiteman |
| | Paul Eshelby | | Gordon Keates | Piano | Geoff Eales |
| Trombones | Derrick Tinker | Tenor Saxes | Peter Warner | Bass | Roy Babbington |
| | Brian Kershaw | | Nigel Nash | Guitar | Graham Atha |
| | Eddie Lorkin | Baritone Sax | Derek Hyams | Drums | Paul Brodie |
| | Tom Cook | Flute | Kenny Dryden | Percussion | John Chambers |
| | | | | Harp | John Marson |

**Dixieland Quartet**

| | |
|---|---|
| Trumpet | Kenny Baker |
| Trombone | Roy Williams |
| Tenor Sax | Danny Moss |
| Clarinet | Henry MacKenzie |

Towards the late 80's, New Orleans and Dixieland jazz in America was on its knees and owed its survival to a handful of dedicated musicians still playing in the Crescent City, together with a strong British contingent resident there.

Fairfield Halls, Croydon
20th October, 1983

In England, few jazz recordings were produced, the bulk of the output of albums being opera and classical, which meant that a main marketing shop window for music was closed to Traditional jazz. There were few clubs operating, and those that were invariably did not remain open for long. One standing the test of time was the 100 Club in Oxford Street, London, run by Roger Horton, which, in order to survive, broadened its horizon but always remained dedicated to staging New Orleans, Dixieland and Traditional jazz over the years.

This is not to say that there was a dearth of our kind of jazz about. Jazz musicians are used to coping with hard times. They were very much around, quietly playing, mostly out of the limelight, but nearly all having regular gigs in the pubs dotted around England. It meant, of course, that there were rich pickings for the breweries and publicans who were quite happy to let the musicians enjoy themselves whilst keeping both fans and customers contented. Soon there would be changes as things

Peggy Lee

could not last in the same way for very much longer. The jazz fans of yesteryear began to swell the ranks of those already retired, a number having taken early retirement, which in turn generated time for a greater awareness of the music. As a result, jazz bands playing the circuit rapidly started to increase in numbers, causing speculation that if such an increase continued at the same rate the bubble could burst once more, just as it had done in the days of the first Traditional jazz revival.

It was thought that one way of avoiding this happening again was to involve local government throughout the country, many of which were already supporting other forms of art, and making them aware of the existence of jazz, thus adding to the benefits that would accrue to local communities. If successful, Traditional jazz this time around would stand a better chance of survival by having a stable background in which bands could prosper. There was no procedure in place for getting our message across to those in authority who were best placed to help, and so out of this dilemma Kings Jazz Review (KJR) came into being in October, 1988, with a pledge to convey our cause to the voice of the people nationwide.

The editor of the Croydon Advertiser at the time was Mr Tony Thomas and it is to him that a great deal of credit must be given for getting the Traditional jazz movement rekindled in an organised fashion.

About a month after the appearance of the Count Basie Orchestra, which was led by Frank Foster, at the Fairfield Concert Hall, a letter from KJR was published by Mr Thomas in the Advertiser, which prompted David Shimell, then director of Fairfield, to arrange a meeting which took place on 8th February, 1989, at Fairfield. The Croydon Jazz Society was set up and pencilled arrangements were put in the Director's diary for three Traditional jazz concerts to be held in the Arnhem Gallery on the first Monday of October, November and December that same year, giving 8 months breathing space to make arrangements.

Meanwhile, moves were in progress to set up the Ken Colyer Trust and talks took place in Epsom with Renee and John Long for the newly formed Croydon Jazz Society to stage the Trust band when it had been assembled, a condition being that it should only include jazz artistes who had played with Ken during his lifetime. As it happened, promoter David Hancocks of Leatherhead staged the first Ken Colyer Trust band, giving it special arrangements which set the Trust off on a sound financial footing. During this time, representations were being made by KJR to Croydon Council to present a jazz festival. The KJR/Society team designed a formal flyer and sent it to the Council early in 1989, but no response was forthcoming.

Down in the West country in 1988, John Minnion, who had previously spent a holiday in Bude, Cornwall, realised that the beautiful seaside town was the ideal spot for him to try out Traditional jazz - which he did, with success.

In Leatherhead, David Hancocks had been promoting all-day annual jazz festivals for over a decade, and his involvement in jazz went back twice that period to his Bristol days. He was an obvious contact for John Minnion. Help was also given to John in Croydon and at the South Bank Festival Hall, by spreading his 1989 leaflets throughout, advertising his Second Bude Jazz Festival.

At the Lord Napier, Thornton Heath, David had been showing a strong behind-the-scenes interest in jazz ever since its inception there 21 years before. Kings Jazz Review (February, 1989) highlighted this admirably:

*The idea of having a party (21st) was first thought of a year ago and nothing more had been said about it since.*

*But you know how things are; there is always one outstanding person among us who has the flare, drive and initiative to be able to see that something like this will get off the ground.*

*One such person is David Hancocks. One Friday evening, without warning, there appeared in the saloon this very large poster, a true work of art, measuring about 35 square feet. It hung majestically on the wall at the back of the bandstand. It covered up our beloved mural, perceived by most to be living up to any scene you're likely to encounter along the surrounding countryside which gave birth to jazz music, or even adorning the halls associated with New Orleans jazz, and that goes too, for Preservation Hall, St Peter Street, in the city of enchantment itself."*

The correlation of these handbills is described in the neighbouring text

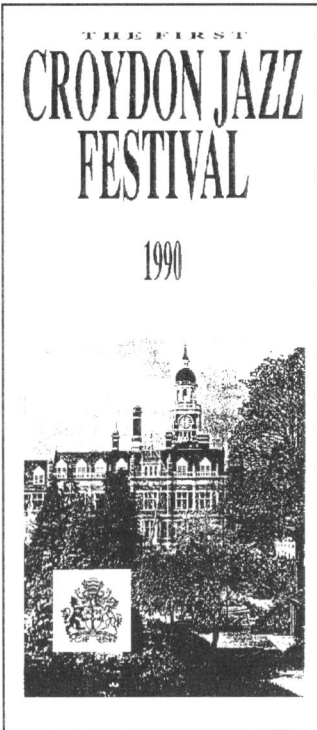

Suggested flyer - KJR Design (1989)

## Croydon Jazz Society

### THE KEN COLYER TRUST ALL STARS

The Ken Colyer Trust was formed just over a year ago and the band which came to life out of it has held several very successful 'Ken Colyer Remembered' concerts over that period. A few changes have taken place to the Line-up since its inauguration, but this All Stars band, as it did then, consists of jazzmen who have played in past Ken Colyer bands. They are Tony O'Sullivan (Trumpet), Colin Bowden (Drums), Dick Cook (Clarinet), Pat Hawes (Piano), Roy Holland (String Bass), Bill Stotesbury (Banjo), Bob Ward (Trombone).

This should prove to be a very popular evening for Ken Colyer fans. It is most fitting that such talented musicians, who play in the New Orleans tradition, should be our first band to grace these Halls in the Arnhem Gallery, as Ken had a regular date here in Croydon, at the Star Hotel for many years.

Tickets £5              Mon 18 Sep'89
Open 8p.m. - Jazz 8.30p.m. to 11.15p.m.

*********************

### MAX COLLIE RHYTHM ACES

Max Collie, president of the Croydon Jazz Society, trombonist, vocals and leader of the Rhythm Aces is a major figure on the British jazz scene. He formed his own band in 1966 and has been associated with jazz in Croydon going back several years. Earlier this year, he toured Germany and has appeared in a number of Jazz Festivals throughout the British Isles. In 1973 he toured the USA and received a rapturous welcome. Max has played with many of the legendary New Orleans jazz figures and was given extensive coverage by the Melody Maker during his American tour, which led to his becoming, winner of a 'World Championship of Jazz' contest.

His 'New Orleans Mardi Gras' presentation created in 1985 is an ongoing success, that, together with his current 'High Society Show'

featuring Blues artist T J Johnson and chanteuse Clare Solomon, which he has staged in various concert halls up and down the country, have given Max Collie a large following.

Max has recorded a string of LP's which are in big demand by all jazz enthusiasts. His Rhythm Aces are, Phil Mason (Trumpet), Trefor 'Fingers' Williams (Double Bass), Paul Harrison (Clarinet), T J Johnson (Piano) and Robert Cotterill (Drums).

A most eagerly awaited event in the Arnhem Gallery jazz calender.

Tickets £5              Mon 16 Oct'89
Open 8 p.m. - Jazz 8.30 p.m. - 11.15 p.m.

*********************

### CUFF BILLET'S NEW EUROPA JAZZ BAND

Cuff Billett began playing trumpet in the Portsmouth area around the mid 50's. He joined the Barry Martin band in 1960 on tour after spending six weeks with the renown trumpeter Henry 'Red' Allen, he visited New Orleans and made recordings with the legendary clarinettist George Lewis. Cuff has led the New Europa Jazz Band since 1972 and is in big demand to guest when the need arises. His band is based in the Southampton area and can be heard playing throughout Hampshire. This will be the band's first visit to the Croydon area.

Cuff's sidemen are; 'Loz' Garfield (Alto and Clarinet), John Wiseman (Trombone), Chris Tilley (Banjo), John Clarke (Piano), Cliff Harper (Bass) & Pete Jackman (Drums). Another great traditional jazz evening is expected and one to look forward to in the Arnhem Gallery. Don't miss this Monday date.

Tickets £5              Mon 13 Nov'89
Open 8 p.m. - Jazz 8.30 p.m. - 11.15 p.m.

ARNHEM GALLERY JAZZ VENUE

For dancing, refreshments or enjoying a chat over a pint of beer when listening to jazz, then check-in at the Arnhem Gallery.

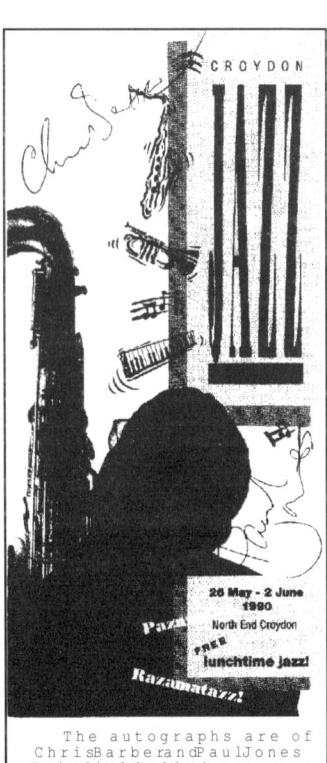

The autographs are of Chris Barber and Paul Jones at Fairfield Halls the same year.

Actual flyer - Croydon design (1990)

The celebratory day at the Lord Napier was an outstanding success and was reported in KJR. Vic Watts, only the fourth landlord of the pub since 1904, proudly received a crystal brandy glass inscribed *Presented to Vic Watts to celebrate his 21st year as guv'nor of the Lord Napier, 1988,* and a large bouquet of flowers was presented to Sheila, the lady who had been his right-hand for seven years.

They were delighted, and six months later they were married.

The Arnhem Gallery winter series of Traditional jazz concerts, far from having the inkwell spilt over the errand writer/organiser, turned out to collect good pass marks. They were every bit worth the cost of the challenge - a challenge of quite formidable dimensions which contained hidden economic formulae in measuring the true worth of success. These concerts became a watershed, not only as to how Traditional jazz could well again establish itself nationwide, but in having brought jazz fans and musicians into Croydon from distant parts of southern England to listen to and play their music in an upmarket venue, albeit creating an informal setting pertinent to their mode of enjoyment. We have been told on several occasions by fans who attended, that their visit to the Arnhem Gallery will always be remembered. Someday we will return.

There were a few regrets. We were unable to persuade Watney Truman Brewery to take an interest in the concerts, bearing in mind that they were the Fairfield suppliers. The BBC declined to record any of our concerts, for the *Jazz In Britain* series being broadcast that summer were said to take priority. Lastly, we had learned just shortly before the last concert that the cost would be beyond us to stage an all-day festival in the Arnhem Gallery the following Easter.

97

Boston Dixielanders

A number of the shopping precincts in the area started losing business and units began to close down. Croydon's Whitgift Centre was no exception, and it too felt the pinch. On Bank Holidays, the North End was virtually empty, with little incentive for the department stores to open over the holiday periods. Clearly, something had to be done to arrest the growing decline.

Towards the end of 1989, Croydon Libraries created a "Town & Country - Exhibition & Festival" taken from its art collection, which was held in the Rothschild Building in the heart of the Whitgift Centre, constructed on the site of the old Whitgift School. There were craft displays and workshops; lunchtime and evening music was performed by various groups and folk singers, plus, street-theatre and entertainments in general. The Croydon Jazz Society was asked to provide groups to play at lunchtime on three Friday's from mid-October to November in the Exhibition area.

Swanee 4

Little were we aware at the time, but the parameters were being set for the first Croydon Jazz Festival the following year. The three quartets chosen were Southern Rag-a-Jazz; the Bill Stagg Quartet, and Boston Dixielanders. It was not surprising that they made a very good impression among the midday shoppers, for they played well. Indeed, so too thought Anna Knox, the main organiser of the exhibition, for we were asked to book another group for the approaching Christmas. This was when the very fine quartet, The Swanee 4, came upon the scene.

The Eighties were to end in good spirits.

## THE FIRST LINE UP

Bob Ward (tmb); Ray Holland (bs); Tony O'Sullivan (tpt); Colin Bowden (drms); Dick Cook (cl).
(Behind Dick Cook is Bill Stotesbury (bjo).)
(Pat Hawes (pno) is out of the picture)

Croydon Jazz Society - October to December, 1989[1]

## THE FAIRFIELD DIARY AND THE CROYDON ADVERTISER

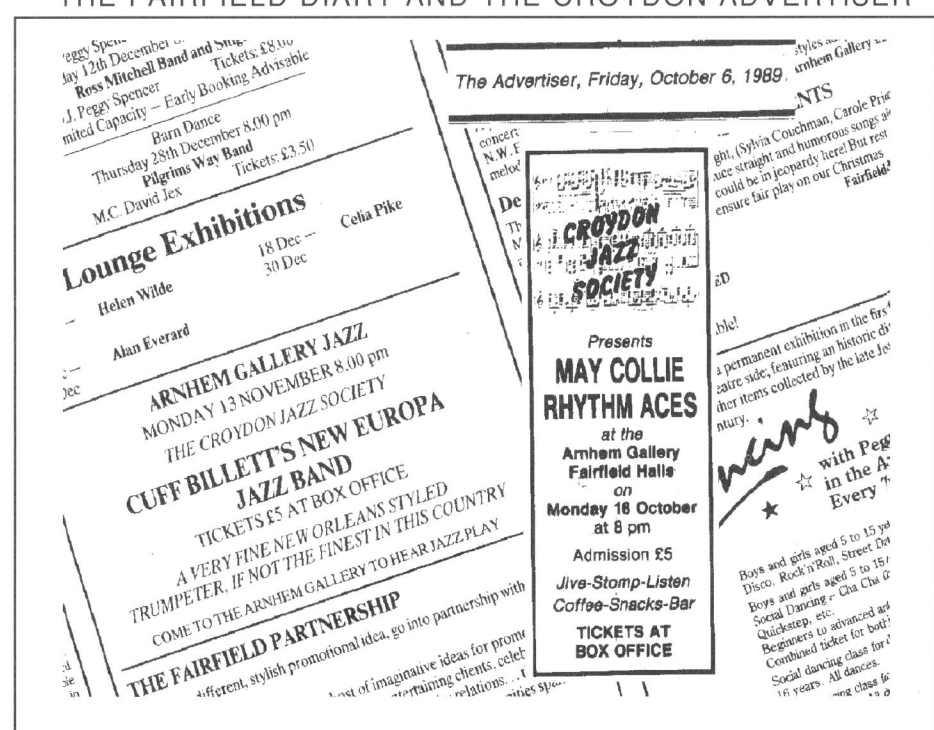

[1] See p 96

21 April, 1989.
Kenny Baker (trumpet) depped for Peter Appleyard

# THE 1990's

"Runnin' Wild"

# 8

The 1990's

Early in the New Year there were clear signs that Croydon would shortly hold its first jazz festival.

The authorities, because of the efforts of local enthusiasts, were beginning to become attuned to the view that the dawning of the 90's was perhaps ripe to include jazz in their entertainment calendar and that a festival would be both fashionable and advantageous in their efforts to improve Croydon's image as a tourist centre.

Elsewhere, Bude was establishing itself as a major Traditional jazz venue; Pontin's Holiday Club had begun to take a greater interest in jazz and had booked the Ken Colyer Trust All Stars Band for an off-peak weekend at their camp in Hemsby, Norfolk; Caister and Pakefield, always sympathetic to New Orleans and Dixieland jazz, were promoting extensively, so why not Croydon, which could boast of a long involvement in the music?

The Croydon Jazz Society was therefore given a grant to start the ball rolling on home territory.

A chance meeting with the Emmanuel Pentecostal Choir Gospel Singers in the studios of Cable Television, which was becoming increasingly active in the Croydon area, resulted in the title of the festival being amended to the *First Croydon Jazz & Gospel Festival,* to include them in the programme of events.

The Holiday Inn (now the Croydon Park Hotel), in Altyre Road, East Croydon, was chosen for the all day festival. The added challenge of persuading one of Croydon's top class hotels to become involved in the venture was to be totally justified.

In July, the whole country was basking in a prolonged heatwave, and the Holiday Inn proved a good place to be on the day, not only for the excellent music which could be heard, but also because the concerts took place in a beautiful and pleasant air-conditioned room.

The Choir sang with great passion, and each of the four bands played their differing styles of jazz in a manner greatly appreciated by the small but enthusiastic crowd. One thing in Croydon's favour, according to Ian King, was that both the Arnhem Gallery and the Holiday Inn venues had the edge over the Grand Hotel, Birmingham as places for listening to Traditional jazz concerts.

The Emmanuel Pentecostal Choir Gospel Singers

Imagine the excitement when, prior to the event, it was learned that there were plans afoot to hold a jazz week covering the May Bank Holiday, in North End, once the main thoroughfare, now the focal point of the shopping centre in Croydon.

Talks soon established that as the Jazz & Gospel Festival had been arranged and settled, it was felt right to go ahead with it in July as planned.

### The Croydon Jazz Week (1990)

With around twenty groups taking part in what was to become known as the Croydon Jazz Week, promoted by Croydon Arts & Libraries, the following extracts from their promotional flyer perfectly summed up the jazz feeling which they hoped to spread through the town:

*"There's nothing like the experience of live jazz to make you feel good to be alive."*

*"The London Borough of Croydon is pleased to present a week of free jazz entertainment in the main shopping street, North End, between Saturday 26 May and Saturday 2 June.*

*Between 11.30 am and 2.30 pm every lunchtime you can enjoy everything from a New Orleans style marching band to a full gospel choir. You can also see veteran dancer Will Gains, who literally tap dances jazz.*

*If you are a jazz fan you will recognise many of the names on our programme, such as Alan Elsdon, Jean Toussaint, Elaine Delmar and Bill Brunskill. If not, here is your chance to sample a selection of acknowledged talent, including a number of up-and-coming local jazz musicians."*

Those well chosen words set the stage to perfection and are as pertinent now as they were then.

The Croydon Advertiser featured Ian King in its publicity for
The Croydon Jazz Week

Earlier in the year, at 6 am on Sunday, 4th March, Diane Luke presented the first all jazz radio station - Jazz FM 102.2, covering Greater London. George Wood and Chris Phillips followed after the hour to when the "First Lady of Jazz," Ella Fitzgerald declared the jazz radio station officially open. Within four years it had dropped *Jazz* from its title and became simply, JFM.

The Excelsior New Orleans Brass Band (England) at the first Croydon Jazz Week

Whilst the story of jazz in Croydon has mainly been one of success, inevitably there have also been disappointments.

Organised by Nikki and Peter Batten, the Bletchingley Jazz Circle, held at the Adult Education Centre, presented top-class jazz for ten years but fell victim to indifferent support and in July, 1993, finally closed its doors. The Circle's resident band, Southland, had accompanied many famous guest jazz musicians during its tenure at Bletchingley.

Bill Newman and Terry Collcutt are endeavouring to re-introduce jazz to the area.

Other worthy but unsuccessful efforts to promote jazz were at the Moonshine Venue Bar, in Park Lane, Croydon, and the Classic Suite in South Croydon.

The Greyhound Hotel, long since gone, but in its day it was a notable Croydon venue for music.

However, although we must be ever-mindful of the history of jazz by glancing back at earlier times, it is the present and future that are of greatest importance to all jazz followers.

l to r
- Allan Bradley
- Dave Hewett
- Alan Littlejohn
- Laurie Chescoe
- Dave Jones

sitting
- Pete Skivington
- Tony Pitt

Bernie Tyrrell's long-established monthly publication, "Jazz Guide," which has its roots back in the 50's when it was part of the West London Jazz Society's magazine, reveals that much quality jazz can be heard both in Croydon and the surrounding areas :- Arkwright's Wheel pub where the local favourite, trombonist Eddie Grover, played his farewell gig with the New Orleans Jazz Men at the end of January, 1995; Carshalton Traditional Jazz Appreciation Society, (Charles Cryer Theatre), Carshalton; Croydon F. C., Woodside; Fox & Hounds, Carshalton; Fox & Hounds, Putney, (Dick Laurie); Grouse & Claret, Addiscombe, (Ken Carter); Gun Tavern, Old Town, (Ken Carter); Hays Galleria, London SE1, (Barry Binch); 100 Club, Oxford Street, London, (Roger Horton); Lord Napier, (Dave Hancocks); Selsdon Park Hotel, Croydon; Sutton Jazz Club, Wallington, (Pat and Neville Dickie); Warehouse Theatre, Croydon; The Woodman, Blackfen (Dick Waterhouse).

Slightly further afield, jazz can be found at the Colchester Jazz Club, Essex; Farnborough Jazz Club, Kent, formerly Badgers Mount J. C. (Diane and Keith Grant); Farnham Maltings, Surrey, (Peter and Jill Lay); Keston Village Hall, (John and Lynn Longley); The Louis Armstrong, Dover, (Bod and Jackie Bowles); Myers Hall, Epsom, (Lorna Corbett); Reading Jazz Club, (Denise and Tony Lawrence); Townhouse, Enfield, and the Tunbridge Wells Jazz Club, Kent.

These are just a few venues; there are, of course, many more the length and breadth of the country.

Goff Dubber (1993)

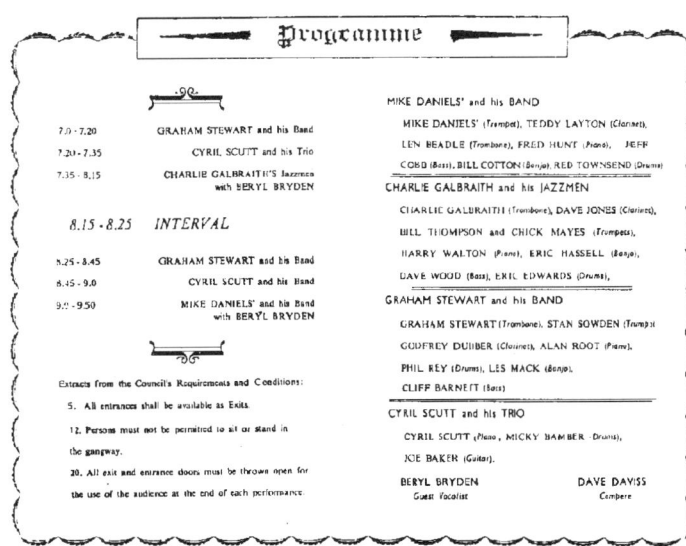

It is heartening to know that a number of musicians who were associated with Croydon in the old days are still playing today with undiminished enthusiasm.

Obviously we cannot include them all in the scope of this book, but older readers will be interested in the reproduction above of the Civic Hall programme for Sunday, 12 October, 1952, which provides a fascinating link with the accompanying photographs of one or two of the musicians involved that evening, showing the dedication of people who years ago decided that music should form a major part of the town's culture.

left
Freddy Legon
George Hopkinson
Micky Ashman
Charlie Galbraith

right
Cyril Scutt

Without them, a very different picture would have emerged, and out of respect for their achievements we should strive to ensure that the tradition is carried on.

What of the future?

Prior to the 30's, Buddy Bolden and Freddy Keppard were creating jazz in New Orleans. Early bands developed with the trumpet taking the melody line, a clarinet providing counter-melodies and a trombone taking up rhythmic slides and punctuating root chord changes. The 30's saw the inclusion of the guitar and saxophone, adding tender rhythms and complicated textures. The 40's witnessed guitarist Charlie Christian who, with others, made changes to the history of jazz. Lester Young's delicate tone lined with Avant-Garde modulations, and Charlie Parker, featured in the creation of Bebop, Rebop or Bop. Cool jazz in the 50's became West Coast jazz, refined by Stan Getz in the 60's. The jazz that remained in the same key, or Modal as it came to be known, blowing monotone for fifteen or so bars non-stop, had a footing on the ground in that period. Following on from that, in the 70's we had Fusion and in the 80's Mainstream.

The Whitehorse Lane Stand at Selhurst Park : part of Crystal Palace F.C.'s dream of the future, with the Holmesdale Stand scheduled for completion by August, 1995.

We are now half-way through the decade; the Millennium beckons.
What will the jazz scene be like in the year 2000?
The London Borough of Croydon has established its annual Jazz Week; Fairfield and the various local pubs and clubs continue to provide jazz on a regular basis.

*John Rickard taking notes for the future with Mike Daniels*

England's only magazine devoted exclusively to New Orleans, Dixieland and Traditional jazz, Kings Jazz Review (KJR), has created the English Traditional Jazz Jazzitoria, which is looking to obtain government grant via the National Lottery Fund, part of the Arts Council of England, so that it can act as "blanket authority" in support of the clubs, bands and musicians involved in these styles of jazz throughout England.

Could the country's first purpose-built Jazzitoria building, be it a castle or castle-like structure, devoted solely to old-style jazz, rise in Croydon before the end of the century, in much the same way that the government over the years has provided for opera and the theatre? To that end we are looking to the Millennium Commission.

Those are some of the questions for the future, but meanwhile . . .

*Let the good times roll!*

Humphrey Lyttelton, Monty Sunshine, Helen Shapiro, Campbell Burnap and the ReBirth Brass Band from New Orleans

Saturday 24 August 1991

Leeds Castle Kent

Max Collie

at the

Trafalgar

200 Kings Road

Chelsea

1973

Dick Charlesworth

Neville Dickie

1995

Chris Barber

Terry Lightfoot

# EXTRA TIME

### "That's 'A' Plenty"

# 9

EXTRA TIME

*Authors' Note*

*Our book is, in the main, home produced. The hardware at our disposal comprised of a Dell 325SX computer with 4 megabyte random access memory; an 80 megabyte hard disk drive, incorporating an intel 32-bit microprocessor; a large number of 3.4", 1.44mb diskettes; a Hewlett Packard Scanjet IIp image maker, and a Brother HL4 laser printer to create the masters, with the aid of JetSetter 6.1 Platinum, Desk Top Publishing software. The animated tools used consisted of ten fingers, free from RSI, to fiddle with the keyboard, and a couple of reasonably compatible brains, one Scottish and one English, to put the whole jigsaw together.*

*As the book progressed, material came into our possession which related to earlier chapters, hence the need for an additional section - 'Extra Time.'*

From Alan Tullett

My recollection of the jazz scene prior to being called-up in November, 1944, is inclined to be hazy, my main interest at that time being the dance orchestras - big bands in today's terminology. Main venue for these performances was the Croydon Empire which booked the likes of Harry Roy, Joe Loss, Oscar Rabin and others, together with supporting acts, for the whole week. The nearest approach to actual jazz was an appearance by Stephane Grappelli's Swingtette which included the formidable presence of George Shearing and Joe Deniz. The combination was completed by two rhythm guitars, bass and drums. A diet of undiluted hot music was not considered acceptable to audiences at this time, so interpolations of popular songs were included, sung by Beryl Davis and drummer Dave Fullerton, as well as a *straight* violin solo from Stephane - Bach's *Air On A G String,* from memory.

Upon being demobbed in January, 1948, I found that Ted Heath was topping the bill at the Empire, whilst a one-night stand by Freddy Randall and Graeme Bell's Australian Jazz Band was scheduled for the Civic Hall. Having carefully counted the small change in my pocket, I was happy to discover that I was just about able to afford four bob (20 pennies) for the former and three and sixpence (approx 17 pennies) for the latter. The Heath show was magnificent, although I thought the inclusion of such forgettable ditties as *Ain't Nobody Here But Us Chickens* were better suited to Billy Cotton than to Britain's No.1 Big Band.

The Civic Hall offering was strictly for enthusiasts of vintage jazz, which was enjoying something of a renaissance. I believe the respective personnel were as follows:-

(a) Freddy Randall (trumpet/leader); Bobby Mickleburgh (trombone); Derek Neville (reeds); Al Mead (piano); Bobby Coram (guitar); Jack Surridge (bass) and Harry Miller (drums).

(b) Graeme Bell (piano/leader); Roger Bell (trumpet); Ade Monsbourgh (trombone/alto saxophone); Lou Silbereisen (bass/tuba). There were also a clarinettist, banjoist and drummer whose names I can no longer remember.[1]

The concert also featured my introduction to a real live Blues singer, the lady concerned being then in her twenties - Beryl Bryden.

The Civic Hall concerts continued at a rate of one per month, staging performances by Mick Mulligan, Mike Daniels, The Temperance Seven and Monty Sunshine. Those appreciating more Modern sounds were catered for by the Ray Ellington Quartet.

In the rather severe winter that followed during the early months of 1949, an ambitious evening was announced - *Jazz In Variety*. The performers scheduled to appear were Adelaide Hall, Harold Berens and the Yorkshire Jazz Band.

On arrival, the audience found that their way to the auditorium was blocked. It seemed that Miss Hall's agent had doubled-booked and she would not be present. The Yorkies van was caught in a snow-drift somewhere in the Midlands, this being before the advent of motorways. The only person on hand was Mr Berens, standing in the foyer wearing an expression more in keeping with an undertaker than a comedian. It was obvious that he had decided that conducting a one-man show was not an option that appealed to him. The prospective customers were then advised to call at the box-office the next day for their money to be refunded.

Another failed venture was a weekly concert at the Pembroke Hall, Wellesley Road, (now an office block). Organised for the Croydon Jazz Club by Harry Randall, brother of Freddy and at that time his manager, the evenings featured the Freddy Randall band with occasional guest artists. The band at this time included in the front

(1) Probably Pixie Roberts, Jack Varney and Russ Murphy (JR)

line Bruce Turner (alto) and Eddie Harvey (trombone), with a rhythm section similar to before. After a week or two Bruce left to join Humphrey Lyttelton and he was replaced by a teenage clarinettist who was later to become noted as Britain's answer to Benny Goodman - Dave Shepherd. Unfortunately, the quality of talent on offer was not matched by a quantity of enthusiasts and when these had dwindled to a mere handful, and the Randalls' had become resultantly poorer, it was decided to close the enterprise down. The Pembroke later became a Theatre-in-the-Round and staged a number of quality plays starring well-known West End performers. Maureen and I remember seeing Andrew Cruickshank as Clarence Darrow in *Inherit The Wind.*

One of the most prolific performers in Croydon was Chris Barber, first at the Civic Hall and later at Fairfield. He has, I believe, appeared in the town every year from the late fifties onwards. During the seventies he seemed obsessed with featuring guest artists, some of whom were ill-chosen from the point-of-view of his audience, most of whom were vintage enthusiasts. Thus when John Lewis of the Modern Jazz Quartet was introduced there was a noticeable exodus to the bar - a pity, because John turned in a first-class performance.

The Fairfield Halls were opened in November, 1962. My first visit to the Concert Hall was when the Duke Ellington Orchestra played in it. Having booked late, the only seats available were in the choir area, on stage behind the orchestra. My memories of the concert include the rich alto of Johnny Hodges, the growl mute of Cootie Williams and the phenomenal dexterity of tenor-saxist Paul Gonsalves.

Other big bands to appear over the years have included Count Basie, Woody Herman and Louis Bellson, as well as the more "commercial" orchestras such as Syd Lawrence, Herb Miller and The Pasadena Roof Orchestra, all returning on a regular basis. In addition to Chris Barber, jazz bands that have been regulars are those of Kenny Ball, Acker Bilk and the Dutch Swing College Band. Stephane Grappelli has delighted devotees of jazz chamber music, and those who prefer the Modern sound have been catered for by the likes of Sonny Rollins.

Being a life-long enthusiast of the music of Paul Whiteman, I was delighted to be afforded the opportunity to see and hear the *New Paul Whiteman Orchestra* at Fairfield in 1975. Conducted by Alan Cohen but actually directed by American cornetist and Bix (Beiderbecke) disciple, Dick Sudhalter, the orchestra concentrated on Whiteman's golden years when Bix, Frank Trumbauer and Bill Rank were all in the band. An all star cast of top session men included Duncan Campbell, Tommy McQuater and Freddy Staff on trumpets; Nat Peck and Harry Roche were among the trombonists; Harry Gold, lurking amid seven other reeds, played bass sax; Reg Leopold led the six violins, and the five-piece rhythm section included pianist Pat Dodd and drummer Jock Cumming. Vocals in the Bing Crosby manner were delivered by

Chris Ellis, then director of the retrieval division of EMI. (Ironically, the LP's on sale in the foyer were on Argo - a Decca label !) A thoroughly brilliant evening, although concentrating on just under two years of the Whiteman band. A definitive Whiteman tribute has yet to be staged.

From Ken Batty

My earliest recollections of jazz in Croydon date back to around 1947-48 when concerts at the Civic Hall featured bands such as Harry Gold and His Pieces of Eight, and I also recall a very youthful Johnny Dankworth playing there with a group led by Cab Kaye.

In 1950 I began visiting the New Addington Rhythm Club, which was run by Frank Getgood and Nobby Clark, with whom I had done my National Service.

From New Addington the jazz club moved to the Pembroke Hall, to the Volunteer, then to The Gun Tavern, and also to a ballroom just off St. James's Road (Unique Ballroom). All of these clubs were run by Frank and Nobby, as were the Civic Hall concerts in the fifties, and Mike Daniels was the resident band, although other bands did play from time to time.

Regrettably, Frank Getgood died some years ago, but I am still in touch with Nobby Clark and spoke to him recently when I told him of your interest.

I enclose a recording made at the New Addington Club about 1951 of *Dr Jazz.* The other side of the record was *Sister Kate,* but regrettably this is no longer available.

The voice on the recording is that of Owen Bryce - although not with his band. I played piano with Owen's band from the mid-to late-fifties, and often played the solo interval spot at The Gun.

I do hope you will find the enclosed of interest. I have many happy recollections of the music scene in Croydon, the last playing piano with the Croydon Dance Orchestra, a 17-piece band under the leadership of Don Weller from Thornton Heath, which I left in 1963 when I moved to Dartford.

From
Graham Langley (Secretary)
The British Institute Of Jazz Studies

With regard to the Croydon scene, I started my jazz club going at the Palm Court in Purley, but too late unfortunately to take part in the famous George Lewis parade round the streets. Apart from Fairfield, my main jazz activity for many years was as a regular at the Star on a Friday. I also tried some of the modern clubs that started out, but the atmosphere they generated at that time didn't really appeal to me.

I was witness to one unique incident which may be a little on the fringe for you, but I believe should be recorded somewhere for posterity. In October 1963 the first American Folk Blues Festival came to Fairfield for two shows on Friday 18th and Sunday 20th, consequently the artists stayed in Croydon over that weekend. Coincidentally, the Star Hotel had decided to choose that Saturday, the 19th, to open a Rhythm & Blues club with the Yardbirds as first act. Partly out of curiosity, and, on the premise that a group who named themselves after Charlie Parker couldn't be all bad, I went along.

I was quite enjoying the music, though the place was half empty, when about nine o'clock, in through the door trooped Big Joe Williams, Otis Span, Sonny Boy Williamson and possibly Lonnie Johnson, plus one or two of the rhythm section from the Festival (Matt "Guitar" Murphy ?) though I can't remember who. (Memphis Slim, Muddy Waters and Victoria Spivey definitely didn't attend). The Yardbirds, who were all about eighteen at the time and included the young Eric Clapton were, to use a horrid modern expression, totally gobsmacked. They faltered, recovered and then enjoyed themselves hugely as the Americans joined in. Big Joe Williams played solo, but the star of the evening, as he had been of the Festival, was Sonny Boy Williamson, who encouraged the boys along singing and swapping harmonica lines with Keith Relf. He was so impressed with the Yardbirds that he used them as a backing group on subsequent tours and even recorded with them. I saw them together again at Fairfield on Friday, 21st February, 1964 at the benefit concert for the late Cyril Davis.

I hope you think this little anecdote worthy of inclusion. I still have Otis Span's autograph from that night. The Sonny Boy Williamson referred to was of course Rice Miller, Sonny Boy II.

Philip F. Dearle
Interviewed by I.K.

In the early 40's, pianist Phil Dearle was living in the USA. It was a time of the Swing bands and Phil became interested in several American groups such as Count Basie, Lionel Hampton and others of the period.

Back in England, living in Southend-on-Sea, whilst attending a record session he heard for the first time *Dr Jazz* by Jelly Roll Morton, and thus began his long association with jazz music.

After much difficulty in finding like-minded chums because of National Service "call-up," he was eventually able to form a band. The band held its first public performance during the Southend Carnival Procession, which they played on the back of a lorry through the town, advertising both it and the opening of their new jazz club.

Members of the Riverside, for that is what they called the band, were:- Phil Dearle (pno); Geoff Pilgrem (1st tpt); Jack Lane (2nd tpt);

Geoff Singer (cl); Len Page (bjo); Dennis Seabrook (tmb); Ian Tickell (tuba) and Johnny Bromley (drms).

The club soon ran into difficulties and a jazz jamboree was organised to help put it on a stronger footing. Billed as "King Of Jazz," Humphrey Lyttelton and his band played, Humph being the president of the club. So too did Mick Mulligan's Magnolia Jazz Band with George Melly, all of which helped the club to survive for a time.

Not long after, the Riverside were impressed by The Crane River Jazz Band, and when word got around that the Cranes were about to split, Phil and banjoist Len Page joined forces with them, whilst trumpeter Geoff Pilgrem, who had made the first approach, kept the Riverside going. The Cranes were to change from being a two-trumpet group, King Oliver style, to one in the line-up.

In the early fifties the Riverside Jazz Band remained a purely local band (Southend-on-Sea area), and the Cranes blossomed, playing throughout the country and at many clubs in and around London: the London Jazz Club/Lyttelton Club in Oxford Street, run by Bert Wilcox; Freddy Randall's Club, Cooks Ferry Inn, amongst them.

During that time Phil produced a double-sided recording on Melodisc Records. Two Rags - *Black & White* and *Blue Goose* played at a nice tempo, but, unfortunately for him, Winifred Atwell brought out the former at the same time, and as a result, Phil's record was not issued.

Nevertheless, it was a very exciting time for Phil, who has great memories of the period when he accompanied Big Bill Broonzy, with the Crane River, at the Cambridge Theatre, Soho, London, about which Steve Race penned a very good review.

Sharing a billing with the Chris Barber Band at the Grosvenor Hotel, Manchester, he recalls when Chris left his trombone at home. (Will he ever be allowed to forget it? *IK*). It was an era when London won the "Jazz Battle." Jazz Band Balls had as many as fifteen groups appearing, with time for each to play but a couple of numbers - great names, Sid Phillips, Eric Silk, Freddy Randall, Ken Rattenbury, Sandy Brown, Harry Gold, all great bands - too many to name all of them.

In 1952 Phil recorded for Parlophone. The days when Hammersmith Palais had its stage in the centre of the ballroom made famous by the Original Dixieland Jazz Band at the turn of the century, Irene Scruggs asked them to play an unrehearsed song during a concert there, about which a reviewer wrote: ". . . that the group went the whole hog, playing an entirely different melody ..." encircled by an audience of 2,500, whilst Irene sang merrily her chosen (forgettable) ballad, but to Phil it was perhaps the worst moment in his musical life.

The following year the Crane River Jazz Band split into three groups out of which came the Phoenix Jazz Band - Ray Orpwood (tmb); Len Page (bjo); Phil Dearle (pno); Geoff Kemp (cl); Arthur Fryatt (drms); Jim Bray (briefly) followed by Don Smith (bs). The Phoenix, Eric Silk,

Bobby Mickleburgh, Freddy Randall and others were featured in concert at the Royal Festival Hall, in aid of the Lord Mayor's Flood Relief Fund. Then during the late 50's, through a couple of decades, Traditional jazz was in decline - Beatlemania - and in any case, Phil was bringing up a family and was out of the scene during that period.

At the dawn of the 70's Phil was asked to join blues singer Myra Abbott as her accompanist at her new Blues Club which, she opened in Southend. Her resident backing group included Phil, Eddie Johnson on bass and Ken Milne on drums. Musicians who sat-in regularly with the group were his clarinettist brother Dave, Digby Fairweather, Eggie Ley, Ray Elliot and John Lancaster.

The band scene began to grow and as a result the Roaring Twenties Jazz Band came into being under the direction of Phil, which brought together his old friend Geoff Pilgrem, his brother Dave, Sam Weller, Brian Fairbanks, Mick Wilkinson and Alun Bundy. The Roaring Twenties lasted several years into the 80's, during which time they played at the Royal Oak in Orpington and at Hilden Manor, Hildenborough. When the band folded up, Phil joined the Washboard Syncopators and has been with them for fifteen years. He also leads the Jazz Bandits, who have been going strong for seven years and have a regular gig at the Liberal Club, Station Road, Orpington, on the first Wednesday of each month. He is obviously in big demand, for he can often be seen at the Lord Napier with the Bill Brunskill Jazzmen (1994), which brings back memories to him of his early Croydon days when he was with the Crane River Jazz Band at the Orchid Ballroom, Purley, as the star attraction band, with a dance band of the period on the same billing.

From Dick Waterhouse (Jazz promoter)

I was born in the mid-thirties and grew up on the sprawling council estate of Downham, near Bromley. All the usual things - dad went off to fight the Hun, mum did munitions work and we went hopping (gathering hops for brewing beer) every August. I went to the local Council school.

I think I was very lucky in my choice of parents. Lou and Dick were, and still are, very enlightened and always sought to improve our living and cultural standards. When WWII ended and life returned to normal, music became an important part of our household. Dad was a fan of the great Ted Lewis Orchestra and Sophie Tucker, and he (dad) and I would spend hours "junk shopping" for the 78" rpm records of these two artists and anything that arrested our attention. Slowly and surely we found records of Fats Waller, Miff Mole, Red Nichols, Benny Goodman, Harry James etc.

Let me quickly add here that we also attended the theatre and opera on a regular basis and I was only nine years old when we first went to the ballet.

Then early in 1948, just past my eleventh birthday, dad won the pools; a small fortune in those days. All sorts of strange gadgets started to appear in our house, including a 9" screen TV. Wonder of wonders.

It was about this time that a neighbour, anxious to obtain a seat to see this novelty, appeared at our door with a large heavy carton saying, " 'ere, you like all this boojie-woojie stuff, don't you?" and deposited some 20 plus records on our mat.

I don't think Fred ever knew or could have imagined what an impact that present would have on my life, for in the carton were 78's by all these strange new names - Jelly Roll Morton, King Oliver, Bunk Johnson and many more.

The record chosen first was *Baby Won't You Please Come Home* by Charlie Lavere's Chicago Loopers. The effect of hearing Joe Venuti's violin and Brad Gowans' valve trombone was electric. Our neighbour was invited back and continued to supply more and more records.

Coming home from school a couple of weeks later, our bus broke down at Bellingham and, seeking shelter from the rain, I found myself in the doorway of a music shop. A departing customer left the door open and this magical sound hit me. Daring to peer round the door I was ordered to come in and shut the door behind me. I found myself in the presence of the lovely Dorothy Guyver, the manageress of Pete Payne's Jazz Record Shop - the only jazz specialist shop in London at that time. "That's Bix Beiderbecke," she said. I just stood there dumbfounded and let Bix and the Wolverines waft over me. All this and only eleven years of age.

It didn't take long for dad to join me on my visits to Pete Payne's shop, and through Peter's guidance we started to frequent the cellar jazz clubs in Soho. I seem to recall that the sessions were often held on Sunday afternoons and I soon found some mates of my own age who were jazz fans, and our little gang travelled all over the London area in pursuit of live jazz. We would go to Cooks Ferry Inn for Freddy Randall, The Refectory in Golders Green to see Mick Mulligan and George Melly, Hounslow to sit enraptured by the Crane River Jazz Band, the Red Lion in Leytonstone to see Eric Silk and his Southern Jazz Band, and Greenford for Steve Lane.

Local promotions were mainly in the hands of Peter Payne who ran clubs at quite a number of pubs in South East London, usually presenting Mike Daniels and his Delta Jazzmen. Concerts at Lewisham Town Hall were also part of Peter's empire and it was at one of these that I first saw and heard Cyril Scutt and his Boogie Woogie Boys. Cyril is today a member of the Tunbridge Wells Jazz Club committee.

I was about 16 when I first met the legendary George Webb (*IK* yes, a living legend) and it was he who first encouraged me to become involved in the promotional side of the business. My first venture, *A Jazz Band Ball,* featured the George Webb Dixielanders and the Mike Daniels band. It was a sell-out and George brought along the singer Neva Raphaello . . . did we have a party !!

Two more dates were scheduled and whilst not such a financial success as the first, they were musically great. Apart from the booked bands - Steve Lane, Eric Silk, George Webb and the River City Stompers - we were joined by members of the Christie Brothers Stompers, the Humphrey Lyttelton Band, Cy Laurie and a host of names who "Webbie" organised during the evening, very much in the style of the Eddie Condon New York Town Hall concerts.

By now our Friday and Sunday evenings were being spent at the Shakespeare pub in Woolwich where George and Minah were running The Hot Club of London and featuring all the great bands of the period and most visiting Americans - Chris Barber; Ken Colyer; Terry Lightfoot; Bob Wallis; Monty Sunshine; Lonnie Donegan - you name 'em and I'll bet they appeared at Woolwich.

National Service interfered slightly. It took me North, where I was able to go and see Bob Barclay's Yorkshire Jazz Band, and to Manchester to listen to the Saints Jazz Band. A short spell in the Wirral gave me a chance to see the Merseysippi Jazz Band. One of the lads in our billet lived in Leicester and I was able to wangle a trip home with him to go and see Sonny Monk and Derek Aitkinson's Dixielanders.

I formed a band at my last camp and managed to get the group some paid work in the Sergeant's Mess.

Civvy street in 1956 found me once again deeply involved in the club scene, although I must confess to having spent quite a bit of the time in the Modern jazz clubs of Soho listening to the likes of Tubby Hayes, Joe Harriot, Ronnie Ross, etc. You can't criticise if you haven't heard the music !!

However, my first love remained the music of New Orleans. I managed one or two not very successful bands, continued to collect records, although by this time Fred had changed his job and my source began to dry up. However, I do remember this guy who used to arrive on his bike with panniers full of the "new-fangled" LPs. I used to give him five bob each for them and sell any I didn't want for half a quid !

Throughout the late 50's I continued to charge around the jazz scene which by now had acquired a new face - "Trad" - it became a bit over the top for me, all those bowler hats and fancy waistcoats were not what it was all about as far as I was concerned. Suddenly, everyone was a jazzer - even tired old dance band musicians who previously had laughed at our music were now forming so-called jazz bands. So I took three paces backwards and concentrated on building up my record collection and corresponding with musicians in America, delving and digging around, finding out more about the early days in the development of jazz.

The 60's were a quiet time for Sheila and I, we had married in 1960 and our daughter Jane arrived in 1963, so our musical activities were of a low profile. We did manage, however, to get to see every visitor to these shores, Eddie Condon, Jack Teagarden, Henry "Red" Allen and all the boys from New Orleans - George Lewis, Louis Nelson and so on, and of course, Louis Armstrong.

A change of job in the early 70's found me with a new chance to explore the live pub scene, as jazz clubs seemed to have disappeared. I started to get to know some of the new faces. Then in 1978 we took a trip to Breda in Holland to attend a jazz festival in that lovely town. On the first evening we met one of our long-time idols, Wally Rose, pianist from the legendary Lu Watters Yerba Buena Jazz Band. Wally introduced us to almost everybody who was anybody, and we became a part of the Breda scene for the next twelve years. I can't remember everybody we had a meal or a drink with, but I certainly recall the wonderful hour we spent with Turk Murphy and the lunch we had with Graeme Bell, also the time we went shopping with Dick Hyman and his wife. It was all glorious days and nights. We were invited to Eindhoven and found ourselves having breakfast with Louis Nelson and Doc Cheatham.

In the early 80's I stopped off in a quiet pub (well it was empty more than quiet) and agreed with the licensee that the place was ideal for jazz presentation, so we started presenting bands one night a week and eventually built it up to seven nights a week. That's how the Prince of Orange became a premier jazz pub in the period 1980-1990.

Quite a bit of my working day now is taken up in corresponding with jazz musicians and fans both here and in the USA. As some of you will know, we are now responsible for the Woodman Jazz Club in Sidcup, Kent, as well as being involved with George Webb and Don Aldridge in the organising of four annual jazz festivals, and this I really enjoy. (Don died in November, 1994. IK).

So here we are, forty seven years on and still in love with the music, still getting goose pimples when I hear Bix and Louis, still collecting records and books, still promoting, still enjoying every minute of it.

From Vic Smith

Whilst I was in the R.E.M.E. regiment of the Army I was transferred, on the 26 November, 1944, from the holding unit in St. Dunstan's School, Catford, to 11 Technical Training Unit at Mitcham Road Barracks, Croydon, to attend a vehicle mechanics course. Firstly, we were sent to an assault course camp in Shirley for a week, and during that time a VI rocket (doodlebug IK) destroyed the cookhouse.

Back at Croydon we were billeted in bombed-out houses, about one and a half miles from the barracks - they said the march would do us good!

I had been there about a week when I saw a notice on the Company Orders board that said "musicians wanted." We all laughed (where did they want the piano moved to?) and the others moved away. But not me; I had played alto and soprano saxophones for a couple of years, in my home town of Rotherham, in a band three or four of us had put together to play in a small dance hall.

So off I went, not knowing what to expect from the sergeant to whom you had to report. I was the only one reporting to him (no piano to move), and I told him all about my playing whereupon out came an alto, which he gave me saying, "play." Now I was not all that good, but he said "OK, you'll do. Report for band practice."

When I approached the practice hall I did not know what to expect and when I opened the door I was taken aback to see a large room containing a dance floor and full size stage on which a crowd of musicians had assembled. I swallowed hard and went in.

As we were tuning up, I looked around and saw that nearly all of the band members were sergeant instructors, and me only a few weeks in the Army! Although they looked after me, I did wonder what the leader, who had auditioned me, really thought when he picked up his alto to start the first time-off. He was superb. The band had a four man rhythm section, three trumpets, two trombones and five saxophones, with me on third alto.

What great dance nights we had; hundreds of girls and all the lads having a great time. It was a marvellous experience for me to sit in with some fine musicians, if only for a short period of my life. The leader, an excellent player, would go off sometimes to record (some of the band told me) with the top bands in London.

It was when I was stationed in Croydon and Catford that the area suffered very badly from the VI and VII rockets, many lives being lost and a great number of people injured.

A VI landed near our billet and later I was on a tram going towards New Cross Gate on the fateful Saturday afternoon when a VII had a direct hit on Woolworths. It was half a mile away, but the tram was blown off the rails and when we eventually got to the scene of the impact there was complete carnage.

One afternoon, on an early pass, (official Army authority to leave barracks) I ran to the railway station and went to London. I visited the Nuffield Centre (some called it the Queensbury Club) to see Glenn Miller and the Allied Expeditionary Force Band.

As you can see, my fourteen weeks in Croydon and two in Catford were eventful, to say the least, but a part of my life I will never forget - I still have my Army pay book, so the dates are correct (not bad for an eighteen year old).

I must come back and see Croydon again.

## Eric Silk's Southern Jazz Band

l to r
Tony Budd (drms); Ken Shepherd (tmb); Eric Silk (bjo); Alan Littlejohn (tpt); Lester Roberts (bs); Dennis Field (tpt); Don Simmons (cl); Peter Rees (pno).

John Rickard's "Jazz Band"

# CODA
# by
# John Rickard

Over two years have elapsed since Ian King penned the Introduction to this book, and as forecast in the opening paragraphs of the Early History chapter, the story is far from complete. The time that we had allocated ourselves to produce the finished article did not allow the depth of research necessary for a full study and we have therefore only been able to give a brief idea of the jazz music which could be heard in Croydon during the period under review.

We hope that you do not mind that we have occasionally strayed from the jazz path to include other elements of the Croydon scene. We felt that it was important to recall the *flavour* of those distant times, and how better to do this than to remember some possibly time-misted events, and also a few places from the past, many of which no longer exist but will always be associated with Croydon.

During the researching of material for the book we found that the names of many jazzmen repeatedly appeared in newspapers and programmes etc and we have included them wherever possible. It is, however, inevitable and regrettable that there may be some jazz musicians who have played in the town but have not been mentioned; hopefully, we will have opened some avenues leading down to memory lane, where others will later stroll and perhaps produce a more complete record of those early and late days of jazz in our town.

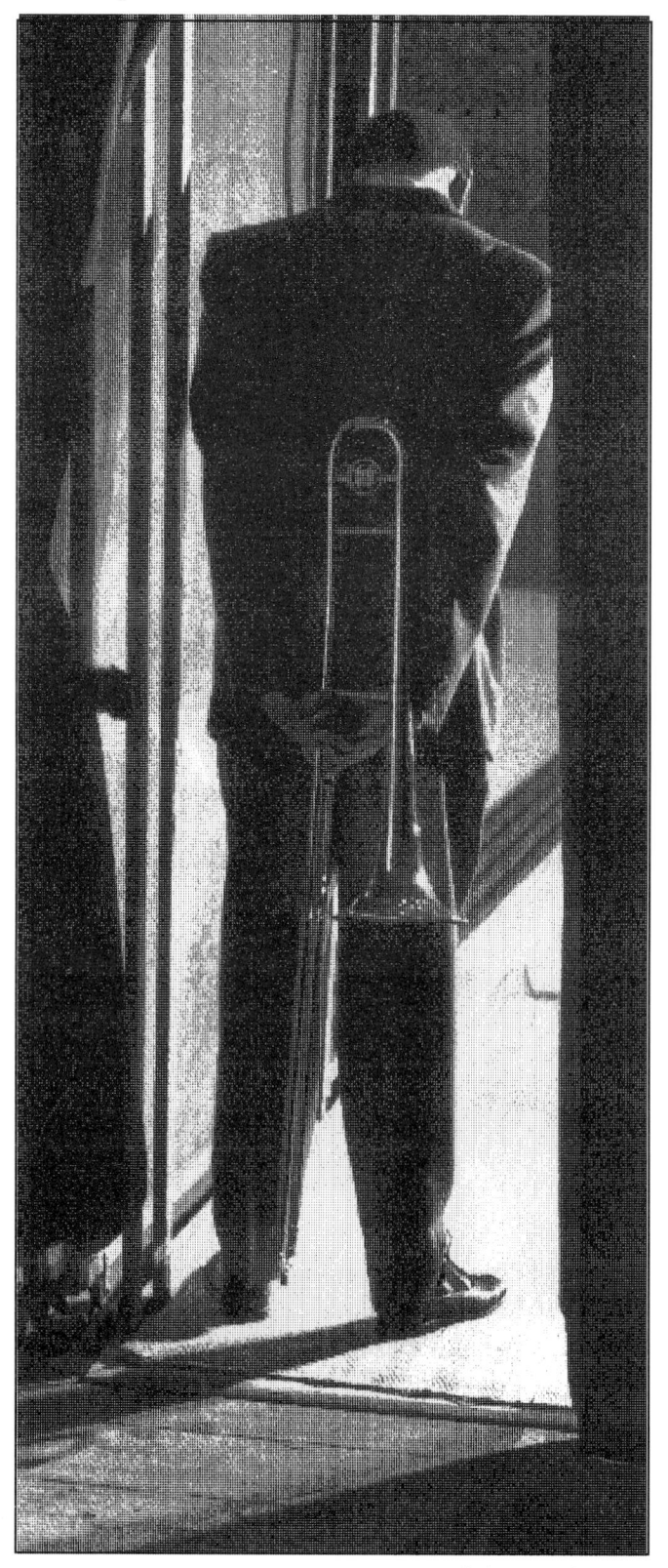

and beyond . . .

# APPENDIX I
## The North End (Civic) Hall

"Where Did The Good Times Go"

APPENDIX I

## THE NORTH END HALL

### CROYDON'S FINE NEW BUILDING ACCOMMODATION FOR 1,400 PEOPLE

From tomorrow (Sunday), thanks to private enterprise, Croydon will be in the possession of a hall worthy of its importance as a County Borough. Ever since the town has acquired immensity in regard to population - now bordering on two hundred thousand - there has always been a serious obstacle in the want of a hall of sufficiently large proportions to meet the requirements all the year round, but now the palatial North End Hall has come into being this reflection on otherwise, perhaps, the most progressive residential Borough in the country, no longer exists. The handsome structure which has sprung up during the past few months, absolutely unobserved by the general public, will undoubtedly become the principal place over a wide area for the holding of the more important social functions and public meetings of national and municipal interest. It would require a strong imaginative mind to picture the elaborate design and vastness of the main hall, especially when one considers its situation.

Encircled by commodious corridors, which open out from splendidly arranged vestibules, the hall is approached from North End and Crown Hill, and the entrances themselves are worthy of a close description. One enters from the North End under a massive domed porch - adjacent to Messrs Kennard's premises - leading to swing doors, which open into a long and broad passage floored with green and white marble in mosaic pattern.

The artistically designed ceiling and walls are of the same ivory tint, relieved with gold and empanelled with rose coloured satin paper. Another swing door breaks the draught that a direct communication might permit and through this one enters a vestibule, similarly decorated, and ending in an entrance to the hall, with corridors in close proximity. With a similar arrangement of doors everywhere, the possibility of draughts is prevented.

The corridor on the left of the North End entrance leads the visitor - beneath the balcony - past the public cloakrooms and into the columned "crush-hall," quite a feature of the building, which will prevent the possibility of confusion. Special attention has been paid to the electric lighting of this department, wherein is situate the box office, and an elaborate cut-glass bowl design electric light has been centrally installed. The box-office faces Crown Hill, and to the right and left there are corridors, each leading to entrances to the ground floor of the hall, while others serve to flights of stairs to the balconies, which have been constructed on each side of the hall. The Crown Hill approach is similar in practically every detail to that on the North End side; the adornment of walls and ceiling and the design of the floor are quite as elaborate, and there will be the added advantage that the pavement in front of it and along the whole length of the Brotherhood Institute will be covered in.

Without doubt the hall will compare favourable with some of the principal of those constructed for similar purposes in the provinces. It affords accommodation for between eleven and fourteen hundred, according to circumstances, and there are fixed seats for considerably more than a thousand. There is no distinction in the matter of comfort, for much thought has been given to procuring the best possible arrangements. The flooring throughout is of polished teak, provided for warmth and hygienic purposes, and every seat is richly upholstered in rose plush, framed in light satin wood, to tone with the general colour scheme, which has been admirably and effectively maintained. The aisles and passage-ways are thickly carpeted and the seats have been so arranged that an excellent view of the proscenium is afforded from all parts. The stalls are on a "raked" floor, which assures an uninterrupted view, and behind is the grand circle, arranged in tiers. Every part communicates easily with the others, and the balconies, running the full length of the hall on each side, are a prominent and unique feature of the building, which has been so constructed that unsightly columns have been found unnecessary. The embellishments are on a magnificent scale, and the lofty domed ceiling, delightfully designed in white and gold, should ensure, without structural obstructions, perfect acoustic properties. In lighting, heating and ventilation the arrangements are of the most modern type; the main illumination is furnished by eight electric pendants diffusing a soft light from the ceiling, while all round the hall are handsome bronze flambeaux, set in the centre of gold coloured laurel wreath designs, which produce an elegant effect. The system of heating consists of underground pipes, as well as radiators, which give a uniform warmth to the hall and corridors, and the hygienic ventilating apparatus, with the advantage of electric fans being in the roof, will prevent stuffiness and ensure a delightful temperature being maintained, both for winter and summer evenings.

The stage is what is termed a chamber stage, and is fronted with oak panelling. The proscenium, decorated in cream and gold, will be draped with rich rose coloured plush, embroidered with satin, and ornamented with gold, while the background will also be a plush curtain of the same colour surrounded by a scroll design in ivory and gold. At each side there are dressing and retiring rooms and with the ample provision of exits from all parts of the hall no confusion can result from the dispersal in a very few minutes of the largest of audiences.

Although the North End Hall owes its inception in a great measure to the growth of the North End Brotherhood, it should not for one moment be thought that the building is to be solely confined to being a meeting place for that progressive movement. The hall is controlled by a company of local gentlemen, whose ambition it is to make it the centre of all Christian and social enterprise in the borough, for everything that will make for the uplifting and happiness of the people. Recognising what an influence upon thought environment has, Mr Elwin Wrench, the President of the Brotherhood, told an "Advertiser" representative this week that those responsible for the origin of the hall have seen to it that it shall combine beauty and elegance with every advantage of utility. Believing that the cinematograph in the future will play an important part in the education, as well as the entertainment of the people, the promoters have installed the latest apparatus in a fire proof room at the rear of a recess above the grand circle, and equipment has been provided at enormous cost for every form of entertainment and meeting.

The third anniversary of the Brotherhood is being celebrated in the new hall tomorrow (Sunday) afternoon, when the speaker will be the Right Hon. Arthur Henderson, M.P., President of the National Brotherhood Council. On Wednesday the Right Hon. Dr T. J. Macnamara, M.P. Secretary to the Admiralty, will address a men's mass meeting, and the following Wednesday a grand evening concert will be given in aid of the distressed Belgians on the Continent.

The Croydon Advertiser and Surrey County Reporter - Saturday, 20th February, 1915

# APPENDIX II
### Fairfield

"Blue Skies"

APPENDIX II

## FAIRFIELD

On Friday, 2 November, 1962, the BBC Symphony Orchestra played in the Concert Hall at the opening ceremony of the Fairfield Halls and the Croydon Schools Orchestra took to the stage the following day.

Although little, if any, information is available about the shows, all credit to Fairfield for retaining their records and to the new Director, Derek Barr, for allowing access to the register to obtain details of the jazz concerts.

Further details were obtained for the years 1971/72 and 1976-1979 from photostat copies of the Croydon Advertiser held in Norbury by the Croydon Local Studies Library.[1]

The swing and dance bands have been included in our listings as they were an important part of the early history and development of British jazz. A number of the orchestras/bands still retain the names of their erstwhile leaders, such as Count Basie and Ted Heath, in order to continue with the style of music for which those band leaders became famous.

### 1962

Friday, 9 November, - *A Festival of Jazz - Mr Acker Bilk;* Monday, 19 November, Dave Brubeck - Harold Davison Promotions; Monday, 10 December, Frank Getgood presented Kenny Ball; Monday, 17 December, John Smith presented the Chris Barber Band.

### 1963

Friday, 22 February, Acker Bilk; Sunday, 21 April, Harold Davison presented Gerry Mulligan; Friday, 7 May, John Smith presented Acker Bilk; Saturday, 7 September, the Beatles; Wednesday, 18 September, Count Basie; Saturday, 2 November, Earl Gardiner; Tuesday, 26 November, Stan Kenton; Friday 6 December, the National Jazz Federation presented the Chris Barber Band.

### 1964

Monday, 27 January, Frank Sinatra with the Tommy Dorsey Orchestra; Wednesday, 19 February, Duke Ellington; Friday, 21 February, Sonny Boy Williamson & The Yardbirds and Chris Barber's Jazz Band; Friday, 13 March, Kenny Ball; Monday, 6 April, Ella Fitzgerald; Sunday, 12 April, the Rolling Stones; Sunday, 19 April, the Modern Jazz Quartet; Friday, 1 May, Shirley Bassey; Friday, 5 June, Acker Bilk; Wednesday, 8 July, Woody Herman; Monday, 20 July, Ray Charles; Monday, 19 October, The Blues Festival.

(1) The Local Studies Library moved to the main Croydon Library building in October, 1994.

## 1965

Wednesday, 17 February, the Duke Ellington Band; Sunday, 14 March, the United States Third Air Force Band (Jazz Concert); Saturday, 17 April, Oscar Peterson and Ella Fitzgerald; Friday, 10th September, an Oxfam Jazz Concert; Monday, 20 September, Count Basie; Monday, 11 October, the National Jazz Federation; Thursday, 21 October, a Jazz Quartet; another National Jazz Federation concert on Sunday, 24 October; Wednesday, 1st December, Dizzie Gillespie.

## 1966

*Jazz On A Summer's Day* on Saturday, 12 March; Friday, 6 May, Jimmy Witherspoon, George Melly and Diz Disley; Thursday, 12 May, the Ornette Colman Trio; Thursday, 9 June, Earl Gardiner; Friday, 10 June, the United States Air Force Band; Sunday, 25 September, the Modern Jazz Quartet; Friday, 21 October, the National Jazz Federation; Wednesday, 2 November, Dave Brubeck.

## 1967

Wednesday, 25 January, Woody Herman; Wednesday 22 March, *Jazz From A Swingin' Era;* Monday, 22 May, Count Basie; Monday, 16 October, the Max Roach Quintet; Harold Davison presented Dave Brubeck on Thursday, 26 October; Wednesday, 1st November, *Jazz Tête a Tête;* Thursday, 14 December, the Modern Jazz Quartet.

## 1968

Wednesday, 7 February, Woody Herman and His Orchestra; Wednesday, 19 June, *Jazz On A Summer's Day;* Monday, Thursday, 26 September, Buddy Rich & His Orchestra; 7 October, the Oscar Peterson Trio; Thursday, 24 October, The Earl Hines All Stars featuring Budd Johnson, Booty Wood, Maney Johnson, Bobby Donovan, Bill Pemberton, Oliver Jackson; Thursday, 12 December, Harold Davison presents The Jimmy Smith Trio.

## 1969

Friday, 24 January, The Roy Budd Trio, Roy Budd (piano), Jeff Clyne (bass), Chris Karan (drums); Sunday, 9 February, *Premier Percussion* The Kenny Clarke - Francy Boland Big Band; The Roland Kirk Quartet; The Philly Joe Jones Group; Thursday, 13 March, The Modern Jazz Quartet; Thursday, 24 April, Count Basie; Sunday, 18 May, Woody Herman; Thursday, 5 June, Edmundo Ros; Monday, 22 September, United States Air Force Band; Thursday, 25 September, The Oscar Peterson Trio; Wednesday, 19 November, Buddy Rich & His Orchestra.

## 1970

Thursday, 8 January, Edmundo Ros; Wednesday, 29 April, Glen Miller Orchestra; Sunday, 10 May, New Jazz Orchestra; Thursday, 14 May, Count Basie; Sunday, 17 May, Syd Lawrence Orchestra; Friday, 16 October, Edmundo Ros; Monday, 2 November, Dave Brubeck; Thursday, 10 December, Oscar Peterson; Friday, 18 December, Cat Stevens; Sunday, 20 December, John Smith presented Fleetwood Mac.

## 1971

Thursday, 11 March, *A Tribute To Glen Miller,* featuring the Clive Sharrock Orchestra; Sunday, 9 May, The Syd Lawrence Orchestra; Thursday 15 May, Count Basie and His Orchestra, featuring Mary Stallings; Friday, 15 October, Edmundo Ros and His Latin-American Orchestra; Monday, 1 November, Harry James and His Orchestra; Wednesday, 10 November, Buddy Rich and His Orchestra; Monday, 13 December, The World's Greatest Jazz Band of Yank Lawson and Bob Haggart.

## 1972

Thursday, 10 February, Stan Kenton and His Orchestra; Friday, 7 April, Jack Jones with Ronnie Scott and His Orchestra, featuring Tina Charles; Thursday, 4 May, *Spring Collection*, with Cleo Laine and the John Dankworth Quartet; Wednesday, 17 May, Mr Acker Bilk and His Paramount Jazz Band; Friday, 22 September, The Syd Lawrence Orchestra; Friday, 20 October, Edmundo Ros and His Orchestra; Wednesday, 1 November, Buddy Rich and His Orchestra; Wednesday, 15 November, Cyril Stapleton and His Showband.

## 1973

Friday, 23 February, Stan Kenton & His Orchestra; Friday, 16 March, the Glenn Miller Orchestra featuring Buddy de Franco; Wednesday, 23 May, Cleo Laine's *Spring Collection* with the John Dankworth Quartet; Tuesday, 28 August, Acker Bilk & His Paramount Jazz Band; Tuesday, 4 September, Georgie Fame and the Harry South Band; Tuesday, 18 September, The Ramsey Lewis Trio : Ramsey Lewis (piano), Cleveland Eaton (bass), Maurice Jennings (drums); Sunday, 23 September, The Syd Lawrence Orchestra; Thursday 4 October, Marian Montgomery and Her Musicians; Friday, 14 October, Ray Conniff & His Orchestra; Thursday, 25 October, Edmundo Ros & His Latin American Orchestra; Friday, 21 December, Joshua Rifkin.

## 1974

Thursday, 24 January, Woody Herman & His Orchestra; Tuesday, 5 February, George Melly & The Feetwarmers with special guest Peter Skellern; Monday, 25 March, The Tommy Dorsey Orchestra featuring Sy Oliver, The Pied Pipers & The Clambake 7; Friday, 31 May, Kenny Ball & His Jazzmen; Thursday, 4 July, The Chris Barber Band - Stephane Grappelli & the Diz Disley Trio; Sunday, 4 August, The Ted Heath Orchestra directed by Stan Reynolds M.C.; Tuesday, 10 September, *A History of Jazz Piano,* featuring Tom Bridges, Lennie Felix, Pat Hawes, Ray Smith, John Taylor and Stan Tracey, with Dave Green (bass) and Trevor Tomkins (drums); Thursday, 10 October, The World's Greatest Jazz Band of Yank Lawson & Bob Haggart with special guests Billy Butterfield and Maxine Sullivan; Sunday, 20 October, *The Ambassadors Of Jazz* featuring Lionel Hampton (vibes), Teddy Wilson (piano), Buddy Rich (drums), George Duvivier (bass); Sunday 27 October, George Melly & The Feetwarmers; Monday, 28 October, The Syd Lawrence Orchestra; Sunday, 1 December, Ray Conniff, His Singers and Orchestra; Friday, 6 December, Edmundo Ros & His Latin American Orchestra; Sunday, 15 December, *The Kings Of Jazz* with Pee Wee Irwin, Bernie Priven, Kenny Davern, Johnny Mince, Cliff Leeman, Dick Hyman, Ed Hubble and Major Holley.

## 1975

Wednesday, 15 January, Kenny Ball & His Jazzmen; Thursday, 6 February, Stan Kenton & His Orchestra; Friday, 14 February, The Paul Whiteman Orchestra with leader Richard Sudhalter; Thursday, 20 February, Humphrey Lyttelton and His Band and the Eddie Thompson Trio; Wednesday, 26 February, The Pasadena Roof with Joan Morris and William Bolcom; Friday, 28 February, The Syd Lawrence Orchestra; Thursday, 3 April, Oscar Peterson; Tuesday, 13 May, Cleo Laine and the John Dankworth Orchestra; Thursday, 29 May, *The Story Of Ragtime* : Neville Dickie assisted by Norman Davey (drums), with Keith Nichols & His Original Ragtime Orchestra with special guest Geoff Love; Thursday, 5 June, Chris Barber's Jazz & Blues Band with special guests, Lonnie Donegan and Monty Sunshine; Friday 27 June, The Pasadena Roof Orchestra; Sunday, 6 July, *An Evening With Spike Milligan & His Friends* : Dave Start, Wild Bill Davison and the Eddie Thompson Trio; Friday, 18 July, *A Tribute To Ted Heath* : The British All Stars Orchestra; Saturday, 2 August, Edmundo Ros & His Latin American Orchestra; Sunday, 13 September, Chris Barber's Jazz & Blues Band; Wednesday, 24 September, The Syd Lawrence Orchestra; Tuesday, 2 November, Kenny Ball & the Jazzmen : The Neville Dickie Boogie Woogie Quartet : Johnny Parker.

## 1976

Monday, 2 February, Woody Herman and His Orchestra; Friday, 27 February, The Syd Lawrence Orchestra, featuring Roy Marsden with Eleanor Keenan and the Serenaders; Thursday, 11 March, Acker Bilk and His Paramount Jazz Band; Monday, 23 March, Dave Brubeck Quartet, featuring Paul Desmond; Friday, 23 March, Geraldo's Concert and Dance Orchestra; Wednesday, 28 April, Chris Barber's Jazz and Blues Band; Tuesday, 11 May, George Melly and John Chilton's Feetwarmers; Thursday, 17 June, Kenny Ball and the Jazzmen; Tuesday, 6 July, *Louis Armstrong Anniversary Concert* : Alex Welsh and His Band, Humphrey Lyttelton, the Lennie Hastings Trio, Ruby Braff; Saturday, 17 July, National Youth Jazz Orchestra directed by Bill Ashton; Thursday, 9 September, Pasadena Roof Orchestra; Friday, 24 September, The Syd Lawrence Orchestra, featuring Sue Adams; Thursday, 30 September, Stan Kenton and His Orchestra; Tuesday, 9 November, The Ted Heath Band; Thursday, 2 December, *Major Glenn Miller Tribute Concert,* featuring Peanuts Hucko.

## 1977

Monday, 14 February, The Dutch Swing College Band with American pianist, Dick Wellstood; Thursday, 24 February, The Syd Lawrence Orchestra, featuring Roy Marsden, Jan Butler and the Serenaders; Thursday, 10 March, Oscar Peterson; Thursday, 21 April, Jazz Suite *Under Milk Wood* The Stan Tracey Quartet; Tuesday, 24 May, Chris Barber's Jazz and Blues Band; Thursday, 16 June, Stephane Grappelli in concert with The Diz Disley Trio; Wednesday, 6 July, Acker Bilk and His Paramount Band; Saturday, 10 September, Big Band Night : *Berlin Greets Croydon* : Caterina Valente with Paul Kuhn and the SFB Big Band; Thursday, 15 September, George Melly with John Chilton's Feetwarmers; Thursday, 22 September, The Syd Lawrence Orchestra, featuring Jan Butler; Monday, 26 September, Woody Herman and His Band; Thursday, 27 October, *Salute To Satchmo* : Alex Welsh and His Band with guest stars Humphrey Lyttelton, George Chisholm and Bruce Turner; Thursday, 3 November, The Barney Kessel Trio and Dick Wellstood; Monday, 7 November, Tony Bennett in concert with The Syd Lawrence Orchestra; Thursday, 10 November, *A Concert Tribute To Errol Garner* : Alan Clare, Lennie Felix, Dave Lee, Bill McGuffie, Eddie Thompson, supported by Lennie Bush (bass) and Bobby Orr (drums); Wednesday, 23 November, The National Youth Jazz Orchestra directed by Bill Ashton.

## 1978

Tuesday, 14 February, Dutch Swing College Band with pianist Dick Wellstood; Monday, 3 April, *Jazz On Film* : (Duke Ellington, Tommy Dorsey, Henry Hall, Debroy Somers and Harry Roy); Thursday, 20 April, Chris Barber's Jazz & Blues Band with American guests John Lewis (piano) and Trummy Young (trombone); Wednesday, 3 May, The Syd Lawrence Orchestra featuring Roy Marsden and Marie Toland; Friday, 12 May, George Melly with John Chilton's Feetwarmers; Tuesday, 21 May, Don Lusher Big Band with Valerie Masters; Wednesday, 31 May, Joe Pass; Thursday, 8 June, The Pasadena Roof Orchestra; Thursday, 22 June, Mr Acker Bilk and His Paramount Jazz Band; Thursday, 13 July, Kenny Ball and the Jazzmen; Thursday, 20 July, Bill Evans Trio : Bill Evans (piano), Red Mitchell (bass), Philly Joe Jones (drums) with guest Lee Konitz (alto sax); Friday, 8 September, Chris Barber's Jazz & Blues Band with guests Alvin Alcorn and Tommy Tucker; Tuesday, 24 October, Buddy Rich Band featuring Steve Marcus (ten sax); Friday, 3 November, Oscar Peterson with John Heard (bass) and Louie Bellson (drums); Tuesday, 21 November, *Salute To Satchmo* : Alex Welsh & His Band with guests George Chisholm (trombone) and Colin Smith (trumpet).

## 1979

Wednesday, 24 January, *Gershwin Evening* with the London Concert Orchestra; Thursday, 25 January, *Hot Jazz Spectacular* : Max Collie Rhythm Aces, The Midnite Follies Orchestra, Monty Sunshine's Jazz Band; Thursday, 8 March, *Basin Street To Harlem* : Humphrey Lyttelton & His Band; Tuesday, 10 April, Stephane Grappelli with the Diz Disley Trio; Thursday, 3 May, Syd Lawrence & His Orchestra with Roy Marsden and Angela Christian; Thursday, 7 June, Mr Acker Bilk & His Paramount Jazz Band; Friday, 15 June, The Pasadena Roof Orchestra; Friday, 20 July, Woody Herman & His Orchestra; Friday, 6 September, Kenny Ball & the Jazzmen; Friday, 12 October, Freddie Hubbard Quintet with guest Leon Thomas; Tuesday, 23 October, Gerry Mulligan & His Concert Big Band; Tuesday, 6 November, *Basin Street To Harlem* : Humphrey Lyttelton & His Band with American guest singer Joe Lee Wilson; Friday, 16 November, The Syd Lawrence Orchestra; Monday, 17 December, *A Tribute In Concert* : The Ted Heath Orchestra directed by Don Lusher.

## 1980

Thursday, 6 March, Chris Barber; Friday, 14 March, Buddy Rich; Tuesday, 8 April, Stephane Grappelli; Sunday, 20 April, Cleo Laine; Wednesday, 30 April, Pasadena Roof Orchestra; Thursday, 10 July, Mr Acker Bilk; Friday, 18 July, Jazz Class Concert; On Monday, 4th August, work started on the safety barriers; Thursday, 11 September, Preservation Hall Jazz Band; Wednesday, 1 October, Humphrey Lyttelton; Thursday, 23 October, Louis Bellson Band; Friday, 7 November, Joe Pass; Friday, 28 November, Geoff Love.

## 1981

Thursday, 8 January, The Pasadena Roof Orchestra; Saturday, 17 January, *A Cole Porter Evening* : The London City Orchestra; Thursday, 22 January, Matt Munro with the Eric Delaney Band; Wednesday, 4 February, Dutch Swing College Band with special guest, multi-instrumentalist Wout Steenhuis; Thursday, 5 March, *Take Me Back To New Orleans* : Chris Barber & His Jazz & Blues Band with special guests from the USA : Dr John and Freddie Kohlman; Saturday, 4 April, Geoff Love & His Orchestra; Friday, 1 May, Radio Big Band conducted by Barry Forgie, George Chisholm and his Gentlemen of Jazz, Rosemary Squires and Vince Hill; Monday, 4 May, Stephane Grappelli with Diz Disley (guitar), Martin Taylor (guitar), Jack Sewing (bass) and David Grisman and His Band; Friday, 8 May, The Midnite Follies Orchestra, Velvet, Sweet Substitute; Thursday, 14 May, Art Pepper Quartet; Friday, 15 May, The Ted Heath Orchestra directed by Don Lusher, with Dennis Lotis. The Dave Shepherd Sextet. Carole Carr; Friday, 5 June, Lonnie Donegan Jubilee Concert; Tuesday, 16 June, *All That Jazz;* Wednesday, 8 July, Kenny Ball; Monday, 13 July, Film - *The Jazz Singer;* Tuesday, 22 September, Preservation Hall Jazz Band; Thursday/Friday, 8/9 October, Geoff Love & His Orchestra; Friday, 27 November, Syd Lawrence and His Orchestra with Jeff Hooper and Eleanor Keenan; Tuesday, 1 December, Mr Acker Bilk.

## 1982

Thursday, 7 January, Midnight Follies; Monday, 11 January, Bob Kerr's Whoopee Band; Thursday, 14 January, Jazz Presentation by Digby Fairweather; Thursday, 4 February, Pasadena Roof Orchestra; Friday, 23 April, The Radio Big Band conducted by Billy May, with Matt Monro. The Dixieland Quartet (Kenny Baker - trumpet, Roy Williams - trombone, Danny Moss - tenor saxophone, Henry MacKenzie - Clarinet); Friday, 30 April, The Don Lusher Big Band Show, with Angela Christian; Monday, 3 May, Stephane Grappelli; Tuesday, 4 May, King Singers; Thursday, 20 May, Chris Barber's Jazz & Blues Band; Friday, 11 June, The Music of Fats Waller & Louis Armstrong, with Humphrey Lyttelton, Keith Smith & Hefty Jazz. Sweet Substitute; Wednesday, 14 July, Kenny Ball; Friday, 17 September, Arnhem Link: Dutch Swing College Band; Thursday, 23 September, Preservation Hall Jazz Band; Thursday, 11 November, *A Tribute To Alex Welsh;* Tuesday, 21 December, Cleo Laine & John Dankworth.

## 1983

Thursday, 13 January, Mr Acker Bilk; Thursday, 27 January, Pasadena Roof Orchestra; Wednesday, 27 April, Ted Heath; Tuesday, 3 May, Humphrey Lyttelton Band with guests Wally Fawkes, John Picard and Kathy Stobart; Wednesday, 14 September, Kenny Ball; Thursday, 20 October, *100 Years of American Dixieland Jazz* featuring the American All Stars : Johnny Mince (clarinet), Eddie Hubble (trombone), Johnny Guarnieri (piano), Arvell Shaw (bass), Barrett Deems (drums) with Britain's Keith Smith (trumpet); Friday, 28 October, Stephane Grappelli with Martin Taylor (electric guitar), Marc Fosset (acoustic guitar), Jack Sewing (bass); Thursday, 10 November, Rosemary Clooney and Buddy Greco; Friday, 18 November, Syd Lawrence.

## 1984

Wednesday, 8 February, The Temperance Seven; Thursday, 8 March, The Chris Barber Jazz & Blues Band with guests Ottilie Patterson, Ken Colyer and Monty Sunshine; Tuesday, 20 March, Jazz on Film; Wednesday, 9 May, Pasadena Roof Orchestra; Saturday, 26 May, *An Evening With* Miss Peggy Lee *And Her Musicians*; Monday, 12 July, Mr Acker Bilk & His Paramount Jazz Band; Tuesday, 18 September, *Mardi Gras* : Max Collie, Cy Laurie, Ken Colyer; Friday, 19 October, The Buddy de Franco Quintet featuring Martin Taylor (guitar), Alex Shaw (piano), Ron Rae (bass) and Clark Tracey (drums); Wednesday, 31 October, *75th Anniversary Tribute to Benny Goodman* featuring Billy Butterfield (trumpet), Abe Most (clarinet), Urbie Green (trombone), Hank Jones (piano), Slam Stewart (bass), Don Lamond (drums) and Peter Appleyard (vibraphone) with special guest star Jack Brymer (clarinet); Friday, 16 November, Syd Lawrence & His Orchestra; Tuesday, 29 November, George Melly and John Chilton's Feetwarmers.

## 1985

Tuesday, 29 January, The Humphrey Lyttelton Band with Bruce Turner, John Barnes, Pete Strange, Mick Pyne, Paul Bridge, Adrian MacIntosh, and special guest Wally Fawkes; Thursday, 7 February, Chris Barber's Jazz & Blues Band with Pat Halcox, John Crocker, Ian Wheeler, Johnny McCallum, Roger Hill, Vic Pitt, Norman Emberson and special guest Ken Colyer; Sunday, 17 February, The Stan Tracey Quartet, with Sal Nisto; Friday, 29 February, The Dutch Swing College Band - 40th Anniversary Tour; Tuesday, 7 May, Anne Shelton and the Squadronnaires; Saturday, 22 June, Pasadena Roof Orchestra; Friday, 28 October, *South Rampart Street Parade* with the Bobcats : Yank Lawson (trumpet), Bob Haggart (bass), Bob Havens (trombone), Abe Most (clarinet), Nick Fatool (drums), Marty Grosz (guitar/vocals), Lou Stein (piano), Eddie Miller (tenor sax); Friday, 1 November, Stephane Grappelli with Martin Taylor (electric guitar), Marc Fosset (acoustic guitar), Jack Sewing (bass) and special guest Jean-Loup Longnon (trumpet); Friday, 15 November, The Syd Lawrence Orchestra featuring Jeff Hooper; Wednesday, 4 December, Joe Loss & His Orchestra - 55th Anniversary Celebration Concert.

## 1986

Tuesday, 11 February, George Melly with John Chilton's Feetwarmers; Thursday, 6 March, Chris Barber's Jazz & Blues Band; Thursday, 17 July, *100 Years of Dixieland Jazz* with George Chisholm, Keith Smith and Hefty Jazz; Friday, 10 October, Cleo Laine and the John Dankworth Quintet; Thursday, 16 October, George Melly and John Chilton's Feetwarmers, Mr Acker Bilk and his Paramount Jazz Band, Kenny Ball and his Jazzmen; Sunday, 2 November, Sonny Rollins; Friday, 21 November, Syd Lawrence & His Orchestra featuring Jeff Hooper and Angela Christian; Saturday, 6 December, The Ted Heath Band directed by Don Lusher with Lita Roza and Dennis Lotis.

## 1987

Friday, 16 January, The Pasadena Roof Orchestra; Friday, 30 January, 4th International Guitar Festival starring Barney Kessel and His Trio (USA), Juan Martin (Spain), Jorge Morel (Argentina), Vic Juris (USA), Antonio Forcione (Itay), Martin Taylor (UK), The Bireli Largrene Trio (France); Thursday, 5 March, Chris Barber's Jazz & Blues Band; Thursday, 16 April, Courtney Pine in Concert; Tuesday, 21 July, George Melly and John Chilton's Feetwarmers; Friday, 2 October, *Swing On Tenth Avenue* : A tribute to the music of George Gershwin, featuring Georgie Fame, Elaine Delmar, Keith Smith and Hefty Jazz; Friday, 23 October, *American Festival Of Jazz* with Peanuts Hucko and Yank Lawson; Saturday, 24 October, Mike Brecker Band and the Andy Sheppard Band; Wednesday, 4 November, Syd Lawrence Orchestra featuring Jeff Hooper and Tracy Miller; Friday, 4 December, The Don Lusher Big Band with Kenny Baker and Tommy Whittle.

## 1988

Wednesday, 6 January, The Pasadena Roof Orchestra; Friday, 12 February, *The Fabulous Forties Show* with George Chisholm, Maxine Daniels and the John Petters Swing Band; Friday, 4 March, Tony Bennett in Concert with the Ralph Sharon Trio; Friday, 25 March, Dutch Swing College Band; Thursday, 7 April, Chris Barber's Jazz & Blues Band with special guest Ottilie Patterson; Wednesday, 20 April, Lonnie Donegan with Max Collie & His Rhythm Aces; Saturday, 23 April, Mr Acker Bilk & His Paramount Jazz Band; Saturday, 18 June, *BBC Radio 2 Festival Of Music - Concert 4* : The Syd Lawrence Orchestra featuring Angela Christian and Jeff Hooper, with The Danny Moss Quartet and Jeanie Lambe; Friday, 30 September, Kenny Ball & His Jazzmen; Saturday, 29 October, Shades of Kenton Orchestra; Friday, 11 November, Syd Lawrence & His Orchestra; Friday, 2 December, Don Lusher Big Band with Kenny Baker, Tommy Whittle, Henry MacKenzie.

## 1989

Wednesday, 8 February, Count Basie Orchestra led by Frank Foster; Tuesday, 14 February, Pasadena Roof Orchestra; Thursday, 13 April, Chris Barber's Jazz & Blues Band (35th Anniversary Tour), Special guests, Monty Sunshine, Lonnie Donegan, Pat Halcox, Ron Bowden and Jim Bray; Friday, 21 April, *When The Swing Comes Marching In* : The Dutch Swing College Band, The Central Band of the RAF, and special guest, Kenny Baker; Tuesday, 23 May, An Evening With Courtney Pine Quintet; Saturday, 17 June, Tony Kinsey All Star Band featuring vocalist Lois Lane; Saturday, 22 July, Mr Acker Bilk & His Paramount Jazz Band; Monday, 18 September, Croydon Jazz Society presented the Ken Colyer Trust Band in the Arnhem Gallery; Tuesday, 26 September, Humphrey Lyttelton & His Band *Echoes of the Duke* with Helen Shapiro; Saturday, 30 September, Cleo Laine with John Dankworth & The Quintet; Saturday, 14 October, The Ted Heath Band directed by Don Lusher; Monday, 16 October, Croydon Jazz Society presented the Max Collie Rhythm Aces in the Arnhem Gallery; Tuesday, 31 October, Benny Goodman Alumni; Monday, 13 November, Croydon Jazz Society presented Cuff Billett's Europa Jazz Band in the Arnhem Gallery; Thursday, 23 November, Central Band of the RAF; Saturday, 9 December, The Syd Lawrence Orchestra.

## 1990

Saturday, 20 January, The Pasadena Roof Orchestra; Monday, 5 February, The Glenn Miller Orchestra and special guests the Kaye Sisters; Saturday, 24 February, Shades of Kenton Orchestra; Friday, 9 March, Don Lusher Big Band with special guest Sheila Southern; Tuesday, 10 April The Legendary Eartha Kitt; Friday, 20 April, The Dutch Swing College - 45th Anniversary Tour; Monday, 23 April, George Melly and John Chilton's Feetwarmers; Thursday, 17 May, Chris Barber's Jazz & Blues Band; Thursday, 24 May, *The Great Guitars* : Barney Kessel (USA), Charlie Byrd (USA), Martin Taylor (UK), The Gypsy Magic of Boulon and Elios Ferre (France), Jan Davils (Spain); Thursday, 7 June, *Stepping Out* : Graham Dalby ad the Gramophone 1930's Orchestra with the Jiving Lindyhoppers; Friday, 21 September, Don Lusher (trombone) with the Upper Norwood S.A. Band; Tuesday, 25 September, The Glenn Miller Orchestra (UK); Friday, 12 October, *Humph 'n' Helen* : Helen Shapiro with Humphrey Lyttelton & His Band; Wednesday, 14 November, Oliver Jones Trio : Oliver Jones (piano), Spike Heatley (bass), Malcolm Mortimer (drums); Friday, 23 November, Ted Heath Band directed by Don Lusher; Saturday, 8 December, The Syd Lawrence Orchestra.

## 1991

Friday, 18 January, Pasadena Roof Orchestra; Thursday, 18 April, Kenny Ball, Kenny Baker & George Chisholm; Thursday, Friday, 10 May, Len Phillips Big Band, with Dennis Lotis (Arnhem Gallery); Monday, 13 May - Wednesday, 15 May, Bertice Reading (Ashcroft Theatre); 13 June, Stephane Grappelli; Tuesday, 9 July, *Jazz All Stars 'In Session'!* - Spike Robinson, Kenny Baker, Roy Williams, Ellen Rucker, Dave Green, Jack Parnell; Tuesday, 23 July, *Mardi Gras* : Bo Dollis and the Wild Magnolias with the ReBirth Brass Band; Friday, 25 October, The Ted Heath Orchestra directed by Don Lusher featuring Lita Rosa, Dennis Lotis, Kenny Baker, Jack Parnell, Tommy Whittle; Saturday, 7 December, The Syd Lawrence Orchestra; Monday, 30 December, The Glenn Miller Orchestra directed by John Watson featuring Tony Mansell and Donna Canale, with the Moonlight Serenaders and the Uptown Hall Gang.

## 1992

Saturday, 11 January, The Pasadena Roof Orchestra; Friday, 28 February, The Don Lusher Big Band; Thursday, 19 March, Chris Barber's Jazz & Blues Band; Friday, 27 March, Danish Radio Big Band; Sunday, 5 April, *In The Mood* : A Tribute to Glenn Miller; Friday, 24 April, Jeff Hooper's *A Swing Affair* with Freddy Staff's All Star Big Band; Tuesday, 12 May, The Dutch Swing College Band; Saturday, 27 June, *Jazz Platform* (sponsored by Jazz FM 102.2) : The Jack Parnell Quintet, The Ronnie Scott Sextet, Kenny Baker; Sunday, 28 June, Grand Union Band, *Jazz And World Music,* Arnhem Gallery; Tuesday, 14 July, *The Great Guitars* featuring Charlie Byrd, Barney Kessel, Martin Taylor and Louis Stewart with Dave Green (bass) and Martin Drew (drums); Thursday, 13 August, Bob Wilber and Kenny Davern *Summit Re-Union,* with the Oliver Jones Trio; Friday, 4 September, *Humph "n" Helen* : Helen Shapiro and the Humphrey Lyttelton Band; Friday, 2 October, The BBC Big Band conducted by Barry Forgie, with special guest Selina Jones; Friday, 9 October, The Modern Jazz Quartet (40th Anniversary); Wednesday, 21 October, Cleo Laine & The John Dankworth Quintet; Saturday 24 October, *Ted Heath Memorial Concert* : The Ted Heath Band conducted by Don Lusher; Saturday, 5 December, The Syd Lawrence Orchestra; Wednesday, 30 December, The Glenn Miller Orchestra directed by John Watson.

## 1993

Wednesday, 13 January, The Pasadena Roof Orchestra; Wednesday, 20 January, National Youth Jazz Orchestra directed by Bill Ashton; Saturday, 30 January, Harry Stoneham - Jazz Organist, Arnhem Gallery; Wednesday, 17 February, *In The Mood* The Herb Miller Orchestra and singers; Friday, 5 March, The Don Lusher Big Band with Sheila Southern, Kenny Baker and Tommy Whittle; Thursday, 18 March, Chris Barber's Jazz & Blues Band, with special guest Lonnie Donegan; Thursday, 20 May, The Bert Kaempfert Orchestra directed by Tony Fisher; Friday, 28 May, Jeff Hooper's *Swing Affair,* directed by Freddy Staff; Tuesday, 22 June, George Shearing with Neil Swainson and Louis Stewart (guitar); Wednesday 14 July, *Jazz On A Summer's Night* with Acker Bilk & the Paramount Jazz Band; Friday, 23 July, *The Jerome Kern Song Book;* Thursday, 9 September, Stephane Grappelli with Marc Fosset and Jean Philippe Veret; Sunday, 10 October, Gershwin's, Ashcroft Theatre; Saturday, 16 October, The Ted Heath Band directed by Don Lusher; Saturday, 4 December, The Syd Lawrence Orchestra, with Tony Jacobs, Sarah Gilbert, with compère Alan Dell; Thursday, 30 December, The Glenn Miller Orchestra directed by John Watson, featuring Tony Mansell and Donna Canale with The Moonlight Serenaders and The Uptown Hall Gang.

## 1994

Saturday, 15 January, The Pasadena Roof Orchestra directed by John Arthy, with singer Duncan Galloway; Saturday, 29 January, Harry Stoneham, *The Great Name of British Organ Jazz,* Arnhem Gallery; Sunday, 6 March, Band Of The United States Airforce In Europe, featuring a special 50th Anniversary tribute to the music of Major Glenn Miller; Sunday, 27 March, *Big Band Orchestral Sounds of the 60's & 70's* : The Bert Kaempfert Orchestra directed by Tony Fisher; Friday, 15 April, Chris Barber's Jazz & Blues Band, 40th Anniversary Concert, with Lonnie Donegan, featuring the original 1954 Chris Barber Jazz Band; Wednesday, 20 April, The Very Best of Mr Bilk and Mr Ball; Sunday, 5 June, *Finale to Croydon Jazz Week* : A Tribute To Benny Goodman, with Bob Wilber and the All-Star Big Band featuring Joanne Horton, including repertoire from the 1938 Carnegie Hall concert; Thursday, 16 June, The Joe Loss Orchestra and singing stars; Saturday, 25 June, Don Lusher Band with Kenny Baker, Tommy Whittle and special guest star Sheila Southern; Wednesday, 13 July, Gail Thompson's Gail Force Big Band; Tuesday, 20 September, *Big Band Special.* The BBC Big Band conducted by Barry Forgie, with special guest Bobby Shew - trumpet (USA); Friday, 23 September, *The Ella Fitzgerald Songbook Show* , featuring Rosemary Squires, Maxine Daniels, Barbara Jay, with Tommy Whittle - tenor saxophone, - Brian Dee - piano, Jim Richardson - bass and Bobby Worth - drums, at the Ashcroft Theatre; Friday, 18 November, The Ted Heath Band directed by Don Lusher, with Jack Parnell, Dennis Lotis, Kenny Baker and Tommy Whittle; Saturday, 3 December, The Syd Lawrence Orchestra : *Moonlight Serenade* - a 50th anniversary tribute to Glenn Miller, with The Minting Sisters.

# APPENDIX 111

## Kings Jazz Review

"Wrap Your Troubles In Dreams"

APPENDIX III


KINGS JAZZ REVIEW


The Croydon Jazz Society was formed by Ian King in 1989 and in that year presented three concerts in the Arnhem Gallery, Fairfield Halls.[1]

>Monday, 18 September, The Ken Colyer Trust Band.
>Monday, 16 October, The Max Collie Rhythm Aces.
>Monday, 13 November, Cuff Billett's Europa Jazz Band.

Prior to the formation of the Society, Ian had started to publish Kings Jazz Review (KJR), the first edition being in November, 1988, and later it was intended that it would become the Society's house magazine. However, due to lack of public support, both for the concerts and the Society in general, a decision was taken in 1990 to suspend the Society and maintain publication of KJR with the help of my wife, Donna, and myself.

Although it was a great struggle in the early years, subscribers to the magazine gradually increased over the years and its acceptance in the initial stages can be put down to a series of articles which Ian wrote between February, 1989, and September, 1991. These articles were, in essence, appraisals of the recordings made by Louis Armstrong and his Hot Five.

As the survival of KJR in its formative years was mainly due to these "reviews," their importance is such that they are re-produced in the following pages.

Today, KJR is flourishing, with readers as far afield as America, Germany, Holland and New Zealand. The Assistant to the Curator of the Tulane Jazz Archive in New Orleans, Alma D. Williams, has recently requested a complete set of back issues of the magazine, and we have been happy to supply them.

KJR is Croydon's only home-based periodical, and one of the very few in England, devoted solely to the New Orleans, Dixieland and Traditional styles of jazz.

John Rickard

(1) See pages 94 & 96

KJR No. 2. (February, 1989)
Louis Armstrong and his Hot Five - 1925

PERSONNEL

Louis Armstrong (cornet, vocals); Kid Ory (trombone); Johnny Dodds (clarinet, alto); Lillian Hardin (piano); John A St Cyr (banjo).

In Chicago, on the 12 November, 1925, Louis Armstrong recorded *My Heart; Yes, I'm In The Barrel; Gut Bucket Blues* and *Come Back Sweet Papa.* This was his first date during the formation of his now famous Hot Five.

This young 25 year old cornettist to whom we are listening on his first tune, *My Heart,* is talking about (if 'talking' is the right expression to use) Lillian Hardin. They had not long been married when Louis cut this record, and the result is that here we have a charming harmonic number. He plays with an easy swing not often heard on his other early recordings. Take a crack at standing on one spot and not moving from it in any jazz dance square, and swing your body, alternating the heel and toes from foot to foot, and you'll see what I mean. The 'Scat-Tapping Jive.'

*Yes, I'm In The Barrel* and *Come Back Sweet Papa* are tributes to Joe Oliver (Papa Joe), whom he left in the summer of 1924. It was during the two years with King Oliver that Louis picked up valuable points of rhythmic phrasing, although he spent four years perfecting his style, and with the Joe Oliver band, Louis learned the technique of how to take the lead in melody.

*Gut Bucket Blues,* on the lyrics *Oh play that thing, everybody in New Orleans can do it* was one of Louis' early attempts at vocals and his public came to like his garbled words and appealing shouts. This blossomed, and later the important quality and feeling of tenderness came into his singing.

KJR No. 3. (Apr/June '89)
Louis Armstrong and his Hot Five - 1926

The place, Chicago; the date, 26th February, 1926, an epoch now well known in the annals of Dixieland jazz. Louis Armstrong recorded *Georgia Grind; Heebie Jeebies; Cornet Chop Suey; Oriental Strut; You're Next* and *Muskrat Ramble.*

Louis was by then well known, by way of his many recordings, produced whilst working third chair in the new three-man trumpet section of the Fletcher Henderson band in New York. These records were made in collaboration with pianist Clarence Williams and soprano-saxophonist Sidney Bechet. But his Hot Five series were the first expression of him as a soloist musician.

Above all, the Hot Five sessions have become special masterpieces, among this vast Armstrong output, notably for the particular style, which came about by playing with his fellow New Orleanians who understood exactly what the musical situation demanded. More remarkable because by this time Louis had outgrown his early ideas and was then beginning to make less use of the plunger mute, an Oliver trademark. He had moved over to playing the trumpet, but for these occasions, in order to obtain the New Orleans sound, he bowed to tradition and played cornet.

Lil (Lillian) Armstrong (née Hardin) could see the potential in her husband's rapidly expanding abilities. It was largely through her influence that the Okeh record company offered the contract for these dates. Louis gave notice to Henderson and came to Chicago to be with Lil, who was sharing the Dreamland bandstand with trombonist Kid Ory. Clarinettist Johnny Dodds and banjoist John A St Cyr, both Oliver alumni, were in town and therefore there were no adjustments needed for the recording and there was little requirement for rehearsals. Interestingly, the group assembled for the sole purpose of cutting these records and never played together as a band elsewhere.

A prime element in the success of these recordings was that Louis learned, when playing with King Oliver, the value of discretion and restraint, working to create the best image and sound for his band, rather than seeking outright attention for the individual soloist.

However, in later years the public was to demand more of his individual talents and it was virtually impossible for him not to oblige.

The first of the six recordings is *Georgia Grind,* a minor performance by Louis, for it features mainly some beautiful blues clarinet and positive, punchy trombone playing. Clearly, Louis' devotion on this record centres on the catchy, chanting love-call tune sung between Lil and himself. Lil leads the way with *Papa, Papa, just look at her, out in the backyard shaking like tha'a,* with a return call from Louis, *Come in here now girl - come in here right now. Georgia Grind* makes one want to listen to it over and over again.

*Heebie Jeebies* put Louis into the best seller category by his impromptu scat vocals; the question is, did he drop his song lyrics during recording? The great thing about jazzmen is their ability to improvise, and I get the feeling that that may have happened in this case, to marvellous effect. The tune has a lovely lilt to it, embracing a nice swing.

*Cornet Chop Suey* is a powerful exposition of Louis' ever expanding musical imagination. A crisp three bar cornet opening solo, and later much higher register playing. There is some nice lead timing on banjo and a long piano solo, for a lovely balancing effect. The main bedrock of New Orleans bands has always been sensitive ensemble playing, and while Ory and Dodds were perhaps in praise of Armstrong's abilities they were, at times, ill at ease with his soaring digressions.

*Oriental Strut* is a St Cyr tune, one which all banjo lovers should listen to. It is one of my favourite numbers. I'll call it a singing cornet melody. I say this because Louis gives us an unhurried cornet melody full of song. On Lil's *Your Next,* one can detect the Armstrong innovative style which later he was to develop to the full. But to bring it all into perspective *Muskrat Ramble* is an early number, credited to Kid Ory, and features splendidly the Louis New Orleans lead cornet.

## KJR No. 4. (July/Sept '89)
## Louis Armstrong and his Hot Five - 1926

I am to apologise. It was pointed out that the date referred to in the previous quarterly should have read 16th June and not the 14th June, 1926, as written. This is correct, for on that day Louis Armstrong and his Hot Five recorded *Don't Forget To Mess Around; I'm Gonna Gitcha; Droppin' Shucks* and *Who's It*.

Any jazz trumpeter who has not listened to any one of those records is missing an invaluable element in the playing of their chosen music, as those records are part of a collection which is unique in history and never to be repeated. They chart Louis' progress from his first realisation of his own potential and show how he was able to remain a true New Orleans musician, whilst upholding his position in the advance guard of other progressive trumpet players around Chicago and New York at the time.

Although Louis worked creatively within the constraints of the gutbucket atmosphere of the Hot Five session period, one can feel that there was a natural inclination in him to exploit his abilities exhibitionistically. Today, we are the beneficiaries of those rigid rules of New Orleans playing. The musicians anticipated each other's move in turn, as each one passes the parcel, and they play with joyous movements of expression and extraordinary unity, with spontaneous creativeness and astonishing rapport. As a result of these sessions, we are rewarded by many appealing components of magnificent cornet solos.

To the Armstrong follower, it must be very difficult to deflect attention to the other members of his Hot Five ensemble. That is to say from the listeners's point of view. In *Don't Forget To Mess Around, When You're Doing The Charleston . . . don't forget to do your stuff, with the jazzband men around,* Louis is inviting his fans to take heed of the talent that he has around him. In so doing, one will be able to hear some of the most beautiful jazz co-ordinated playing one is ever likely to encounter.

It was a period in which jazz undertook some dramatic changes, significantly so when one begins to realise that few jazzmen of prominence recorded any records of any standing prior to 1924.

Yet without Armstrong during this period of white band expansion, there would not have been any correct balance of advancement in the musical development of jazz.

In *I'm Gonna Gitcha,* Louis is out on his own and portrays beautifully the novel creations that we were to hear coming from his horn in later years. He holds the listener's interest with phrases, unhurried and timely, in anticipation of the melodic passages which he mirrors are to follow. An accomplished first foot on the platform for the Armstrong vocals in *Hey Mama . . . I'm gonna gitcha . . . some sweet day . . . you can't get away* make listening to this one all the more enjoyable, but to overlook the Dodds alto saxophone and the 'Dut dut, te dut ta' clarinet playing would be most unforgivable, for it really is enchanting.

The tempo on *Droppin' Shucks* is much slower, with the piano and banjo controlling the mood most of the time. One can savour some of the best of Johnny Dodds' blues clarinet playing. As with several New Orleans tunes, there are musical phrases which intermingle in various tunes and the vocals here could quite easily fit in comfortably with the previous number. *Sweet Mamma . . . droppin' shucks . . . I'm gonna droppin' on you . . . roses are red, violets are blue . . . what's the matter with you.* It would not be complete without a mention that there cannot be many trombone players around today who have not at one time or another emulated note for note Kid Ory on this tune.

On *Who's It* one can listen to some clear, beautifully articulated piano and a composition of perfectly formed blues clarinet of opulence in the low register, in accompaniment to a Louis novel slide-whistle. Now, just listen to Kid Ory. In no way does Louis outshine his Hot Five sidemen. Yes, Louis is playing full bodied, yet with rounded cornet tone and a profound feeling in line for the blues; it is his kind of blend of musical creation and an acknowledgement form of entertainment that has kept for him a tremendous global following of listeners, sympathetic to jazz music.

## KJR Vol.2 No.1 (Oct/Dec '89)
### Louis Armstrong and his Hot Five - 1926

With no quarrel about the dates mentioned in the last quarterly to contend with, I can without any more ado name the four tunes that the Hot Five recorded in Chicago on 23 June, 1926: *King Of The Zulus; Big Fat Ma And Skinny Pa; Lonesome Blues* and *Sweet Little Papa.*

It was a year during the first golden age of jazz, the second age coming on from that period in New York some twenty years later. But, for the moment, Chicago was the place where much progression was taking place and new ideas in jazz were being developed and created.

Having been refused more money from Bill Bottoms, owner of Café Dreamland, Lil Armstrong and her pieces of eight band (group) had quit playing at this venue. Louis having been persuaded by Earl Hines to join the "Young Ones" was by now holding a chair in the Carol Dickerson Sunset Café Orchestra. It is perhaps important to mention that it was during Louis' stint at Dreamland that he was at his most creative and where he gained his reputation as being the best jazz trumpeter around, with several notables in challenge for the title. Thus, Armstrong was beginning to live up to his billing, insisted upon by Lil on his starting work at the Café, as the "World's Greatest Trumpet Player."

Kid Ory had recently moved to Chicago and was with King Oliver's "Dixie Syncopators." At the Dreamland Café Ballroom, Doc Cook had put together an orchestra with John A St Cyr in the line-up. In the more intimate surroundings of the Nest Club the Dodds brothers were in residence, so that the Hot Five jazz musicians were all readily available and on hand to make these historic recordings.

During this period, Louis kept playing for Erskine Tate, a popular orchestra conductor of the theatre, and it was during his days at the Vendome Theatre under Tate that he acquired a vast young audience from those who could not afford the high entrance prices to the nightclubs, but who could afford a box office ticket to watch a film show. Indeed, many of them went to the place for the sole purpose of listening to the great man himself, and so the Hot Five recordings present only a small but important picture of the complete Armstrong musical activities.

We can now turn to the first of our four tunes mentioned above. Apart from the opening few bars of ensemble playing, there is a very fine cornet solo on *King Of The Zulus,* with much feeling and emotion, taking in a meteoric scream on a seven pulse High C, not to mention some beautiful banjo accompaniment, marred by a short interaction by the other instruments. I cannot help feeling that the cornet and banjo alone were all that was required of this recording to make it stand out as one of *the* greats among the great Armstrong classics in this series.

Presumably, in sympathy with the title, but with what certainly seems to have been an afterthought, the intrusive, strange incantations, *chippling row from Jamaica . . . interruption of the solo . . . wait, man, wait,* somehow seem not right and sounds utterly misplaced. Since recordings were limited to three minutes in those days, this one just short of that, I get the feeling that the slot-in chanting was for commercial reasons, to appeal to the great influx in the Chicago population coming up from the South, for it is certain that Armstrong could have extended his solo threefold as he was accustomed to when playing in the clubs.

With an audible blow and whistle sown into his instrument, Kid Ory leads in with a full bodied rounded tone trombone on a commanding four, five pulse, 2 bar repeat introduction to *Big Fat Ma And Skinny Pa,* as if to announce without ambiguity to which side on the dance display lay his support. In this second tune of the four in question, Louis concentrates on vocals turning the lyrics into song, more tuneful than his earlier garbled vocals, *Everybody fall in line, grab your partners and get back on time,* creating for the first time a new tone and melodic musical expression on the Hot Five recordings.

There is a marked sign that the musicians are now moving onwards from the New Orleans style of playing, following the Louis lead, yet very much retaining that competent, collective, improvisatory movement, pertinent to their music. Dodds shines on the blues style of playing and, with a lovely piano rhythm, this number makes one want to join 'Ma and Pa' on the dance floor, doing the Kings Jazz Review Scat-Tapping Jive.

Louis takes a back seat on instrumentation, sticking mainly to vocals, yet through his special phrasing he obviously had a great deal of influence on the new swing movement of the tune, much of that stemming from the fact that he had accompanied many of the great variety of blues singers of the day, prior to making this unique Hot Five series.

*Lonesome Blues* is perhaps one of the finest of early blues recordings ever made. A lilting, clear and well articulated movement on piano gives this number an air of aplomb and dignity. Johnny Dodds takes over in one of the most beautiful blues clarinet solos I've ever heard, making it a must for all lovers of blues clarinet to listen to. Then comes a taste of the Armstrong vocals, sung in a noticeable stage of development, setting out parameters and laying the groundwork which made Louis become in later years a masterly jazz singer of character, with a style and manner whom many were attempting to copy and still try to emulate to this very day.

There's everything right with that.

*Aye-e mama I'm so sad and lonely, just for you only, I'm blue, Ohhhh mama, won't you write me-e, that will enlight me, to go through with this misery-ee . . . I don't know - what to do.* Real tear-jerker words, yes, but singing and the music does not in any way leave the nation or its people listening to it in a crying state of depression. The blues 'is' jazz and jazz is a music created to get the limbs moving and free one from the blues; whatever other and higher achievements jazz also has to its credit, and it has many, jazz is a music that makes one feel happy and want to get up and dance. Even with an apple a day, come to the Arnhem Gallery and listen to hear jazz play. A Dodds number.

*Sweet Little Papa* is a well rehearsed number, and every New Orleans jazzman should if they have not already done so, get hold of *Cornet Chop Suey* (see No 3 issue or visit James Asman's record centre) the forerunner to *Sweet Little Papa,* and listen to them in concert. We can learn a little of how Louis' progression materialized by introducing pre-determined phrases, superbly intertwined to produce a melodic structure of 'perfect' timing, exciting behind the beat and before the featuring jazzman's end of phrasing in take-up of the solo for the next musician in line. Any jazzband that can effectively master that technique will, notwithstanding the jivers and tappers, have its listeners, if sitting, wear out the seats of their knickers and pants as they involuntarily bounce, rock and roll in time to the music, as the leader increases the rhythm to such a pitch that his band ends in a climax, causing the kind of listener's applause commensurate with something commonly referred to as bringing the house down in ecstasy.

Courtaulds will not be rubbing their hands together with the prospects of a share price increase, for with Ken Colyer no longer with us, there are few jazz bands around today able to play that way.

KJR Vol.2 No.2 (Jan/Mar '90)
Louis Armstrong and his Hot Five - 1926

Nearly all the big names in jazz in the mid 20's were centred in or around the "Windy City." Jelly Roll Morton the self-styled creator of stomps and rags, always willing to teach and encourage new talent; King Oliver's Dixie Syncopators, consisting of Kid Ory, Albert Nicholas and Darnell Howard, held a spot at the Club Plantation, and at Dreamland there was Doc Cook's Orchestra with Freddie Keppard, George Mitchell, Jimmie Noone and John A St Cyr. The Dodds brothers and Natty Dominique in trio played the West Club and finally, at Sunset Café, the greatest attraction of all was Louis Armstrong fronting the Carroll Dickerson Orchestra. Louis started at the Sunset in 1926 and stayed there for 18 months when jazz then moved to New York. Whilst at the Sunset only one known recording was ever made, which was *Chicago*

*Breakdown*, and that was cut between two Hot Seven sessions in May, 1927. By now, towards the end of the Hot Five series, Louis in some respects learned from Oliver and was beginning to show us just how jazz could retain its spontaneity and emotional power, even when played with a large measure of control, for he was playing with a nonchalant innocence that he was about to lose, for the group was soon to enlarge by taking on the drums and tuba, a change which I hope to cover in future issues.

It becomes noticeable from the following four recordings, cut on the 16 November, 1926, with variations in playing on each one of them, whereas the previous numbers nearly all had phrasing very much alike, with slight differences throughout, never ever since to have been quite matched, and that is what makes them unique and charming as the major block of the Hot Five series.

The four records as mentioned are:- *Jazz Lips; Skid-Dat-De-Dat; Big Butter And Egg Man From The West* and *Sunset Café Stomp.* The latter two records have May Alix on vocals.

*Jazz Lips* is perhaps the start of the new phase for Armstrong. Tension is created by a *call and response* routine between the cornettist and the trombonist on opening, following through to all jazz artists, stilted, yet creating some beautifully timed musically facetious harmony. The sheer power and drive of Louis' playing provides a new dimension for young jazzmen to get excited about, and *Jazz Lips* becomes the touchstone for others to experiment upon.

Louis was playing superbly during his recording sessions on this day, for on *Skid-Dat-De-Dat,* by way of some fast thinking, he was able to turn this beautiful blues number into a polished performance by the Hot Five. Dodds was in his element having all but succeeded in turning *Jazz Lips* into a blues, won the day on this tune with some fine low register improvisations, aided by trombone, piano and banjo, during which time Louis was occupied on scat vocals . . . Da, de do da da, dey de da dey, de da del la. Not so easy.

*Big Butter And Egg Man,* a descriptive term for the wealthy farmer, possibly from Iowa and Missouri who came to Chicago to do business and spend his leisure time in the night clubs, a tune popular among traditional bands of today, composed by Lucius Venable (Lucky Millinder). A much faster tempo with a beautiful ensemble opening, commanded by some lovely accentuated piano, following on with joyous vocals by May Alix as if the two ladies together firmly aimed at putting their stamp on this number. Clearly, Louis was revelling in the attention paid to him by those two fine artistes, yet holding his own well in response to the leg pulling coming from the chanteuse as he refers to himself in song as becoming *her* "big butter and egg man" from away down South, other than from the West, as the lyrics go. Indeed, he'll even play a solo in minor G or even hit a high C for her. We are now beginning to get the picture as to why Louis' performance on this number in particular was truly outstanding and perfect. If only our society in the late 60's and early 70's had listened more to those Hot Five recordings, it would have learned much that is good from them and perhaps would have saved face and been less susceptible to being duped into a confused neutered state of confusing play acting, for it was nature's true difference and complexities that inspired Armstrong to produce his masterpiece of trumpet playing on this number, for without Lil and May playing their natural uninhibited roles, it would have undoubtedly turned out to be a mere orchestrated chorus of precision; instead, what we have on *Big Butter And Egg Man* is the work of a natural musical genius, inspired by woman.

*I want a butter and egg man, away out in the West; 'Cause I'm getting tired of working all day, I want somebody who wants to play; Pretty clothes, have never been mine, but if my dreams come true, the sun's gonna shine; Cause, I want, some butter and egg man, some great big butter and egg man, for me.*
There is everything that is pure in those words, but what is all the more wonderful is that the simple format of them formed the basis of one of Armstrong's best solos on this series. His rhythmic composition of melody made up of triplets, eights and sixteenths, with over and underlapping measures in strict two four timing, and his curtailing notes far removed from his earlier New Orleans style, are played without stumbling the imagination of the listener, whose ear denotes all the marvels and intricacies about them, yet deceptively creating an unique swing movement. How did he do it? Passionate feeling for his music coupled with emotion aroused by his ladies! Dodds was overshadowed.

*Sunset Café Stomp* is a number based on Joe Glaser's night spot of the same name, where musicians among the clientele came to study Armstrong. Although the main attraction of the club was the floor show and chorus line, Louis was regarded as an entertainer, even whilst he was a sideman in the orchestra. This recording opens with a five bar honky-tonk piano intro, moving into a screaming Dodds clarinet, settling down nicely into a lovely bluesy piece, only to be rounded off by the cabaret shout song, sung by May Alix (Liza Mae), who was the singer with the Sunset orchestra (Dickerson's). Dodds takes this number. That makes two each.

To avoid the impression that a battle for supremacy was raging between Armstrong and Dodds, created by myself, on these four recordings, indeed throughout the series, I ought to mention that Dodds was leading Freddie Keppard's house band at Kelly's Stables and that all five musicians were key players in their own field who had come together, not only for their own enjoyment, but because they knew exactly the importance of setting a high standard on their recordings. After all, they were the best musicians around at the time. Although Armstrong was much later to gain in stature over Dodds, a point on which I hope to expound upon at a later date, there was still a full year's enjoyable recordings ahead of them, taking in the Hot Seven series.

*Sunset Stomp, got folks jumping, Sunset Stomp, got folks bumping, up and down, all around; They yell man, play some more, Charleston, Charleston, I'll stay in town; But the Black Bottom - its got 'em, With all that Sunset Stomp. Now - let's go in - there are people crying, Created in that crazy house, that's what folks are saying; Gentlemen, Ladies too, rush around and romp, They lose their heads, just out there; Doing the Sunset Stomp - out there, Doing the Sunset Stomp.*

The Charleston was a dance of the 20's which appeared in the musical "Liza" (1922), later becoming a popular dance song used in other dances, notably the "Black Bottom," a dance which came out of the Eubie Blake/Noble Sissle revue, *Shuffle Along,* introducing dancing to jazz music.

In our next issue, I will cover the two numbers recorded on 27th November, 1926, which concludes the first group in the Hot Five series giving a total of 24 in all. Interestingly, the "New Grove" mentions a figure of 26 but does not list them, so I will do just that and make a point of sorting out the variance. I will also cover three of the nine sleeves cut between September and December, 1927, in which I am in agreement with this figure.

## KJR Vol.2 No.3 (Apr/June '90)
### Louis Armstrong and his Hot Five - 1926

*As mentioned in the last edition, I said that I would list the 22 tunes so far covered in this series and so here they are:- My Heart; Yes, I'm In The Barrel; Gut Bucket Blues; Come Back Sweet Papa; Georgia Grind; Heebie Jeebies; Cornet Chop Suey; Oriental Strut; You're Next; Muskrat Ramble; Don't Forget To Mess Around; I'm Gonna Gitcha; Droppin' Shucks; Who's It; King Of The Zulus; Big Fat Ma And Skinny Pa; Lonesome Blues; Sweet Little Papa; Jazz Lips; Skid Dat De Dat; Big Butter And Egg Man; Sunset Café Stomp.*

On the 27th November, 1926, the Hot Five recorded *You Made Me Love You* and *Irish Black Bottom,* making a total of 24 in the premier group.

In approaching these two numbers, it becomes clear that we are entering into the end of the beginning of what was perhaps one of the most important periods of jazz history. At the tail-end of the nineteenth century, more than just the knowledge to write a score was needed by the Downtown New Orleans Creole jazz musician if he was to make a living from playing jazz music.

The powerful feeling for the blues and the head arrangements adopted by the Uptown blacks were beginning to take precedence, a tenet that was to hold good a quarter of a century later when one Louis Armstrong was to make a profound change in concept and style to the Fletcher Henderson band when he joined it at the Roseland, an event which was to turn the tables on the New York jazz scene.

Yet, understandably so, it was from such bands as Henderson's, with arrangers, that Louis was able to make his living in those days, just as it is so today for the musicians playing the works of the great classical composers of the past. The Hot Five series recordings were noted for the pleasure they brought to the jazzmen taking part.

Today, Britain is seeing a revival in Armstrong's early jazz music. Not a great deal has been written about the potent power of jazz being able to sustain the onslaught of the commercial trappings that were being gained by dropping it in favour of embracing the rag-doll (RD) syndrome towards the pop artist, when jazz was at its height in this country in the 50's and 60's. KJR hopefully tempers the taste buds.

Jazz, if it is not to fall victim again during this current, 'throwaway RD sleepy-time' truce or vacuum must, as it enters into the last decade of the century, prepare itself now for a jazz work of art, based on Louis' Hot Five series. It is hoped that KJR will still be around when jazz celebrates the centenary of the birth of its greatest artist, appropriately with an overture entitled 'Armstrong's two dozen Hot Five Overture,' for in doing so, non-metronome jazz will be given a new lease of emoluments life, providing it adheres to the basic Armstrong principles.

It is not necessarily true to say that the greatest achievements in any art form came about because of the love for it, and that abject poverty is thought synonymous with inventiveness, regardless of whether such talent make a sound living at what they are trying to create. In other words, the small jazz group, recognised by the establishment, will not feel any less passionate for the love of their music.

It has, therefore, for far too long now gone unnoticed by those to whom it should be of concern, that it is the warm instrument that makes the sweetest note. That brings me on to Louis' number, *You Made Me Love You*.

Dodds was at his bluesy best on this number, but was no match for Louis' power and creativeness. Armstrong's ability to read had by this time much improved, which came about during the time he spent with the Henderson band, and this was very much in evidence. The tune is not the popular one of later years and apart from the title and the sad and glad line, the similarity ends.

*Please Mama won't you listen to what I want to tell you, You made me love you when I saw you cry; I didn't know till I saw tears in your eyes, That you're just like a baby as sweet as can be, And you made me want to kiss your tears away: My Little Darling: Don't mean to hurt you, meanwhile, when I made you cross, And to make you forgive me, I will cry; Oh, You made me sad, but in a way I'm glad, I'm glad you'll be so now, Cause you made me love you, when I saw you cry.*

This tune was perhaps the turning point in Louis' musical career. On piano the recording was Lil's finest so far, a superb performance, and it was little wonder that the title of the tune was used at a later stage, although one wonders how this was allowed to come about.

*Irish Black Bottom* opens with a passage sounding something like Easter Bonnet, moving on to a smooth, effortless composition quite indistinguishable from any of Louis' previous ones in the series, showing just how much of a grand master he had become - not only as a master of his horn, but also as a 'bandleader' and entertainer, or 'solo artist,' as he was later to become.

It is apparent that this recording was meant as a 'fun' record, cut every bit for commercial purposes. Armstrong was perhaps now feeling that this would be his last get-together in the studio with this small group, and thus set about stretching his talents to the utmost in creating both an hilarious hotchpotch ballad coupled with some very fine inventive playing.

Dodds and Ory were in 'dreamland,' both wrong-footed, perdu, or more regal; an uncustomary lapse had overtaken them, although the former regained control showing some of his true talents as if to remind Armstrong that he was with his old New Orleans friends, or had he forgotten it? Louis was undeterred and rattled on into song by telling us that all over Ireland the people were dancing to a new reel, *Black Bottom,* the new rhythm dance, being the biggest change that he had ever seen whilst wearing of the green. A truly uninhibited masterpiece of entertainment and jazz acumen supreme, by the "World's Greatest Trumpeter."

To conclude on this group of 24, I'll return to the previous number mentioned, that for the first time Louis fitted in a two bar string of high c's which on occasions he would adopt later on in his career. It took some time for the listener (me) to reflect on what he had just heard. It is therefore no blarney that the jazz fan dig's *You Made Me Love You,* Louis Armstrong. The classical musician simply cannot do the things a jazz musician can with his instrument. At this point I call upon a Jelly Roll Morton quote: "there is nothing finer than jazz music, because it comes from the finest class of music." (Was he in fact referring to the European Schottische and Quadrille movements?).

KJR Vol 3 No 3 (Apr/Jun '91)
Louis Armstrong and his Hot Five - 1927

I am now able to return to the Louis Armstrong series, having had to miss out on reviews in the last three issues of KJR due to an increase of live jazz in our area over that period.

The "first group" of the Hot Five recordings was completed in Vol 2 No 3 and this amounted to 24 tunes in total. I promised to try and sort out the variance which exists between those 24 and the figure of 26 referred to in the New Grove dictionary. Brian Rust, in *Jazz Records 1897 - 1942,* published by Storyville, throws some light on the matter. He includes a tune entitled *Leave Mine Alone,* which was rejected, making 25 in his list, thus leaving one tune still unaccounted for in the New Grove.

Another interesting point that comes to light in his *Jazz Records* is that on *You Made Me Love You* and *Irish Black Bottom* Henry Clark allegedly replaces Kid Ory on trombone. In my review, no mention was made about Ory in the former tune, but in the latter it read as follows:- "Dodds and Ory were in 'dreamland,' both wrong-footed, perdu, or more regal; an uncustomary lapse had overtaken them, although the former regained control showing some of his true talents as if to remind Armstrong that he was with his old New Orleans friends, or had he forgotten it?" Could it have been that Kid Ory went to the studios that day only to record *You Made Me Love You,* and for some reason Henry Clark had to take his place on *Irish Black Bottom,* causing a minor upset which Louis Armstrong immediately handles in his usual skillful way?

There are eleven Hot Seven tracks plus *Chicago Breakdown,* recorded in Chicago on the 9th May, 1927, by his Stompers, in the "second group" which I'll be looking at on completion of the Hot Five band series. New Grove gives no figure for this group which was recorded between 7 - 14 May, 1927, but this agrees with the Jazz Records list.

The "fourth group" of this Hot Five 'plus' recordings I'll cover in future issues, but for now I'll start upon the "third group," which returns to the Hot Five band that recorded 9 tunes in Chicago between 2 September and

13 December, 1927. There is no disagreement on this figure, which reads as follows:- *Put 'Em Down Blues* and *Ory's Creole Trombone* on 2/9/27; *The Last Time* on 6/9/27; *Struttin' With Some Barbecue* and *Got No Blues* on 9/12/27; *Once In A While* and *I'm Not Rough* on 10/12/27 and, finally, *Hotter Than That* and *Savoy Blues* on 13/12/27.

We have heard how Armstrong learned the value of discretion in the Oliver band, and of ensemble playing rather than in creating a group of individual soloists, the finer points of rhythmic phrasing and in establishing a positive lead melody. Then, when he was with Fletcher Henderson in 1924/25, how he transformed the popular tunes/arrangements of the day into swinging jazz numbers whenever he was given the chance to solo on them.

We have learned how he varied his playing to the mood of accompanying blues singers; how he exchanged views with the top New York jazzmen, and how they admired his feeling for the blues in his playing when they first met each other. Then how he left Henderson and returned to Chicago, where his wife, Lil Hardin, had a job lined up for him at Dreamland and Okeh Records offered him a recording contract. Within days of the agreement he had started to turn out his Hot Five series.

By way of those November 1925 to December 1927 recordings, we get a good idea or measure of Louis Armstrong's musical development and to appreciate just how much he had moved on to becoming a soloist in the series, one only need listen for comparison to any of the George Mitchell New Orleans Wanderers numbers that were cut in July, 1926, alongside the Hot Five records.

To turn now to *Put 'Em Down Blues,* the first tune of the nine in the "third group." It was when the Sunset job had ended that Louis Armstrong turned to, or more likely was asked, to cut this new Hot Five series. Judging by results, it was all to his credit that he set about these recordings with a willingness akin to his nature of always wanting to achieve his best, no matter in what circumstances he found himself. However, on these 9 tunes there is one big difference and that is he played trumpet on them throughout and did not resort to the cornet as he had done so on the earlier Hot Five tunes already covered in this series, a point which Jazz Records overlooks.

There is a lovely trombone opening with clarinet, and banjo by John A St Cyr follows through accordingly; then Louis takes command with a brilliant, effortless performance, showing the sentimental side of this very fine trumpeter's nature; *Let Him Put You Down L . . . D . . ., I'll pick you up for myself.*

Kid Ory gets a chance to shine, while Johnny Dodds gets cut out early but is rewarded later with a break just prior to vocals, showing just how fine a clarinettist he really was. *I've been looking for a girl like you so long; a girl as nice and gentle with a lovely sweet song.*

There are signs of the beginning of the end of this group as Armstrong moves along in 'swing' four four, over Lil's two four piano, and no doubt Louis would have liked this number to have been, or at least have ended, as such. This was not to be, and Armstrong probably felt that his clarinettist's incursion towards the end of the track was best left out. I expect so, too, did Dodds afterwards on listening to it.

*I for you, you for me; that's the only way two loving hearts should be: So just be glad when he puts you down, I'll pick you up for myself.* An ideal number for any budding trumpeter to learn note for note.

*Ory's Creole Trombone* has been taken up by many a trombonist and to a large extent Armstrong declines to overshadow Ory on this tune, although it is noticeable that the tune becomes lively at his making, and he rounds the number off with some daring experimentations.

KJR Vol 3 No 4 (Jul/Sep '91)
Louis Armstrong and his Hot Five - 1927

Out of the blue, I suddenly stumbled upon the answer to the vexing question of the two extra recordings in the first group of 24 Hot Five tunes, noted as 26 in a publication elsewhere. It happened the day after the evening we had all met at Fairfield to discuss the setting up of a Surrey and Kent Jazz Federation. It was a hot, gloriously sunny day and we were returning from a visit to Tunbridge Wells in Kent, and had just happened to stop by at a beautiful hamlet - Westerham - on the way back home.

As if by a miracle, there, staring us in the face was what I'd been looking for although I did not know it at the time; it occurred literally seconds after we had parked the car in a spot just a few feet away from the sidewalk café bar where we were to take refreshments.

On 28 May, 1926, Lill's (sic) Hot Shots, the same group of jazz artists as the Hot Five above, made two cuts for Vocalion, part of the Brunswick label, *Georgia Bo Bo* and *Drop That Sack,* and those records came to the attention of the Okeh representatives. The story goes that someone from Okeh called Louis Armstrong into their office, played the records and asked him who he thought was the singer on them. Louis replied, "I don't know, but I sure won't do it again."

On April 24th, 1991, the Tunbridge Wells Jazz Club featured George Webb and His Dixielanders with American blues singer Marilyn Middleton Pollock at the town's Corn Exchange, in the Pantiles, and as a point of interest it was on Lil's *Drop That Sack* that George, as it were, cut his jazz teeth on this Hot Shots record, to give Britain its first taste of "trad" in the early 40's that has endured well to this day, sustained by a healthy devoted minority following of the British jazz public.

Resolved, I now return to the Hot Fives series. In vol 3 No 3 where I covered briefly two of the nine tunes in the third group, *Put 'Em Down Blues* and *Ory's Creole Trombone. Put 'Em Down Blues,* as can be gleaned from the lyrics in the last quarterly, is not a blues but 'jazz Louis Armstrong' from a popular song of the day. *Ory's Creole Trombone* is of course a classic New Orleans number, which he himself recorded earlier in 1922 with his own band, the Sunshine Orchestra. (Read article on latest discoveries about this recording in the magazine New Orleans Music Vol 2 No 4 - April 1990).

The other seven tunes in this "third group" are as follows:- *The Last Time; Struttin' With Some Barbecue; Got No Blues; Once In A While; I'm Not Rough; Hotter Than That* and *Savoy Blues.*

"Jazz at the time of Armstrong was a captive of show business, not free to go its own way," states James Lincoln Collier. It was his book, *Louis Armstrong - A Biography,* in paperback form, that the mystery, or should I say the vexing question, in paragraph one above was solved. The book, which was acquired for a peppercorn sum at the stop-over spot on that day mentioned, was the means whereupon reading at the heart of it, my mind was put to rest and the 'records' put to right.

*The Last Time, Honey babe, mean it's the very last time - I mean - mean - it's the very last time,* jumps ahead of its time as a precursor to the 'swing' bands which came much later. Dodds opens the number with Louis leading in on a high note. There is mellow singing by Louis, fine solos by Dodds and Ory, with some beautiful interplay and nice harmonies by Ory, making this number a firm entry to the jazz classics. *I've told you many times before; It's the last time,* but never ever, will there ever, be a last time, to play *The Last Time.*

*Struttin' With Some Barbecue* was recorded on the same day as *Got No Blues,* the 9th December,1927, both tunes having been written by Lil. It would appear that the former was a quick tempo warm up for the latter. This, the former, has a lovely low register, infectious Dodds clarinet chorus, followed by a warm Ory trombone, leading into a heavy off beat piano rhythm which Armstrong, with invention, crisscrossing, alternating, overlapping bars, without losing the basic three note melody, ending up on a neatly worked out ingenious head arrangement. It is little wonder that *Struttin' With Some Barbecue* has now become popular with many "trad" jazz musicians of today.

*Got No Blues* has a nice banjo intro taken up by a smooth gliding 'Very Special Old Phonography Lil/Kid Tone' movement, which is based on the three note - two quarters and a half note, G above the stave - over which the melody intertwines. Louis moves this soaring part from a nice St Cyr banjo solo, relying for timing on Lil's austere, firm left hand one chord piano beat as he explores new realms of his horn, and in turn reins himself in from sailing daringly over the precipice of an 'aglobal' world, *not spherical,* as it was then believed to be by many at the time. Dodds does not quite succeed in turning it into a blues, (it isn't), and there is a wonderful moment when Ory flows in without any stop-time from his solo, blending beautifully in harmony with Armstrong as he, Louis, brings this jazz masterpiece to a close.

For *Once In A While* a repositioning perhaps of the instrumentation facing the recording bell of antiquity from the previous day's sessions could have taken place, lending currency to the improved piano tone, or who knows, maybe it was because of the presence of guitarist Lonnie Johnson, who was to appear on the next record, *I'm Not Rough*, that same day, the 10th December, 1927. Whatever the reason, with Louis playing much within the middle register, *Once In A While* turns out to be a fine New Orleans jazz number. Here we get the feeling of consolidation of all that has gone into the previous strictly Hot Five sessions, leaving us to marvel at the wealth of jazz that has been created by them.

Leaving aside the second group, i.e. the Hot Seven tunes cut for Tommy Rockwell of Okeh, this, the "third group," and in particular the next three Hot Five tunes in it, which include guitarist Lonnie Johnson, mark new horizons in Armstrong's mood and improvisations, heralding the start of a remarkable jazz epoch.

Lil opens on piano on *I'm Not Rough* and the guitarist immediately brings a new tension into the group but they soon settle down to turn tables on the listener who discovers that the tune is a brash blues, relished by Dodds. It is faster than a normal blues as is made apparent by a double time 4 bar movement brought in towards the end. Louis takes no solo on this number, but makes up for it by articulating the lyrics, *I ain't rough, and I don't fight, but the woman that gets me got to treat me right; Cause I'm crazy 'bout my loving, and I must have it all the time.* There is a lovely 11 bar guitar solo with banjo backing, which Johnson and St Cyr most likely had worked out together previously, making this tune overall a Lonnie Johnson country blues number.

*Hotter Than That,* cut on 13 December, 1927, has an exciting introductory ensemble part and the whole tune can be classified as a quite outstanding piece of work. It would seem as though Louis used the two free days following the previous recording session to mastermind a truly jazz classic, for this number is all his doing, although the writing of it is accredited to Lil. Clearly, the inclusion of the guitarist had much to do with it, in as much as that Louis was perhaps determined not to allow the newcomer to the group outshine him. Both Dodds and Ory rose to the occasion and produced some very fine playing. But what is most remarkable is that directly after a superb 32 bar clarinet solo, Louis' scat vocal produces some exquisite acute jazz phrasing that few, if any, instrumentalists would have been able to accomplish so masterfully. Then, within nanoseconds, there is a switch to a duel with the guitarist, when Louis articulates various notations over Lonnie's seemingly standard phrasings until the Armstrong vocals are creatively complementing in identity the sounds produced by this fine guitarist. A piano break to allow Ory to show his skills, then Louis explores new pastures, yet somehow it all fits in beautifully with the theme gone before it, constituting a complete movement that defies the logic of swing. He had set parameters for various versions of existing and new jazz tunes for himself and others to play and record in later years. Louis allows Lonnie to end the recording on a reverent Amen break. It is an outstanding performance of perfection, created by a conductor leading but five musicians with an off the cuff composition which matches the works of any of the grand masters of the classics who passed before him. George Webb, in an interview, referred to Louis Armstrong as a genius, and I doubt if there is anyone to argue with that after listening to *Hotter Than That.*

*Savoy Blues,* the last in the group, was written by Kid Ory and is, on the face of it, a catchy riff tune for trombone made fuller by guitar fill-in. But, underlying this, one detects a change of mood in Louis' playing, which portrays a touch of real tenderness, serenity and calmness about it. Without exception, a monumental day for jazz recording in cylindrical format that is listened to today by an ever growing worldwide circle of jazz followers. □

# Index

**A**
*A Night With The Gershwins*, 100
Aarons, Dave, 86
Abbott, Myra, 115
ABC Cinema, 88
Ace Broadcasting Band, 28
Addington Artisan Jazz Band, 55
Addiscombe Music Shop, 47
Aitkinson, Derek, Dixielanders, 117
Albert Pub, The, 66
Aldridge, Don, 118
Aldridge, Pat, 48
Allandale Eric, New Orlean Knights, 69, 72
Allen, Henry "Red", 47, 96, 117
Allen, Les, 79, 80, 82
Allied Expeditionary Force Band, 119
Ambrose, 23
American Folk Blues Festival, 113
Anderson, Brian, 32
Anderson, Cat, 59
Anka, Paul, 44
Appleby, Pete, 51
Appleyard, Peter, 16, 100
Archey, Jimmy, 47
Arkwrights Wheel Pub, The, 105
Armstrong, Louis, 14, 16, 17, 23, 29, 42, 48, 50, 51, 52, 61, 72, 74, 84, 118
Arnhem Gallery, xii, 94, 96, 97, 99, 101
Arts Council of England, The, 107
Ash, Vic, 75, 86
Ashcroft Theatre, 50, 55, 100
Ashman, Micky, 37, 72, 73, 88, 105, 106
Asman, James, 9, 24
Atha, Graham, 92
Atmospheric Arms Pub, The, 66
Atterbury, Mike, 9
Attwell, Winifred, 33, 114
Avon City Jazz Band, 72
Ayling, Les, Orchestra, 43

**B**
Babbington, Roy, 92
Badgers Mount Jazz Club, 105
Bailey, Bill, 24
Baker, Gordon, Six, 73
Baker, Harold "Shorty," 63
Baker, Joe, 105
Baker, Kenny, 31, 42, 92, 100
Baldry, Long John, 33, 65
Baldwin, Len, Dauphin Street Six, 72,
Baldwin, Ted, 84
Ball, Kenny, 60, 69, 70, 83, 84, 111
Bamber, Micky, 105
Barber, Chris, Jazz & Blues Band, 40, 41, 46, 47, 50, 60, 69, 71, 73, 74, 82, 85, 92, 96, 108, 111, 114, 117
Barcelona, Danny, 50
Barclay, Bob, Yorkshire Jazz Band, 117
Barclay, John, 92
Barnes, Johnny, 91
Barnes, Paul, 82
Barnet, Cliff, 105
Barr, Derek, 9
Barrett, Dave, Cambridge Jazz Band, 97
Barter, Fred, 48
Barton, Ken, 88
Basie, William "Count", 42, 58, 62, 94, 95, 111, 113
Bassey, Shirley, 58
Bastable, John, 57
Bates, Philip, 87
Batiste, Milton, 82
Batten, Nikki & Peter, 104
Batty, Ken, 9, 112
BBC Symphony Orchestra, 34
Beadle, Len, 105
Beatles, The, 70, 115
Beatty, Doreen, 72
Beazley, Graham, 71
Bebop Preservation Society, 86
Bechet, Sidney, 58, 63
Beiderbecke, Bix, 16, 74, 111, 116, 118
Bell, Graeme,
 Australian Jazz Band, xii, 25, 30, 31, 33, 110, 118
Bell, Ian, Jazzband, 45
Bell, Roger, 25, 110
Bell/Holloway Big Nine, 42
Bellson, Louis, 111
Bennett, John, 84
Benson, Ivy, All-Girls Band, 23
Berens, Harold, 110
Bernard, Clem, 43
Berry, Johnny, 37,
Berry, Ron, 47, 55
Bevan, "Count" Clifford de, 69
Bexley Jazz Club, 72
Bilk, Bernard "Acker", 40, 41, 46, 52, 55, 69, 70, 71, 72, 84, 92, 111
Billett, Cuff, New Europa Jazz Band, 96, 99
Binch, Barry, 105
Bird, Ian, Sextet, 75
Bishop, Dickie, 69
Black Boy Pub, The, 66
Black Eagle Band, 51
Black Prince Hotel, 72
Black, Stanley, 30
Blackwell, Martin, 86
Blake, Sue & Robert, 9
Blashfield, Eddie, 88
Bletchingley Jazz Circle, 104
Blount, Chris, 97
Blue Anchor Pub, The, 75
Blue Crow Jazzmen, 47
Blue Room Orpheans Orchestra, 43
Blues Incorporated, 70
Bolden, Buddy, 14, 106
Bolden, Ray, 9
Boston Dixielanders, 98

Boswell, Eve, 83
Bowden, Colin, 48, 71, 96, 97, 99
Bowden, Ron, 40, 84
Bowles, Bod & Jackie, 105
Bowlly, Al, 23
Bradley, Allen, 104
Bray, Jim, 40, 114
Breda Jazz Festival, Holland, 118
Breeze, Alan, 30, 43
Britchford, Ken, 86
British Institute Of Jazz Studies, 58, 112
Brodie, Paul, 92
Bromley Jazz Club, 73
Bromley, Johnny, 114
Broonzy, Big Bill, 53, 71, 114
Brown, Clifford, 41, 42
Brown, Gerry, Jazzband, 55, 57, 72
Brown, Lawrence, 59
Brown, Phil, Band, 59
Brown, Sandy, 41, 114
Browne, Sam, 23
Brubeck, Dave, 53, 83
Brunskill, Bill, 79, 80, 82, 95, 101, 102, 115
Bryant, Ray, 63
Bryce, Owen, 23, 24, 35, 112
Bryden, Beryl, 35, 36, 37, 69, 72, 105, 109, 110
Buck, Jim, 92
Budd, Roy, 60, 120
Budd, Tony, 38, 120
Bue, Papa, Viking Jazz Band, 72
Bundy, Alun, 115
Bunk Johnson Appreciation Society, 48
Burbidge, Graham, 46
Burnap, Campbell, 9, 84, 107
Burns, Clay, Quintet, 45, 50
Burns, Duke, 58, 59
Burns, Tito, Famous Sextet, 31
Burrell, Kenny, 63
Butterfield, Billy, 16, 83
Byas, Don, 63

C
Café de L'Europe, 30
Café Society, 63
Cairns, Forrie, & The Clansmen, 74
Calloway, Blanche, 62
Calloway, Cab, 17
Campbell, Duncan, 111
Canterbury Arms Pub, The, 47, 48, 66
Carey, Dave, Swing Shop, 38, 43, 47
Carpenter, Paul, 28
Carroll, Barbara, 63
Carshalton Traditional Jazz Appreciation Society, 105
Carter, Benny, 17, 62
Carter, Ken, 105
Carter, Nigel, 92
Castle Pub, The, Tooting Broadway, xi

Castle, Roy, 100
Celestin, Papa, 82
Cellarmen, The, 44
Central Band of the RAF, 100
Chambers, John, 92
Chapman, Don, 55
Charles Cryer Theatre, 105
Charles, Ray, 58
Charles, Rob, Rhythm Group, 75
Charlesworth, Dick, City Gents, 41, 48, 50, 55, 72, 97, 108
Cheatham Doc, 118
Chescoe, Laurie, 91, 104
Chesterman, Chez, 80
Christian, Charlie, 106
Christie Brother Stompers, 117
Christie, Ian, 51
Christie, Keith, 29
Civic Hall/North End Hall, Croydon, 25, 32, 34, 35, 36, 37, 38, 43, 44, 46, 47, 52, 55, 56, 57, 69, 70, 71, 76, 105, 110, 111, 112, 123-125
Clapton, Eric, 58, 113
Clark, Charles 'Nobby', 9, 32, 33, 36, 112
Clarke, John, 96
Classic Cinema, 55
Classic Suite, 104
Clayton, Buck, 62
Clayton, Peter, 70
Clubmen, The, 75
Clyde Valley Stompers, 72
Coach and Horses Pub, The, 66
Cobb, Jeff, 105
Cobblestones Pub (Streatham), The, 86
Codd, Johnny, 38
Coe, Tony, 87
Cohen, Alan, 111
Colar, George 'Kid Sheik', 83
Colchester Jazz Club, 72, 105
Cole, Bill, 75
Cole, Geoff, 57, 97
Cole, Nat King 42
Collcutt, Terry, 104,
Collie, Max, Rhythm Aces, 33, 72, 96, 99, 108
Collier, Mike and His Band, 37
Collin, Tom, 73
Collins, Mick, 48
Colyer, Ken, Jazzmen, xii, 33, 40, 47, 48, 55, 57, 65, 69, 72, 73, 74, 75, 94, 96, 97, 117
Colyer, Ken, Trust All Stars, xii, 40, 96, 99, 101
Condon, Eddie, 16, 62, 117
Condon, Les, 42
Conniff, Ray, 83
Connor, Charles, 36
Cook, Dick, 96, 99, 101
Cook, Eddie, 73
Cook, Tom, 92
Cooks Ferry Inn, 114, 116
Coon, Jackie, 16
Cooper, Alan Swainston, "Henry MacHooter", 69

Cooper, Andy, 84
Cooper, Buster, 59
Coram, Bobby, 110
Corbett, Lorna, 105
Corfield, Loz, 96
Cornish, Willie, 14, 51
Corrie, Ed, Concord Jazz Band, 72, 73
Cotterill, Robert, 96
Cotton, Bill, 36
Cotton, Billy, 17, 23, 30, 38, 43, 47, 105, 110
Cotton, Mike, Jazzmen, 75
Coulsdon Jazz Club, 72
Count Rudolph Jazz Band, 72
Courtley, Bert, 42, 75
Covington, Warren, 84
Cox, Mel, 73
Crane River Jazz Band, 38, 40, 114, 115, 116
Crawford, Paul, 82
Crimmins, Roy, 38, 50, 51, 91
Cristo and His Stardusters, 34
Croham Valley Stompers, 49
Crooked Billet Pub, The, 42
Crosby, Bing, 111
Crowcombe, Pete, 47
Croydon Advertiser, ix, xii, 17, 18, 30, 34, 45, 52, 54, 58, 82, 94, 99, 103, 123-125
Croydon Airport, 68
Croydon Arts & Libraries, 102
Croydon Dance Orchestra, 59, 112
Croydon Empire, 17, 22, 23, 25, 28, 30, 31, 33, 38, 109, 110
Croydon Express, 18
Croydon F. C., 105
Croydon Guardian, 18
Croydon Jazz Club, The, 32, 37, 38, 41, 45, 46, 50, 55, 57, 60, 65, 68, 69, 70, 77, 110
Croydon Jazz & Gospel Festival, First, 101
Croydon Jazz Society, 12, 94, 96, 98, 99, 101
Croydon Jazz Week, 102, 103, 107
Croydon Palais, 42
Croydon Park Hotel, 101
Croydon Pub, The, 86
Croydon Times, 36, 43, 46, 65
Croydon Traditional Jazz Festival, 32
Crozier, Hugh, 79, 80, 82
Crystal Palace F.C., 26, 30, 68, 92, 106
Cumming, Jock, 111

## D

Dale, Roy, 79, 80
Daniels, Mike, Delta Jazzmen, 32, 33, 35, 36, 37, 38, 41, 43, 45, 46, 53, 55, 57, 69, 72, 73, 105, 107, 110, 112, 116
Dankworth/Laine, John/Cleo,
  Big Band, Quartet, Seven, 42, 55, 59, 73, 92, 112
Davenport, Bob, 83
Davies, John R T, "Sheik of Wadi el Yadounir", 69
Davis, Beryl, 109
Davis, Cyril, 71, 113
Davis Theatre, 17, 18, 39, 42, 44, 48, 50
Davison, Harold, Promotions, 50, 61, 74
Davison, Wild Bill, 16, 68, 83
Dawbarn, Bob, 38
Day, Jimmy, 31
Dearle, Dave, 115
Dearle, Philip F., 9, 113, 114
Dee, Brian, Trio, 100
Deems, Barrett, 93
Defferay, John, 75
Dejan, Harold, 82
Dell, Alan, 83
Delmar, Elaine, 102
Delta Rhythm Kings, 73
Demond, Frank, 90
Deniz, Joe, 109
Dennis, Denny, 23
Dent, Alan, Jazz Band, 73
Derby Arms Pub, The, 34, 48, 66
Deuchar, Jimmy, 42
Devon, Terry, 31
Dickenson, Vic, 62, 64, 84
Dickie, Pat & Neville, 105, 108
Dickie, Neville,/
  Keith Nichols Ragtime Orchestra, 92
Disley, William "Diz", 40, 87
Dobbs, Jack, 92
Dodd, Pat, 111
Dodds, Johnny, 14, 61
Dodsworth, Norman, 38
Donegan, Dorothy, 63
Donegan, Tony "Lonnie", 40, 41, 117
Dorsey, Tommy, 58, 62, 84
Douglas, Jim, 91
Downs, Geoff, 88
Drakestein, Henk Bosch van, 87
Dryden, Kenny, 92
Dubber, Goff, 105
Duff, Ronald, 71
Duke Of Clarence Pub, The, 48
Duke's Head Pub, The, 59
Duncan, Fiona, 74
Durbridge, Don, 92
Durrell, Kenny, 63
Duncan, Mac, 47, 82
Dutch Swing College Band, (DSCB), 25, 72, 87, 92, 100, 111
Dutrey, Honoré, 47
Dutton, Lyn, Agency, 72

## E

Eagle Pub, The, 66
Eales, Geoff, 92
Ealing Club, The, 71
*Easter Jazz In Croydon*, 50
Eckman, Sharon, 100
Edwards, Eddie, 15
Edwards, Eric, 105

157

Eel Pie Island, 75
Eighth Cavalry Mexican Band, 66
Eisen, Irvin, 82
Eldridge, Roy, 61, 63, 64
Ellington, Duke, 17, 58, 59, 61, 63, 74, 111
Ellington, Mercer, 59, 63
Ellington, Ray, Quartet, 110
Elliot, Ray, 115
Ellis, Chris, 112
Elsdon, Alan, 8, 9, 33, 41, 57, 70, 82, 91, 92, 102
Emberson, Norman, 83
Emmanuel Pentecostal Choir Gospel Singers, 101, 102
English Traditional Jazz Jazzitoria, The, 107
Eshelby, Paul, 92
Etheridge, John, 87
Evans, Bill, 84
Evans, Dave, 48, 75, 83,
Excelsior New Orleans Brass Band (England), 103

## F
Fairbanks, Brian, 115
Fairfield Halls, 25, 32, 55, 56, 58, 59, 61, 63, 64, 75, 77, 82-84, 88-94, 96, 99, 100, 107, 111-113
Fairweather/Brown All Stars, 73
Fairweather, Digby, 91, 92, 115
Fame, Georgie,
Farnborough Jazz Club, Kent, 105
Farnham Maltings, Surrey, 105
Fawkes, Wally, 23, 24, 29, 37
Feather, Leonard, 62, 74
Field, Dennis, 38, 120
Fighting Cocks Pub, The, 79
Fitzgerald, Ella, 44, 50, 58, 103
Five Pennies, The, 52
Focus Cinema, 88
Forino, Vic, 37
Forsyth, Bruce, 42
Foster, Frank, 94, 95
Foster, Geoff, 55
Fountain Pub, The, (Garratt Lane, Wandsworth), 86
Fox and Hounds Pub, The, Carshalton, 105
Fox and Hounds Pub, The, Croydon, 34, 42, 66
Fox and Hounds Pub, The, Putney, 105
Foxley, Ray, 97
Franc, Rene, 43
Frazier, Joseph, "Cie," 89, 90
Freeman, Bud, 16, 62, 64
Fryatt, Arthur, 114
Fullerton, Dave, 109

## G
Gains, Will, 102
Galbraith, Charlie, 33, 37, 105, 106
Galloway, Jim, 16
Garfield, Loz, 96
Gay, Al, 73
Gedge, Dave, 48

Gelly, Dave - Art Themen Quintet, 75
George Pub, The, 66
Georgian Club, The, 58, 59
Getgood, Frank, 32, 33, 41, 45, 47, 60, 65, 69, 88, 112
Getz, Stan, 106
Gibbons, Tony, 38
Gibbons, Vic, 9, 85
Gill, Mick, 43
Gillespie, Dizzie, 50, 61, 63
Glass, Papa, 82
Globe Pub, The, 66
Goddard's Band, 17
Gold, Harry, and His Pieces of Eight, 31, 111, 112, 114
Gold, Jack, Band, 17
Gold, Laurie, Boogie Boys, 31
Gonella, Nat, 72, 79
Gonsalves, Paul, 59, 111
Goodman, Benny, 30, 62, 63, 111, 115
Gordon, Dexter, 63
Gordon, Hugh, 71
Gowans, Brad, 116
Grand Theatre, (Facing title page)
Grandison Ballroom, 43
Grant, Diane & Keith, 105
Grant, Sandra, 65
Granz, Norman, 50, 61
Grappelli, Stephane, 87, 109, 111
Gray, Wardell, 63
Green, Benny, 42, 100
Green, Brian, New Orleans Jazz Band, 80
Greenow, Bill, 48, 75
Greig, Stan, 40
Gresty, Alan, 88
Greyhound Hotel, 17, 43, 100, 104
Greyhound Theatre, 18
Groom, Chris, 9
Grosvenor Hotel, Manchester, 114
Grouse & Claret Pub, The, 77, 105
Grover, Eddie, 105
Grute, George, 47
Guarnieri, Johnny, 93
Gubbay, Raymond, 89
Gun Tavern, The, 32, 33, 37, 38, 41, 42, 48, 59, 77, 81, 105, 112
Guthrie, Jimmy, 26
Guyver, Dorothy, 116

## H
Hague Orchestra, The, 25
Haim, John, 43
Halcox, Pat, 40, 46
Hall, Adelaide, 110
Hall, Reg, 82
Hammersmith Palais, 114
Hampton, Lionel, 63, 113
Hancocks, David, 94, 95, 105
Hanna, Jake, 16
Harper, Cliff, 96
Harriott, Joe, 75, 117

Harrison, Paul, 96
Harvey, Eddie, 23, 24, 111
Hassell, Eric, 105
Hastings, Jimmy, Quintet, 86
Hastings, Lennie, 38
Hatton, Jeff, Manhatton Jazz, 101
Hawes, Pat, 38, 96, 97, 99
Hawkins, Coleman, 17, 63
Hayes, Tubby, 42, 75, 117
Hays Galleria, London SE, 105
Heath, Ted, Orchestra/Band, 28, 30, 42, 44, 110
Heckstall-Smith, Dick, 71
Hemsby Holiday Camp, Pontin's, 101
Herbert, Mort, 50
Herman, Woody, 58, 63, 83, 111
Hewett, Dave, 104
Hibbler, Al, 44
High Society Jazzmen, 42
Hilden Manor Hotel, Hildenborough, Kent, 115
Hill, Norman, College Boys, 32, 35
Hilversum, Holland, xii, 25
Hines, Earl "Fatha," 61, 63, 64
Hippodrome Cinema, 17
Hoare, Geoff, 42
Hodges, Johnny, 59, 63, 111
Hodier, André, 74
Holiday Inn, Croydon, 101
Holland, Ray, 96, 99
Holloway, Denny, 9, 41, 45
Holly, Buddy, 44
Holmes, Jim, 48, 75, 95
Hone, Ged, Ragtime Jazz Band, 73
Hooker, Chris, 92
Hooter Jazz, 58, 59
Hopkins, Claude, 62
Hopkinson, George, 37, 106
Horton, Roger, 93, 105
Hot Club de France, xi, 29
Hot Club of London, 117
Hot Five, 23
Hot Rods, Skiffle, The, 44, 45
Howard, Avery "Kid", 48, 50
Howard, Cephas, "Capt", 69
Howard, Johnny, and His Orchestra, 52, 68
Hucko, Peanuts, 16, 50, 83
Hughes, Spike, 32
Hull, Pete, 37, 38
Humble, Derek, 42
Humphrey, Percy, 90
Humphrey, Willie J., 89, 90
100 Club, Oxford Street, London, 59, 93, 105
*Hundred Years Of American Dixieland Jazz*, 92, 93
Hunt, Don, 42
Hunt, Fred, 36, 38, 50, 51, 105
Hyams, Derek, 92
Hyman, Dick, 83, 118

I
Ingram, Gerry, 48
Innes, Brian, "Professor Emeritus", 69

J
Jackman, Pete, 96
Jackson, Haydon, 86
Jackson, Oliver, 63, 64
Jacquet, Illinois, 63
Jaffe, Allan, 90
James, Harry, 115
Janssen, Huub, 87
*Jazz At The Philharmonic,* 44, 50, 61
Jazz Bandits, 115
Jazz Beat, 73
Jazz Book Club, 74
Jazz Centre Society, 86
Jazz FM 102.2, 103
*Jazz From A Swingin' Era,* 61, 63, 64, 65
Jazz Guide, 97, 105
Jazzhouse, The, 75
Jazz Journal, 73
Jazz News, 73
*Jazz On A Summer's Day,* 55
Jazzshows Jazz Club, 72
Jazz Times, 73
Jefferson, Andrew, 82
Jefferson, Thomas, 83
Jenkins, John, 92
Johnson, Albert "Bud," 63
Johnson, Bert, Metro Band, 43
Johnson, Eddie, 115
Johnson, Johnny, 88
Johnson, Lonnie, 58, 113
Johnson, Ron, 42
Johnson, T. J., 96
Johnson, Willie "Bunk", 33, 47, 116
Johnstone, Mark, 84
Jolson, Al, 17
Jones, Dave, 104, 105
Jones, Paul, 96
Jones, Philly Joe, 84
Jordan, Louis, 82
Jubilee Bridge, 66

K
Kaart, Dick, 87
Kaminsky, Max, 16, 74
Kanal, Toni, 100
Kaper, Bob, 87
Kaye, Cab, 112
Kaye, Danny, 52
Keates, Gordon, 92
Keen, Jim, 9
Keene, Ronny, and His Orchestra, 44
Keir, Dave, 41, 71

Kelly, Chris, 51
Kelly, Joanne, 33
Kemp, Geoff, 114
Kempen, Jaap van, 87
Kenton, Stan, 83
Keppard, Freddy, 16, 106
Kerr, Bob, 92
Kershaw, Brian, 92
Keston Village Hall, 105
Keyes, Phylis, 35
Kimball, Narvin, 90
King, Miff, 83
Kings Jazz Review, xii, 94, 95, 97, 107
Kingwell, Colin, Jazz Bandits, 72
Knight, Terry, 82
Knox, Anna, 98
Konitz, Lee, 84
Korner, Alexis, 70, 71
Kort, Bert de, 87
Kyle, Billy, 50, 63,
Kymbrell, Peter, 86

## L

Ladnier, Tommy, 47
Lager, Max, 97
Laine, Cleo, 42, 92
Laine, "Papa" Jack, 14
Lamb, John, 59
Lancaster, John, 115
Lane, Jack, 113
Lane, Steve, 73, 80, 116, 117
Lang, Don, 45
Langley, Graham, 9, 58, 112
Lantern Hall, The, 47
Lanza, Mario, 44
La Rocca, Nick, 15
Lateef, Yusef, 63
Latus, John, 47
Laurie, Cy, 33, 72, 117
Laurie, Dick, 105
Lavender, Johnny, 38
Lavere, Charlie, Chicago Loopers, 116
Lawrence, Denise & Tony, Storeyville Tickle Band, 97, 105
Lawrence, Syd, Orchestra, 31, 111
Lawson, Yank, 16, 97
Lay, Peter & Jill, 105
Layton, Teddy, 105
Lazy Ade's Late Hour Boys, 31
Lee, Davy, 17
Lee, Peggy, 92, 93
Leeds Castle, Kent, 107
Leggett, Max, 83
Legon, Freddy, 37, 106
Leicester Square Jazz Club, 30
Lemon, Brian, 91
Lennon, John, 70
Leonard, Jo, 37

Leopold, Reg, 111
Lesberg, Jack, 16
Lewis, Father Al, 82
Lewis, Frank, 14,
Lewis, George, 40, 47, 48, 50, 51, 96, 112, 117
Lewis, John, 111
Lewis, Ted, Orchestra, 115
Lewis, Terry, 73
Lewis, Vic, 43
Ley, Eggie, 55, 115
Lightfoot, Terry, Jazzmen, 45, 46, 47, 50, 55, 57, 72, 74, 108, 117
Lil's Hot Shots, 23
Lister, Eric, 71
Littlejohn, Alan, 9, 38, 104, 120
Lomax, Alan, 74
London City Stompers, 72
London Jazz Club, 114
Long, Don, 45
Long, John & Renee, 94
Longley, John & Lynn, 105
Lord Napier Pub, The, 41, 77-81, 83, 95, 97, 105, 115
Lorkin, Eddie, 92
Loss, Joe, Orchestra, 23, 28, 109
Louis Armstrong Pub, The, 105
Lounge Lizards, 80
Lovatt, Harry, 58, 59
Lowrie, William E, "Empire" Dance Band, 18
Lowther, Henry, 86
Luke, Diane, 103
Lyttelton, Humphrey, Band, 29, 33, 35, 37, 41, 60, 72, 74, 92, 94, 107, 111, 114, 117
Lyward, Rodney, 44

## M

MacDonald, Sally, 9
Mack, Bob, 38
Mack, Charles and His Band, 30
Mack, Les, 105
MacKenzie, Henry, 92
McCartney, Paul, 70
McDowell, Paul "Whispering", 69
McKenzie, Mike, 72
McKinley, Ray, 50
McKrell, Mac, 42
McQuater, Tommy, 111
Maddock, Owen, 38
Mann, Manfred, 33
Mann, Tony, Trio, 87
Marks, Jon, 83
Marquee, The, 73
Marsh, Johnny, Trio, 75
Marson, John, 92
Martyn, Barry, 48, 75, 96
Mascal, Roy, 75
Mason, Phil, 96
Mason, Rod, 69
Masso, George, 16

May, Billy, 92
Mayes, Chick, 105
Mead, Al, 110
Mears, Alan, 83
Melachrino, George, 23
Melbourne New Orleans Jazz Band, 72
Melly, George, 31, 32, 35, 41, 79, 114, 116
Melody Maker, 32, 60, 73
Merseysippi Jazz Band, 72, 117
Mickleburgh, Bobby, 110, 115
Middleton, Velma, 50
Miles, Butch, 16
Miller, Colin, 71
Miller, Ernest "Punch", 48
Miller, Gary, 44
Miller, Glenn, 30, 50, 83, 100, 119
Miller, Harry, 110
Miller, Herb, 100, 111
Miller, James "Sing", 89, 90
Miller, Mike, Swanee Syncopators, 101
Miller, Rice, 113
Millinder, Lucky, 63
Milliner, Tony, 38
Million Airs Concert Orchestra, 83
Mills Brothers, The, 17
Milne, Ken, 115
Mince, Johnny, 93
Minnion, John, 95
Minor, Anderson, 82
Minter, Brian, 82
Modern Club, The, 45
Modern Jazz Quartet, The, 111
Mole, Miff, 16, 115
Monk, Sonny, 117
Monro, Matt, 92
Monsbourgh, Ade, 25, 110
Moonshine Venue Bar, 104
Moran, Eddie, 93
Morris, Sonny, Jazzmen, 46
Morrissey, Dick, 47, 75
Morton, Jelly Roll, 74, 82, 113, 116
Moss, Danny, 91, 92
Moten, Bennie, 62
Moull, Jimmy, 73
Muddy Waters Pub, The, 34
Mullen, Jim, 86
Mulligan, Gerry, 58
Mulligan, Mick, and His Magnolia Jazz Band, 32, 35, 37, 38, 41, 110, 114, 116
Munnery, Paul, 97
Murphy, Matt, 113
Murphy, Russ, 25, 110
Murphy, Turk, 16, 118
Myers Hall, Epsom, 105

# N
Nance, Ray, 59
Nash, Nigel, 92

Nelson, Dave, Marlborough Jazz Band, 72
Nelson, Louis, 117, 118
Neville, Derek, 110
Nevard, Don, 73
New Addington Artisan Jazz Band, 55
New Addington Rhythm Club, The, 32, 35, 37, 38, 41, 49, 112
New Addington Youth Club, 32
New Jazz Orchestra,
New Orleans Jazz Men, 105
New Orleans Stompers, 51
New Regent Dance Orchestra, 17
Newman, Bill, 104
Nicholls, Alan, Dixieland Band, 87
Nicholls, Nick, 69
Nichols, Keith, 92
Nichols, Loring "Red", 16, 52, 62, 115
Noble, Ray, 62
Nomads, The, 44, 50
Noone, Jimmie, 61
North End Hall - see Civic Hall
Nowhere Inn Particular Pub, The, 66

# O
Odeon Cinema, 52, 88
O'Donnell, Eddie, 40
Oliver, Joe "King," 14, 16, 23, 61, 71, 82, 114, 116
Oliver, Sy, 84,
Olympia Brass Band of New Orleans, 82
Omega Brass Band, 74
Orchid Ballroom, Purley, xii, 30, 42, 43, 52, 115
Original Dixieland Jazz Band, (ODJB), 15, 114
Orpwood, Ray, 114
Ory, Edward "Kid", 14, 47
O'Sullivan, Tony, 96, 99
Otis, Big Bill, 58

# P
Pacific Brass Band, 51
Paddock Pub, The, 66
Page, Len, 114
Page, Tom, 38
Pakefield Holiday Camp, Pontin's, 101
Palais de Dance, Thornton Heath, 17
Palladium Cinema, 28
Palm Court - Purley, 44, 53, 75, 112
Palmer, Harry, and His Orchestra, 30
Palmer, Roy, 47
Panama Jazz Kings, 97
Panassié, Hugues, 29, 74
Park Lane Ballroom, 42, 45, 50
Parker, Charlie, 63, 106, 113
Parker, Frank, 90
Parker, Johnny, 37, 38, 69, 84
Parr, Bobby, 79, 80, 82
Parry, Harry, 28
Pasadena Roof Orchestra, 92, 111
Pass, Joe, 100

Paterson, Graham, 48
Patterson, Ottilie, 46, 50, 71, 73, 74,
Pavageau, Alcide, 50
Paverty, Franklin D, "Steve Powers", 69
Pavilion Cinema, Thornton Heath, 28
Payen's Mexican Military Band, 66, 67
Payne, Peter, Jazz Record Shop, 43, 116
Peck, Nat, 111
Peerless, Clive, 48
Pemberton, Bill, 63, 64
Pembroke Hall, 17, 27, 32, 33, 110, 111, 112
Pembroke Theatre, 27, 111
Perdido Street Six, 48
Perez, Manuel, 14
Peterson, Oscar, Trio, 50, 83
Petit, Buddy, 51
Phillips, Chris, 103
Phillips, Sid, 114
Phoenix Jazz Band, 114
Piccadilly Jazz Club, 72
Pilgrem, Geoff, 113, 114, 115
Pitlake Arms Pub, The, 66
Pitlake Bridge, 66
Pitt, Terry, Jazz Band, 72
Pitt, Tony, 104
Pitt, Vic, 84
Ploughboy Jazz Band, 97
Pointon, Mike, Jazzmen, The, 9, 47, 48, 75, 95
Pond Music Shop, The, 47
Porcupine Pub, The, Great Newport Street, London, 48
Potter's Music Shop, 43, 47
Preservation Hall Jazz Band, 89, 90
Prince Albert Pub, The, 48
Prince of Orange Pub, The, 118
Procope, Russell, 59
Purley Hall, 48
Pyke, Tony, 65
Pyne, Chris, 86
Pyramid Record Shop, 48

## Q
Queen's Surrey Military Band, xi, 66, 67
Queen Victoria Pub, The, 66

## R
Rabin, Oscar, 109
Racehorse Pub, The, (Carshalton), 86
Race, Steve, 114
Radio Big Band, 92
Ragas, Henry, 15
Rainey, Hugh, 73
Ralfini, Jan, Band, 17
Randall, Freddy, xii, 27, 30, 38, 110, 114, 115, 116
Randall, Harry, 110
Rank, Bill, 111
Rankine, Brian, 92
Raphaello, Neva, 31, 37, 72, 116

Ratcliffe, Stan, 73
Rattenbury, Ken, 114
Reading Jazz Club, 105
ReBirth Brass Band of New Orleans, 107
Red Barn, The, (Barnehurst), 23
Red Barn, The, (Blindley Heath), 87
Red Deer Hotel, The, 59, 86
Red Lion Pub, The, (Leytonstone), 116
Red Onions Jazz Band, 33
Red River Jazzmen, 73
Rees, Peter, 38, 120
Refectory, Golders Green, 116
Reid, Bill, 50
Relf, Keith, 113
Reliance Brass Band, 14
Rena, Kid, 51
Rendall, Ron, Alhambra Jazz Band, 72
Rendell, Don, Quintet, 73
Renshaw, John, Jazz Band, 72
Rey, Phil, 105
Rich, Buddy, 83
Richardson, Johnny, 50
Richford, Doug, London Jazz Band, 47, 72
Richmond Jazz Club, 73
Ridge, Pete, 57
Rifkin, Joshua, 83
Rigden, Reg, 23, 24, 29
Rimington, Sammy, 48, 57, 75, 79, 83, 97
Ritz Ballroom, Thornton Heath, 30
River City Jazzmen, 46, 47
River City Stompers, 117
Riverside Jazzmen, 72, 113, 114
Roaring Twenties Jazz Band, 115
Roberts, Joan, 43
Roberts, Lester, 38, 120
Roberts, Pixie, 25, 110
Robichaux, Joe, 48, 50
Robinson, Barry, 92
Robinson, Duggie, 92
Robinson, Jim, 47, 48, 50
Roche, Harry, 111
Rodber, John, 48
Rolands, Bill,
Rollins, Sonny, 111
Root, Alan, 105
Rose and Crown Pub, The, 66
Rose, Wally, 118
Ross, Ronnie, 72, 73, 117
Rowlands, Bill, 37
Roy, Harry, 23, 28, 109
Royal Engineers Drill Hall, 17
Royal Festival Hall, 115
Royal Oak Pub, The, Orpington, 115
Royston Ballroom, Penge, 52
Rudolph's Jazz Bar, 86
Ruskin Hall, 17
Russell, Pee Wee, 75
Russell, Ron, 68

## S

Saffron Valley Boys, 50
Saints Jazz Band, 117
Salisbury, Gerry, 37, 69
Savannah Band, 17
Savory, Peter, 55
Savoy Cinema, 26, 44, 45
Sbarbaro, Tony, 15
Scala Cinema, 17
Schilperoort, Peter, 25, 26, 87
Scobey, Bob, 16, 23
Scott, Don, Dance Orchestra, 30
Scott, Keith, 71
Scott, Ronnie, 73
Scruggs, Irene, 114
Scutt, Cyril, Boogie-Woogie Boys, 31, 37, 105, 106, 116
Seabrook, Dennis, 114
Selhurst Picture Theatre, 17
Selsdon Park Hotel, 105
Semple, Archie, 38, 50
Serter, Gordon, 86
Shakespeare Pub, The, Woolwich, 117
Shannon, Kevin, 72
Shapiro, Helen, 107
Sharp, Jackie, 42
Shavers, Charlie, 63
Shaw, Arvell, 93
Shearing, George, 109
Sheik, Kid, 83
Shelley, Jim, 'Frisco Band, 97
Shelton, Anne,
Shepherd, Dave, 111
Shepherd, Jim, 71
Shepherd, Ken, 38, 120
Sherbourne, Mike, 79, 80, 82
Shields, Larry, 15
Shillito, John, & The Rhythm Aces, 97
Shimell, David, 94
Shirley Parish Hall, 30
Short, Tony, 24
Silberiesen, Lou, 25, 110
Silk, Eric, Southern Jazz Band, 33, 38, 72, 114, 116, 117, 120
Simmons, Don, 38, 120
Sims, Ken, Vintage Jazz Band, 72
Sinclair, Bob, 38
Sinclair, David, 9
Sinclair, Nigel, 38
Singer, Geoff, 114
Six Bells Pub, The, 66
Skivington, Pete, 91, 104
Skrimshire, Neville, 51
Slim, Memphis, 58, 113
Smith, Bessie, 74
Smith, Carrie, 16
Smith, Dick, 40, 46
Smith, Don, 114

Smith, Eddie, (banjo), 46
Smith, Eddie, (violin), 63
Smith, Keith, 48, 72, 75, 80, 93
Smith, Roy, 73
Smith, Terry, 86
Smith, Vic, 9, 118
Smith, Willie, 62, 64
Smoky City Stompers, 73
Solomon, Clare, 96
South, Harry, 86
South Bank Concert Hall, 35
South London Jazz Federation, 86
Southern Rag-A-Jazz, 98
Southland, 104
Sowden, Geoff, 69, 73,
Sowden, Stan, 105
Span, Otis, 113
Spanier, Francis "Muggsy", 16
Spencer, Frank & Peggy, 52
Spivey, Victoria, 113
Spree City Stompers, 72
Squadronaires, The, 30
Stackyard Stompers, 97
Staff, Freddy, 111
Stagg, Bill, 47, 48, 79, 80, 82, 98
Stahl, Josie, 45
Stamford, Bob, 71
Stanley, Mike, 47, 48
Star Hotel, The, 33, 41, 42, 45, 46, 48, 50, 52, 53, 55, 57, 58, 60, 65, 69, 72, 77, 86, 112, 113
State Cinema, 28
Stephens, Doreen, 43
Stewart, Graham, 33, 37, 41, 105
Stewart, Pete, 42, 50, 55, 65
Stobart, Kathy, 42, 86
Stone, Lew, 23
Stotesbury, Bill, 96, 97, 99
Streatfield, Art, 23, 24
Streatham Locarno Ballroom, xi, 17
Studio 51 Club, The, 48
Sudhalter, Dick, 111
Sunshine, Monty, 40, 42, 46, 69, 70, 72, 85, 88, 97, 107, 110, 117
Surridge, Jack, 110
Sutton Jazz Club, Wallington, 105
Sutton, Ralph, 16
Swanee 4, 98
Swing Shop, The, 38, 47

## T

Tabor, Al, Trans-Atlantic Band, 17
Tamworth Arms Pub, The, 66
Tatum, Art, 63
Taylor, Bert, 31
Taylor, Brian, Jazz Band, 50
Teagarden, Jack, 42, 51, 117
Teale, Michael, 91
Temperance Seven, 69, 110
Ternent, Billy, 23, 28

Terry, Sonny, 58
Thatcher, Norman, 97
Themen, Art, 75
Thomas, Tony, 94
Thompson, Bill, 105
Thompson, "Sir" Charles, 63
Thompson, Colin, 35
Thompson, Frank, 51
Thomson, Eddie,
Thornton Heath Sports Club, 17
Tickell, Ian, 114
Tilley, Chris, 96
Tinker, Derrick, 92
Tio, Lorenzo, (jnr), 14
Tobin, Louise, 16
Torff, Brian, 16
Torregano, Joseph, 82
Tough, Dave, 16
Toussaint, Jean, 102
Townhouse, The, Enfield 105
Townsend, Red, 36, 105
Tracey, Stan, Quartet, 86
Trafalgar Pub, The, (Chelsea), 108
Traill, Sinclair, 74
Tropicana, 75
Trumbauer, Frank, 111
Tucker, Sophie, 115
Tullett, Alan, 9, 109
Tunbridge Wells Jazz Club, 105
Turner, Bruce, 27, 111
Tyrrell, Bernie, 73, 105

## U
Unique Ballroom, 33, 34, 112

## V
Valentine, "Kid" Thomas, 89, 90
Vallis, Buddy, 23, 24
Varney, Jack, 25, 110
Varro, Johnny, 16
Vas, Olaf, 86
Vaughan, Roy, 43
Vaughan, Sarah, 58
Venuti, Joe, 116
Verris, Marjorie, All-Ladies Orchestra, 30
Vink, Frans, 25
Vintage Jazz Band, 95
Volunteer Inn, The, 33, 47, 66, 112

## W
Waller, Ed, 42
Waller, Thomas "Fats" 17, 115
Wallington Public Hall, 30, 68
Wallis, Bob, 55, 73, 117
Walton, Harry, 105
Ward, Bob, 96, 99
Ward, Ron, 57
Warehouse Theatre, 105

Warner, Peter, 92
Warren, Earle, 62
Washboard Syncopators, 115
Waterhouse, Dick, 9, 105, 115, 117
Waters, Muddy, 58, 71, 113
Watkins, Joe, 50
Watson, John Grieves, 69
Watters, Lu, Yerba Buena Jazz Band, 16, 23, 118
Watts, Vic & Iris, 78
Watts, Vic & Sheila, 97
Webb, George, 9, 23, 24, 25, 29, 116, 117, 118
Webber, Michael, Promotions, 91
Webster, Eric, 83
Weir, Frank, 88
Weller, Don, 86, 112
Weller, Ed, 45, 47
Weller, Jim, 42, 55
Weller, Sam, 115
Wellington Pub, The, 66
Wellstood, Dick, 87
Welsh, Alex, Dixielanders, 33, 38, 46, 50, 51, 60, 69, 72, 75, 86, 87, 91
Wesson, Don, 59
Westbrook, Mike, Band, 75
West London Jazz Society, 73, 105
Weston, Humph
White, Brian, Magna Jazzband, 97
Whiteman, Brian, 92
Whiteman, Paul, 111, 112
Whittam, Ray, 69
Wilcox, Bert, 114
Wilkins, Geoff, Diplomats, 72
Wilkinson, Mick, 115
Williams, Big Joe, 58, 113
Williams, Cootie, 59, 111
Williams, Roy, 16, 91, 92
Williams, Trefor "Fingers," 96
Williams, Vaughan, 53
Williamson, Sonny Boy, 58, 113
Wilson, Dave, Dixielanders, 73
Wilson, Eric, 37
Wilson, Frank, 47, 48
Wilson, Teddy, 63, 83
Wilton Arms Pub, The, 34
Winnick, Maurice, 30
Winstone, Eric, 23, 28
Winstone, Norma, 75
Winter Gardens, The, 17
Wiseman, John, 96
Wolverines, The, 16, 116
Wood, Dave, 105
Wood, Diggie, 35
Wood, George, 103
Woodman Pub, The, Blackfen, 105, 118
Worlds Greatest Jazz Band, 83, 84
Wray, Ken, 73
Wren, Andy, 70
Wrightson, Tony, 55
Wurr, John, 73, 97

Wykes, Roy, 23

X -- -- -- --

Y
Yardbirds, The, 58, 113
Yarra Yarra Jazz Band, 78
Yerba Buena Jazz Band, 16
Yorkshire Jazz Band, 110, 117
Young, Lester, 63, 106
Young, Trummy, 48, 50

Z
Zenith Hot Stompers, 97

THE TUNES

A Pound Of Blues, 46
Ace In The Hole, 80
Ain't Nobody Here But Us Chickens, 110
Air On A 'G' String, 109
All I Do Is Dream Of You, 80
All Of Me, 57
Apex Blues, 25, 35, 61
At The Jazz Band Ball, xii, 116
Baby Won't You Please Come Home, 116
Basin Street Blues, 35, 82
Beale Street Blues, 46
Bessie's Blues, 35
Big Butter And Egg Man, 35
Big Cat, Little Cat, 37
Big House Blues, 46
Black And Blue, 35
Black And White, 114
Blue Goose, 114
Blue Turning Grey Over You, 46
Bobby Shaftoe, 46
Bogolousa Moan, 57
Bourbon Street Parade, 46, 80
Brownskin Mama, 37
Bucket's Got A Hole In It, 35, 37
Buddy Bolden's Blues, 35
Buddy's Habits, 37
Burgundy Street Blues, 46
Bye And Bye, 46
Cake Walking Babies, 37
Careless Love, 46
Cater Street Rag, 35
Ce Moissieu Qui Parle, 37
Chimes Blues, 57
China Boy, 35
Chinatown, 46

Clarinet Marmalade, 35
Climax Rag, 46
Corinne Corinna, 57
Dallas Blues, 57
Decent Woman, 35
Deep Bayon Blues, 46
Dippermouth, 57
Doctor Blues, 37
Doctor Clayton's Blues, 46
Doctor Jazz, 46, 112, 113
Double Check Stomp, 46
Do What Ory Say, 35
Down In Honky Tonk Town, 37
Drop That Sack, 23
Fidgety Feet, 35, 46
Fish Face, 35
Froggie Moore, 35
Georgia Bo Bo, 23, 35
Georgia Cake Walk, 35
Get It, 37
Get Out Of Here And Go On Home, 35, 37
Gettysburg March, 69, 80
Goin' Home, 57
Good Time Tonight, 46
Graveyard Words, 35
High Society, 46
Hilarity Rag, 57
Hollywood Hangover, 62
Hotter Than That, 35
Hush-a-Bye, 46
I Can't Escape From You, 46, 57
Ice Cream, 46
Ida, Sweet As Apple Cider, 38
I Love My Baby, 46
I'll Build A Stairway To Paradise, 38
In The Mood, 23
It's Magic, 63
It's Tight Like That, 46
Jelly Roll, 35
Jet Black Blues, 35
John Henry, 57
Judge, 35
Just A Closer Walk With Thee, 35, 57
K. C. Rider, 46
Keep Your Feet Still, Geordie Hinnie, 83
King Size Papa, 35
Kitchen Man, 35
L'annee Passe, 37
Lawd, You Sure Been Good To Me, 46
Little Lawrence, 35
London Blues, 37
Lonesome Road, 46
Mahogany Hall Stomp, 35
Mama Don't Allow, 46
Market Street Stomp, 46
Maryland, My Maryland, 46, 57
Melancholy Blues, 57
Michigan Water, 57
Midnight In Moscow, 70, 84

165

Miss Otis Regrets, 80
My Monday Date, 61
New Second Line, 82
1919 Rag, 35, 37
9.20 Special, 62
Nobody But My Baby, 35
Nobody Knows The Way I Feel Tonight, 35
Of All The Wrongs You've Done To Me, 35
Oh, Didn't He Ramble, 46, 57
Ole Man Mose, 46
Olga, 46
One O'Clock Jump, 62
One Sweet Letter, 57
Original Jelly Roll Blues, 35
Over The Waves, 57
Panama Rag, 35, 46
Perdido Street Blues, 80
Petite Fleur, 70
Red Hot Poker Rag, 35
Rent Party Blues, 46
Revolutionary Blues, 35
Robbin's Nest, 63
Rock Island Line, 35, 41
Rockin' Down The River, 55
Rockin' In Rhythm, 46
Rockin' The Blues, 62
Rosetta, 61
Runnin' Wild, 57
St. Louis Blues, 37
St. Philip Street Breakdown, 46
Samantha, 70
Saratoga Swing, 46
Sheik Of Araby, 57
Shine, 46
Sister Kate, 112
Snag It, 37, 57
Snake Rag, 35
Song Of India, 84
South, 35
Stop Now It's Praying Time, 46
Straight From The Wood, 37
Strange Blues, 35
Strange Peach, 25
Strutting With Some Barbecue, 35
Stuffy, 63
Summertime, 35
Sunset Café Stomp, 35
Swannee River, 57
Sweet Georgia Brown, 46
Sweet Substitute, 37
Sweet Sue, 46
Tar Paper Stomp, 35
The Duck's Yas Yas, 82
The Grey Goose, 57
The Martinique, 46
The Old Rugged Cross, 35, 46, 57, 80
The Onions, 37
Tia Juana, 37
Tiger Rag, 38, 46
Tishomingo Blues, 35, 57, 80

Tom Thumb, 62
Trog's Blues, 37
Trouble In Mind, 35
Wa Wa Wa, 37
Wang Wang Blues, 35
Washington And Lee Swing, 35
Weary Blues, 35, 46
Weather Bird, 61
We Shall Walk Through The Streets Of The City, 57
When I Leave The World Behind, 80
When I'm Sixty Four, 70
When My Sugar Walks Down The Street, 35
When You And I Were Young Maggie, 46
Whistlin' Rufus, 46
Wild Cat Blues, 46
Wild Man Blues, 61
Willie The Weeper, 46, 80
Yaka Hula, 57
Yama Yama Man, 46
Yes, Lord, I'm Crippled, 46
Yes, Yes, In Your Eyes, 80
You Took Advantage Of Me, 46

The Frontispieces

Chapters

1 Way Down Yonder In New Orleans
2 You Tell Me Your Dreams
3 Lonesome Road
4 Goin' Home
5 Back In Your Own Back Yard
6 Beautiful Dreamer
7 When You're Smiling
8 Runnin' Wild
9 That's A Plenty

Appendices

{i} Where Did The Good Times Go
{ii} Blue Skies
{iii} Wrap Your Troubles In Dreams

166